GLOBAL ECONOMIC STUDIES

SELECT FOREIGN MARKETS AND INDUSTRIES

POLICIES AND INSIGHTS

GLOBAL ECONOMIC STUDIES

Additional books in this series can be found on Nova's website under the Series tab.

Additional E-books in this series can be found on Nova's website under the E-book tab.

GLOBAL ECONOMIC STUDIES

SELECT FOREIGN MARKETS AND INDUSTRIES

POLICIES AND INSIGHTS

PETER M. LUJÁN
EDITOR

NOVA

Nova Science Publishers, Inc.
New York

Library of Congress Cataloging-in-Publication Data

Select foreign markets and industries : policies and insights / editor, Peter M. Lujan.
p. cm.
Includes index.
ISBN 978-1-62100-133-1 (hbk.)
1. Industrial policy--Developed countries. 2. Trade regulation--Developed countries. 3. Industries--Developed countries. I. Lujan, Peter M.
HD3616.D4553S45 2011
338'.01--dc23

2011031103

Published by Nova Science Publishers, Inc. † New York

CONTENTS

PREFACE

This book explores policies and insights from select foreign markets and industries. Topics discussed include mortgage markets in selected developed countries; tax administration information on selected foreign practices that may provide useful insights; U.S. postal service and foreign posts' strategies that could inform U.S. postal service's efforts to modernize food safety, as well as selected countries' systems that can offer insights into ensuring import safety and response to food-borne illness.

Chapter 1 - The United States, Canada, Denmark, and Australia are advanced economies that share many features, but their approaches to financing homeownership have differed. As the U.S. Congress considers housing finance reform, the experiences of these other nations may suggest some potentially useful policy approaches. In recent years, homeownership rates in the United States, Canada, and Australia have been similar: 66.9% in the United States, 68.4% in Canada, and 69.8% in Australia. Denmark's homeownership rate of 54.0% is low for this group of nations and for countries with developed economies.

Chapter 2 - The Internal Revenue Service (IRS) and foreign tax administrators face similar issues regardless of the particular provisions of their laws. These issues include, for example, helping taxpayers prepare and file returns, and assuring tax compliance. Understanding how other tax administrators have used certain practices to address common issues can provide insights to help inform deliberations about tax reform and about possible administrative changes in the U.S. existing system to improve compliance, better serve taxpayers, reduce burdens, and increase efficiencies. GAO was asked to describe (1) how foreign tax administrators have approached issues that are similar to those in the U.S. tax system and (2) whether and how the IRS identifies and adopts tax administration practices used elsewhere. To do this, GAO reviewed documents and interviewed six foreign tax administrators. In some cases, GAO also interviewed tax experts, tax practitioners, taxpayers, and trade-group representatives who were selected based on their expertise or involvement in developing or using the foreign systems. GAO also examined documents and met with IRS officials.

Chapter 3 - The foreign postal operators (foreign posts) in industrialized countries in GAO's review have been experiencing declining letter mail volumes and have modernized their delivery and retail networks to address this challenge. As requested, GAO reviewed the innovations and initiatives that foreign posts are using and the lessons the U.S. Postal Service (USPS) might learn to help it address plummeting mail volumes and record financial losses. This report examines initiatives foreign posts have implemented to improve mail delivery and retail networks and related results, and modernization strategies used by foreign posts that can inform consideration of proposals to improve USPS's financial condition and customer service. GAO selected foreign posts in Australia, Canada, Finland, Germany, Sweden, and Switzerland as case studies based on characteristics, such as delivery and retail changes and country size and location. GAO reviewed foreign posts' documents, including annual reports and strategic plans related to delivery and retail network changes and innovations. GAO met with foreign post officials, toured their retail facilities, received briefings on their delivery and retail networks and other areas, and met with regulators, labor unions, and mailers to obtain their views on the effects of their posts' modernization efforts. USPS generally agreed with GAO's findings and mentioned both its own modernization efforts and the barriers it faces.

Chapter 4 - Like other nations, the United States faces growing food safety challenges resulting from at least three major trends. First, imported food makes up a growing share of the food supply. Second, consumers are increasingly eating foods that are raw or have had minimal processing and that are often associated with foodborne illness. Third, changing demographic patterns mean that more of the U.S. population is, and increasingly will be, susceptible to foodborne illness. In 2005, GAO reported on the approaches and challenges seven countries faced in reorganizing and consolidating food safety functions. Since then, the European Union (EU) has taken on a larger role in overseeing food safety within its 27 member states. GAO was asked to describe how Canada, the EU, Germany, Ireland, Japan, the Netherlands, and the United Kingdom (UK) (1) ensure the safety of imported food, (2) respond to outbreaks of foodborne illness, and (3) measure the effectiveness of their reorganized food safety systems. GAO also asked experts in these countries and the EU to identify emerging food safety challenges that they expect to face over the next decade. In doing this work, GAO did not evaluate the countries' management of their food safety systems or explicitly compare their efforts with those of the United States.

In: Select Foreign Markets and Industries
Editor: Peter M. Luján

ISBN: 978-1-62100-133-1

Chapter 1

MORTGAGE MARKETS IN SELECTED DEVELOPED COUNTRIES*

N. Eric Weiss

SUMMARY

The United States, Canada, Denmark, and Australia are advanced economies that share many features, but their approaches to financing homeownership have differed. As the U.S. Congress considers housing finance reform, the experiences of these other nations may suggest some potentially useful policy approaches.

In recent years, homeownership rates in the United States, Canada, and Australia have been similar: 66.9% in the United States, 68.4% in Canada, and 69.8% in Australia. Denmark's homeownership rate of 54.0% is low for this group of nations and for countries with developed economies.

- Of these four nations, only the United States and Denmark offer mortgages with payments that are fixed for 30 years. In Australia and Canada (and most of the world), mortgages adjust to current interest rates at intervals of one month to five years.
- Of the four nations, between 1991 and 2008, house prices increased the most in Australia and Denmark, but other countries including Ireland, the Netherlands, New Zealand, and Norway had still greater increases.
- Underwriting standards have been the most flexible in the United States and less flexible in Canada and Denmark. Some homeowners in the United States would not qualify for mortgages in Canada or Denmark.
- The United States and Australia have programs to encourage homeownership. Canada offers limited support for home purchases, and Denmark has no homeownership programs. Nevertheless, homeownership rates are similar in the United States, Australia, and Canada.

* This is an edited, reformatted and augmented version of a Congressional Research Service publication, CRS Report for Congress R41432, from www.crs.gov, dated September 29, 2010.

- U.S. and Canadian governments directly or indirectly guarantee most mortgages and assure lenders that mortgage payments will be made in a timely manner. Australia and Denmark have no such government guarantee.
- In Canada, Denmark, and Australia, borrowers who default remain responsible for any unpaid balances, but it is not clear how frequently this is pursued. In the United States, the ability of lenders to seek compensation beyond a foreclosure sale depends on state law and frequently this remedy is not invoked.
- Capital gains from the sale of one's main home are usually tax-exempt in all four nations; all but Canada allow taxpayers to deduct mortgage interest payments.
- Only the U.S. government has a maximum size on the mortgages that it will support. In the other nations, government support is offered to all mortgages.

INTRODUCTION

This report discusses mortgage markets in selected nations[1] and identifies aspects of housing finance that may suggest interesting policy options as Congress debates housing finance reform in the United States. The report describes similarities and differences in a number of countries by comparing homeownership rates and changes in housing prices. It examines features of each country's primary mortgage market, which homebuyers directly experience when applying for and obtaining a mortgage; and it discusses the secondary mortgage market connections that link national mortgage markets and international financial markets. The report concludes by tentatively identifying what may explain why mortgage markets in three of the four countries examined appear to have more differences than similarities, yet have led to similar rates of homeownership.

This report concentrates on the United States, Canada, Denmark, and Australia, occasionally mentioning other nations to provide context. Canada was selected because of its proximity to the United States, similarity of its economy to that of the United Stages, and the distinctive attributes of its housing market. Homeownership rates in Canada and the United States are similar, but Canada has stricter mortgage qualifications (i.e., underwriting standards). Both nations have experienced home price increases over the past 10 years, but Canada has had neither the price level collapse nor the increase in foreclosure rates that the United States has had. Canada funds its mortgages mainly with bank deposits, whereas the United States depends on domestic and international financial markets. The homeowner in the United States typically has a 30-year fixed-rate mortgage (FRM), whereas the Canadian homeowner has a five-year adjustable-rate mortgage (ARM) that is renewed and is designed to be paid in full after 25-30 years. According to the Organization for Economic Cooperation and Development (OECD), Canadian home prices reached a maximum in 2007 that was 60% higher than in 1991, whereas another index developed by Teranet and the National Bank of Canada shows prices continuing to increase.[2] U.S. home prices reached a maximum in 2006 that was 61% greater than in 1991.

Denmark is included because it has very strict underwriting standards and has developed a type of covered mortgage bond with specific collateral to guarantee payment if the bond issuer fails. This is similar to covered bonds throughout much of the European Union (EU), including Germany. Homeowners in Denmark can prepay their mortgages by paying either the unpaid balance (as in the United States), or the market value of the mortgage. This market value will be less than the unpaid balance when interest rates have increased. Denmark and the United States are the only two nations where 30-year fixed-rate mortgages are common.[3] Danish house prices reached a maximum in 2007 that was 150% greater than the 1991 house price level.

Most Australian mortgages have adjustable interest rates. Australian homeowners can make extra payments on their mortgages; these prepayments can be withdrawn, sometimes by a special credit card. Between 1991 and 2009, home prices in Australia increased by 107%.

HOMEOWNERSHIP RATES

Broadly speaking, homeownership rates are determined by the relative costs of housing tenure options (renting versus owning) and the nonfinancial aspects of owning or renting a home. These factors can vary according to a household's income, savings, age, marital status including number of children, the tax system, anticipated house price changes, government regulations such as land use and zoning, building codes, immigrant status, and availability of desirable rental housing. Some factors including income, age, and family status can affect a person's decision to move out from their parents' home and to form an independent household. Because most homebuyers use a mortgage to finance their purchase, mortgage terms can affect homeownership rates.

Homeownership rates vary over time and within a country. For example, in the United States, the national seasonally adjusted homeownership rate reached a peak of 69.4% in the first quarter of 2005; since then, it has trended down with occasional, slight upticks. [4] As an example of regional variation in homeownership rates within the United States, in the second quarter of 2010, the Midwest had the highest rate (70.8%) of any census region, and the West had the lowest rate (61.4%).

As shown in Table 1, homeownership rates for selected developed countries in Europe, North America, Australia, and Asia range from approximately 35% to approximately 97%.[5] The European Union (EU) reports an average homeownership rate of 66.8% with national rates ranging from a low of 43.2% in Germany to a high of 97.0% in Lithuania and Romania. Germany's relatively low homeownership rate is frequently attributed to a policy emphasis on supplying subsidies to rental housing and the integration with the former German Democratic Republic (East Germany).[6] Outside the EU, Switzerland has long had a relatively low homeownership rate (34.6%) that is usually attributed to a high cost of ownership and strong protections for renters, including limits on rent increases. Lithuania and Romania, both EU members, had high homeownership rates following privatization initiatives after their transitions from communism in 1989 and presently lack alternative rental housing.[7] Australia reports a homeownership rate of 69.8%, whereas Japan's homeownership rate is usually estimated around 60%.

Figure 1 displays the homeownership rates, graphically sorted by the rate. A cautionary note: As a result of differences in the ways that countries collect and report data, international comparisons of homeownership rate statistics can be misleading. For example, in the United Kingdom, units with long-term rental contracts are considered to be owner occupied, and in Japan dwellings owned by an occupant's parents are listed as owner occupied.[8]

Table 1. Selected Homeownership Rates Most Recent Year Available

Country	Year	Homeownership Rate
United States	Q2 2010	66.9%
Canada	2006	68.4%
Denmark	2008	54.0%
Australia	2006	69.8%
Austria	2003	57.0%
Belgium	2007	78.0%
Bulgaria	2002	96.5%
Cyprus	2006	68.0%
Czech	2007	58.7%
Estonia	2008	96.0%
Finland	2007	59.0%
France	2007	57.4%
Germany	2002	43.2%
Greece	2008	80.6%
Hungary	2003	92.0%
Iceland	2008	80-85.0%
Ireland	2008	74.5%
Italy	2002	80.0%
Japan	n/a	60.0%
Latvia	2007	87.0%
Lithuania	2008	97.0%
Luxembourg	2008	75.0%
Malta	2006	75.0%
Netherlands	2008	57.0%
Norway	2001	77.0%
Poland	2004	75.0%
Portugal	2007	76.0%
Romania	2007	97.0%
Russia	2003	63.8%
Serbia	2002	89.0%
Slovakia	2008	88.0%
Slovenia	2008	82.0%
Spain	2008	84.5%
Sweden	2007	52.0%
Switzerland	2000	34.6%
United Kingdom	2008	59.0%

Source: United States: U.S. Census Bureau, "Residential Vacancies and Homeownership in the Second Quarter 2010," press release, July 27, 2010, http://www.census.gov/hhes/www/housing

Canada: Statistics Canada, "2006 Census: Changing patterns in Canadian Homeownership and Shelter Costs," press release, June 4, 2008, http://www.statcan.gc.ca/daily-quotidien/080604/dq080604a-eng.htm.

European Union: European Mortgage Federation, *Hypostat 2008, p. 62,* http://www.hypo.org/Objects/6/Files/ Hypostat%202008%20-%20light%20version.pdf.

Switzerland: Swiss Federal Statistical Office, *Taux de logements occupes par leur proprietaire et logement en propriete, en 2000,* http://www.bfs.admin.ch/bfs/portal/en/index/regionen/thematische_karten/maps/bau-_und_wohnungswesen/wohnverhaeltnisse.parsys.0001.PhotogalleryDownloadFile1.tmp/k09.15s.pdf.

Australia: Australian Bureau of Statistics, "Year Book of Australia," press release, 2008, http://www.abs.gov.au/ ausstats/abs@.nsf/bb8db737e2af84b8ca2571780015701e/37171EAC4F4F016ECA2573D20010F849? opendocument.

Japan: Miki Seco, "Transforming Housing Finance in Japan in the 21st Century," in Danny Ben-Shahar, Charles Ka Yui Leung, and Seow Eng Ong (eds.), Mortgage Markets Worldwide (Oxford, England: Blackwell Publishing), p. 75.

Note: In Japan housing is shared by unrelated individuals more frequently than in the other nations, making comparison of homeownership rates difficult. The range of estimates for Japan is from source cited above.

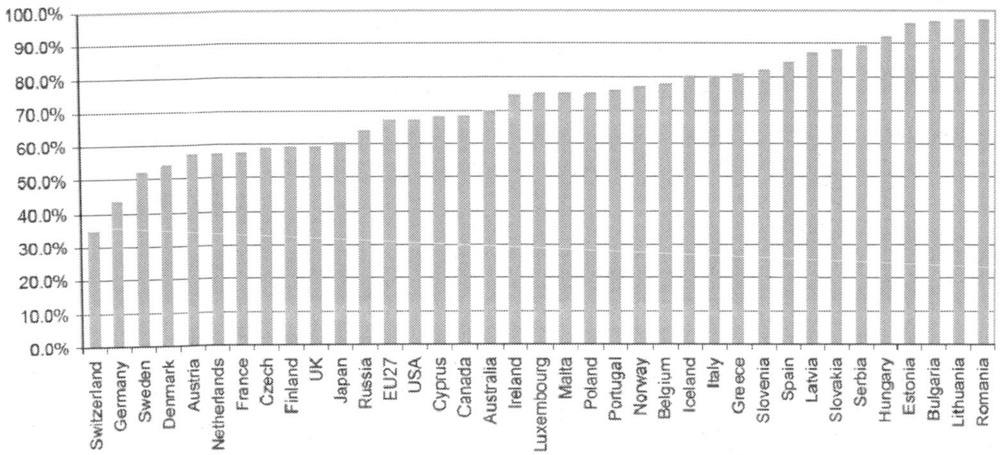

Source: Same sources as Table 1.

Figure 1. Homeownership Rates.

HOUSE PRICE CHANGES

In many countries, real (inflation adjusted) house prices were relatively stable from 1991 until approximately 2000. Between 2000 and 2008, prices increased in real terms, peaked, and declined. In this latter time period, most OECD-member countries experienced at least one year of rapid, real house price increases greater than 10%; the greatest price increase (28%) occurred in Ireland during 1998.[9] The United States' maximum annual price increase was 8.2% (2005), Canada's was 9.8% (2006), Denmark's was 19.3% (2006), and Australia's was 16.0% (2003). Between 1991 and 2008, U.S. house prices increased 50%. House prices in Canada increased 60%, Denmark 150%, and Australia 107%. Nations with the largest house price declines since reaching their maximum were Ireland (-0.53), the United States (-0.16), and Iceland (-0.13).

Real house prices do not always increase. Between 1991 and 2008, real house prices declined in Japan, Korea, and Switzerland.

Figure 2 graphs the price levels for the United States, Canada, Denmark, Australia, Japan, Ireland, and the United Kingdom. The graph emphasizes the point that many other nations had greater increases in housing prices than the United States did.

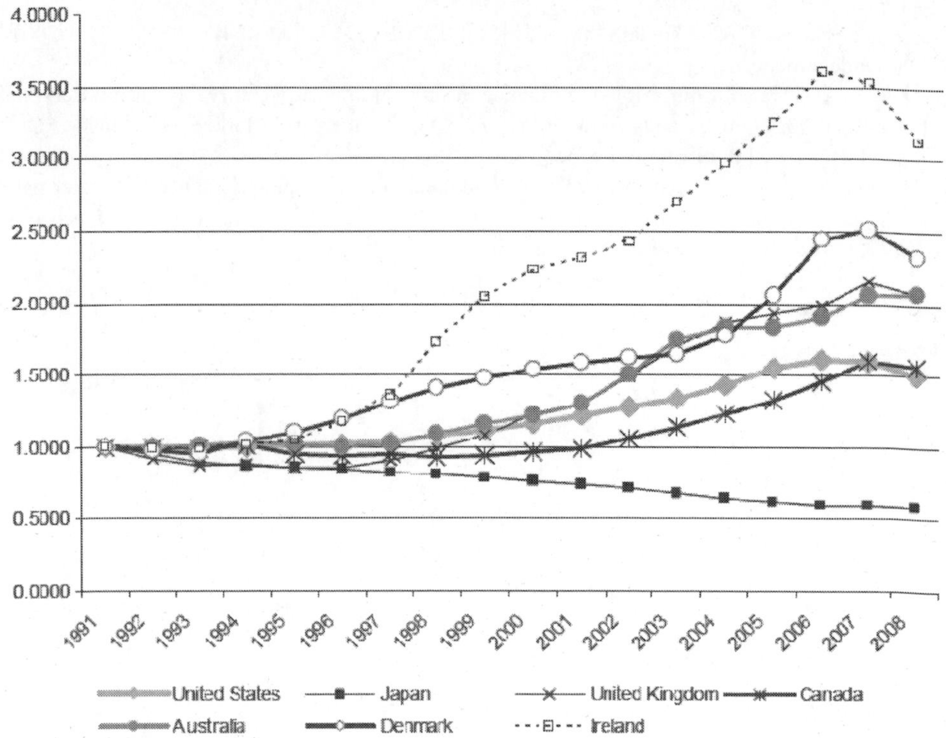

Source: See sources for Table 1.

Notes: Each country's housing price level is set to 1.00 in 1991. The maximum is the greatest price level for the specified nation. For example, the U.S. maximum of 1.62 represents house prices in 2007 that were 1.62 times the level in 1991. Different price series will show somewhat different results. For example, another Canadian house price index (www.housepriceindex.ca) shows prices continuing to increase.

Figure 2. House Price Levels; 1991 = 1.00.

FACTORS AFFECTING MORTGAGE INTEREST RATES

This section discusses how the mortgage interest rate paid by a homeowner is determined in the United States, Canada, Denmark, and Australia. It begins by describing a widely used framework for explaining how mortgage interest rates are determined in the United States and then applies the same framework to the other nations.

United States

In a benchmark competitive economic model, the interest rate on a fixed-rate mortgage (FRM) depends on four sets of factors: (1) the interest rate for a riskless government bond with the same life; (2) adjustments to reflect borrower risk; (3) adjustments to reflect risks associated with the characteristics of the property; and (4) adjustments to reflect the differences between the government bond and the mortgage.[10] The mortgage industry term for the sum of these adjustments to the base rate represented by the riskless government bond to adjust for risks and structural differences is *spread.*

In the United States, the rule of thumb is that a 30-year FRM is paid off in 7 to 10 years.[11] As a result of the 7-to-10-year life, most mortgage calculations are based on the interest rate on a 10- year Treasury bond. For example, a decrease in the interest rate on 10-year Treasuries will lead to lower mortgage interest rates and more prepayments as borrowers refinance their mortgages to take advantage of lower interest rates.

Adjustable-rate mortgages (ARMs) use one of a variety of interest rates plus a mark-up or spread instead of Treasury bonds as the basis for determining the interest rate paid by the borrower.[12] In many economic environments, lenders are willing to offer ARMs with lower interest rates than similar FRMs because the interest rate increases if the index rate or reference increases; this protects the lender against being locked into a loan that pays less than other loans. Borrowers can find ARMs attractive because of the potentially lower interest rates, the chance of future decreases in the mortgage rate, and limits (caps) on the increase in the interest rates. An ARM with a lower or "teaser" initial rate can be attractive to a homebuyer who plans to move before the teaser rate ends.

Borrower risk is typically assessed in terms of credit history (perhaps summarized by the borrower's FICO [formerly Fair Isaac Company] score), and debt-to-income ratio. The better an individual's credit history and the lower the debt-to-income ratio, the lower the spread that will be charged.

Property Characteristics

Property characteristics that influence risk assessments include the loan-to-value (LTV) ratio, and the type of property (owner occupied, investor, condominium, and manufactured housing). In general mortgages, with high LTVs, and mortgages on investor-owned property, on condominiums, and on manufactured housing properties are considered riskier and pay a higher interest rate. Sometimes lenders add a risk premium based on the location of a home.

Home Mortgages and Government Bonds

To a lender, a home mortgage loan is less valuable than a Treasury (or other government) bond of the same risk, maturity, and interest rate because the home mortgage comes with the option to prepay and risk of default.[13] To compensate for the relatively lower value, lenders seek higher interest rates on mortgages than on Treasury bonds. In the United States, the legal ability of lenders to seek full recourse from homeowners who have defaulted depends on state law, but until the recent recession, lenders frequently assumed that defaulters had few additional assets worth pursuing, regardless of state law. [14]

Some of the borrower and property characteristics such as FICO score and LTV jointly determine the mortgage interest rate that is charged.[15]

In the United States, lenders advertise mortgage rates on the internet and in newspapers; this rate is adjusted (usually increased) based on borrower and property characteristics.

Canada

Canadian banks post rates for various types of mortgages. Borrowers with good credit can negotiate appreciable discounts on one type of mortgage (five-year fixed rates, which are explained in the "House Price Changes" section). For example, in 2009, the Canadian Association of Accredited Mortgage Professionals (CAAMP) reported that the average advertised rate on one type of mortgage was 5.97%, but that the average mortgage rate actually paid was 4.74%.[16]

Denmark

In Denmark, mortgage interest rates are fixed at the time of the loan. The bonds financing the loan are pass-through bonds issued on the stock exchange, where the terms of the bonds exactly match the terms of the loan.[17] Thus, the borrowers pay the market interest rate at the time of the loan, and the rates are posted by the stock exchange.

Other European Countries

Recent European interest rates on mortgages with short-term initial fixed period rates have been in the range of 3.04% (Spain) to 4.77% (Netherlands); mortgages with long-term initial fixed period rates and 10-year or more maturities have ranged from 4.30% (Germany) to 5.22% (Netherlands).[18]

Features of Selected National Mortgage Markets: The Homebuyer's View

United States

In the United States, mortgages can be split into three general groups: conforming, government insured, and other.[19] Conforming mortgages are those that meet the government-sponsored enterprises' (GSEs) purchase standards and do not exceed the statutory maximum mortgage amounts known as the conforming loan limits.[20] Government-insured mortgages are those guaranteed by the Federal Housing Administration (FHA), the Department of Veterans Affairs (VA), or the U.S. Department of Agriculture's rural housing program.[21] The other group includes mortgages that do not qualify as conforming and are not government insured;

this can happen if a mortgage exceeds the conforming loan limits (in which case the mortgage is known as a jumbo mortgage), if the borrower's credit quality is too low (in which case the mortgages are called subprime), or the mortgage application lacks full documentation about the borrower's income or assets (in which case the mortgage is called Alt-A, or alternative A).

At present, interest rates on FHA-insured and Veterans Affairs-guaranteed mortgages are not based on risk; every borrower pays approximately the same interest rate.[22] As discussed above, the interest rates for conforming mortgages and those in the "other" category are based on the risk associated with borrower, property, and lender characteristics.

Research at the Federal Reserve suggests that in normal times the GSEs mortgage market activity reduces the interest rate on mortgages by less 0.5% (50 basis points) compared to a world without GSEs.[23] There is no published research on the impact of the GSEs in the current economic environment, but in 2009 Fannie Mae and Freddie Mac issued 72% of all MBS suggesting that without the GSEs, mortgage availability would be lower and interest rates would be higher.[24]

Homeowners pay certain transaction costs that vary across (and sometimes within) nations. In the United States, borrowers frequently pay for real estate appraisals, land surveys, inspections, title insurance (which protects the lenders in case the sellers do not have a clear title to the properties being sold), origination fees (sometimes called *points*), lender services, and recording the new ownership and liens with state or local governments. Closing costs are lower in most other nations.

Loan Limits

In 2010, the conforming loan limit (the maximum mortgage that the GSEs can purchase) is $417,000 except for in high-cost areas in the contiguous 48 states where it varies to a maximum of $729,750. The conforming loan limit in Alaska, Hawaii, Guam, and the U.S. Virgin Islands is $625,500 (50% higher than the regular limit of $417,000), and the high cost maximum is $938,250. The conforming loan limit is reviewed annually.[25] FHA-insured mortgages are limited to $271,050, except for in high-cost areas where the limit varies to a maximum of $625,500. FHA loan limits are set specially in Alaska, Hawaii, Guam, and the U.S. Virgin Islands.[26]

The typical loan-to-value ratio in the United States on a new purchase or refinance money mortgage is 80%. Generally, borrowers who do not make at least a 20% downpayment must either purchase private mortgage insurance (PMI), or they obtain a government-insured mortgage.

Mortgage Payments

In the United States, home mortgages typically are for 30 years and have monthly payments that amortize the entire amount borrowed over the term of the loan. Biweekly mortgage payments, which pay off the loan more quickly, are not as common as they are in some other nations.

At times mortgages have been offered requiring only interest (or sometimes a fraction of the interest) to be paid for a period of time Such mortgages stopped being available at the start of the 2007-2009 recession.

In the United States, most prime mortgages can be prepaid without penalty. This is most commonly done to refinance a mortgage or when the homeowner moves. Many subprime mortgages with adjustable rates had low introductory rates and prepayment penalties to discourage borrowers from refinancing until after the higher rates became effective.

U.S. mortgages can be refinanced to take advantage of lower interest rates or to take equity out of the home. The amount of equity withdrawn increases the size of the mortgage, and it is paid to the homeowner when the refinancing is finalized or *closes*. Refinancing with an equity withdrawal is known as cash *out refinancing*. In a refinancing, most closing costs are incurred again. Prior to the current recession, cash out refinancing for more than the amount owed was common. Recently, Freddie Mac has reported that some homeowners have reduced the amount of the new mortgage by using cash to reduce the balance. On reason for a cash in refinancing is that the homeowner wanted to refinance, but needed more equity (money down) to qualify for the mortgage.

Assumptions

An assumable mortgage allows a new purchaser to take the place of the seller of a home in an existing mortgage. This option would be exercised by the new home purchaser only when it is to his advantage (e.g., can obtain a lower mortgage interest rate than otherwise), and consequently usually a disadvantage to the lender.

Most conforming mortgages are not assumable, although the housing GSEs say they will purchase these mortgages on a negotiated (as opposed to a standard) basis. Government-insured mortgages are assumable if the new borrower meets the current credit standards, and if the original borrower agrees to be responsible if the new borrower defaults. This liability makes assumption rare.

Foreclosure and Recourse

Foreclosure (the forced sale of a house because the borrower is delinquent in making mortgage payments) is governed by state law.[27] In addition to foreclosure and sale of the property to satisfy the debt, some states allow a lender to seek any unpaid balance through the courts (recourse). Even where recourse is permitted, most lenders have rarely exercised this option because most homeowners who default have few additional assets.

Taxation

Home mortgage interest is generally tax deductable for U.S. taxpayers who itemize deductions. There is a 100% capital gains exemption on a home that the owners have lived in for two of the last five years. For married couples filing jointly the maximum exemption is $500,000 and for taxpayers filing individually the exemption is $250,000.

Between April 9, 2008, and June 30, 2010, there were special tax credits ranging from $7,500 to $8,000 for qualifying homebuyers.[28]

Subprime

Subprime mortgages are those made to borrowers with less than prime credit histories. There is not a formal definition of the term. According to Federal Reserve Chairman Ben S. Bernanke, the annual size of the subprime market ranged from $35 billion (4.5% of the mortgage market) in 1994 to $600 billion (20%) in 2006.[29]

Low-Income Homeownership Efforts

In the United States, government policies to increase homeownership by low-income households have been the FHA-, VA-, and USDA-insured loan programs and involved the GSEs' affordable housing goals imposed by statute and regulation. There are also programs to provide downpayment assistance to low-income households and tax-free mortgage revenue bonds that municipalities can issue to reduce the mortgage interest rate paid by low- and moderate-income households.[30]

Other Nations

The only nations in the world offering long-term fixed-rate mortgages are the United States and Denmark[31]. In the other countries, mortgages are for shorter time periods and the interest rates adjust, sometimes monthly, sometimes every few years. This creates the risk that homeowners will not be able to afford the new payments. In Canada, this risk is eliminated by offering adjustable mortgages that extend or shorten the life of the mortgage to reflect the new interest rate.

Denmark and Canada place less emphasis than the United States and Australia on homeownership as an aspiration.[32] These other nations support low-income housing through a variety of programs and, in general, do not place as much emphasis on homeownership.

The amount of government intervention varies. Canada, Denmark, and Australia do not have anything similar to the GSEs in the United States. In Canada, government mortgage insurance (somewhat similar to the FHA's insurance) plays a major role for all borrowers regardless of income or the amount borrowed.

Canada, Denmark, and Australia have some tax support for owner-occupied housing. In Canada and Australia, much of the intervention in the housing markets is to support indigenous and immigrant populations.

Arguably, underwriting standards in Canada, Denmark, and Australia have been stricter than in the United States.

Canada

Key differences between U.S. and Canadian mortgages are as follows:

- Canadian mortgages are more likely to have adjustable rates, prepayment penalties, and are currently easier to obtain with high loan-to-value (LTV) ratios.
- Most Canadian mortgages with less than 20% down are 100% guaranteed under the National Housing Act (NHA) by a government corporation (the Canadian Home Mortgage Corporation or CHMC).[33] In contrast, most U.S. mortgages with less than 20% down are privately guaranteed for the difference between the downpayment and 20%.
- Canadian mortgages typically roll over every five years, even if they amortize over 30 years. If these mortgages are guaranteed by CHMC, the renewal is guaranteed and other banks can take them over. Closing costs are minimal or non-existent for rollovers.
- Canadian policy is to support programs that make rental and owner-occupied housing viable alternatives for all residents. Typically, various levels of government and

nonprofits contribute to reduce the cost of low-income homeownership. In the United States, most government intervention has been to open homeownership to low- and moderate-income households.[34]

- Minimum down payments in Canada have fluctuated in recent years from as little as 0% to 5% at the present time. The minimum downpayment in the United States on an FHA mortgage is presently 3.5%.
- Canadian mortgage payment schedules can be synchronized to one's pay schedule.

Canada supports housing options for low-income households through a variety of rental and ownership programs. Typically, various levels of government, CMHC, and nonprofits contribute to reduce the cost of low-income homeownership.[35]

Comparing mortgage costs in the United States and Canada is difficult, although one IMF study concluded that when interest rates, refinancing costs, and mortgage insurance costs are considered that similar prime borrowers pay similar amounts.[36]

CMHC is a government corporation that is partially supported through appropriations and partially self-funded. Appropriations cover assisted housing, implement other housing policy, and research. Mortgage insurance and securitization are commercially funded through fees, but the government provides the ultimate guarantee. CMHC pays the government for this guarantee.

The role of Canadian mortgage brokers has been growing in recent years. The provincial governments license brokers, and in some provinces brokers have a fiduciary responsibility to borrowers. Brokers are not paid yield spread premiums, which amount to extra payments for higher rate mortgages.

Loan Limits

Unlike the United States, there is no fixed dollar limit on a mortgage that can be securitized with government support. Nor are there any eligibility limits on government mortgage insurance.

In 2008 and 2009, the Canadian government enacted a number of mortgage requirements including limiting LTVs to 95%, prohibiting interest only loans, limiting the life of a mortgage to 35 years, and establishing other standards for government mortgages. The government also intervened in the secondary mortgage market by committing to purchase up to C$ 125 billion of insured mortgage pools. Approximately half that amount was spent.

In Canada, a conventional mortgage is one with an LTV of 80% or less.[37] Low downpayment mortgages are called high-ratio mortgages. By law, federally regulated depositories can hold a high-ratio mortgage only if there is mortgage insurance to protect against default.[38] This mortgage insurance can be provided by a government corporation, CMHC or a private company. CMHC guarantees 100% of the loan amount and private insurers guarantee 90%.[39] The typical new Canadian mortgage has an LTV of 75%.

Types of Mortgages

Interest rates on Canadian mortgages can be fixed for the life of the mortgage, or the interest rate can change. Mortgages with changeable interest rates can modify either the amount paid or the life of the mortgage.

Canadian mortgages that have adjustable rates are called variable rate mortgages and are tied to market rates. When the rate changes, the mortgage payment remains constant, and the amounts going for principal and interest are adjusted, that is, the amortization schedule and life of the mortgage are adjusted to reflect the new interest rate. Variable rate mortgages can have caps, but those with caps usually have higher interest rates.

Based on the length of the mortgage when it was initially taken out, the interest rates on most (62%) Canadian mortgages are fixed for four to five years, but interest rates were fixed for one year or less for 10% of mortgages, and only 12% of mortgages had fixed interest rates for more than five years.[40]

Mortgage Payments

Canadian mortgage payments are frequently weekly, biweekly or monthly and synchronous with one's pay schedule. Canadian mortgages usually have a term from six months to 10 years, but payments are designed so that it will take 25 to 30 years to pay off the mortgage. The homeowner owes the balance of the loan at the end of the mortgage's term. Unless the homeowner opts to pay off the mortgage in whole or part, the outstanding balance is automatically rolled over into a new mortgage without additional fees. If the mortgage is insured, the homeowner has the option to negotiate a better arrangement with another lender and to transfer the mortgage. This refinancing could be problematic if the balance on the mortgage is more than the value of the home or if lenders reduce their lending.[41]

Canadian mortgages can have prepayment penalties (closed mortgages) or not (open mortgages). A closed mortgage prepayment penalty is incurred even if the homeowner moves, although this is frequently waived if the homeowner obtains a new mortgage from the current lender. For closed mortgages, there is a closed period, such as the first three years, during which a certain amount (typically 15%-20%) of the principal can be prepaid. Open mortgages, which are usually for one year, can be prepaid like a U.S. mortgage. If a homeowner moves, the mortgage can be transferred to the new home

Assumption

Some Canadian mortgages are assumable, which reduces the purchaser's appraisal and lawyer's fees. Some Canadian mortgages can be used to purchase a different home. Both these options reduce the burden of any prepayment penalties.

Foreclosure and Recourse

Canadian lenders can force delinquent borrowers into bankruptcy. After foreclosure, Canadian lenders can pursue borrowers for any unrecovered losses.

Taxation

Mortgage interest is not tax deductable in Canada. Capital gains on a principal residence are usually not taxed.

Subprime

Canada has a small Alt-A or "non-prime" mortgage market for borrowers who do not document their income. In 2006, Canadian non-prime mortgage originations were 5% compared with 14- 20% in the United States.[42]

Low-Income Homeownership

The federal and provincial governments have a number of affordable housing programs, which include rental and homeownership. Low-income homeownership programs frequently target indigenous populations.

Denmark

Denmark traces its current mortgage finance system to 1797. The Danish mortgage market is based on underwriting criteria established by law, matching mortgages' terms to bond terms (the balance principle), high securitization rates, and recourse lending which makes a borrower personally liable if foreclosure does not raise sufficient funds to cover the outstanding debt and costs of foreclosure.

Denmark and the United States offer 30-year mortgages with constant (fixed) interest rates. Mortgages in most other nations are fixed for a few years at most.

Mortgages in Denmark are made by specially authorized banks and subject to underwriting criteria established by law. For example, the maximum loan-to-value (LTV) ratio is currently 80% for owner-occupied homes; the maximum LTV on other homes (e.g., vacation) is lower regardless of borrower credit history. Mortgage interest rates are published, and there are no adjustments for borrower characteristics. To qualify for any kind of mortgage, the borrower will typically be required to qualify for a 30-year fixed-rate mortgage. This cost is generally higher than for adjustable-rate mortgages.

Recent legislation, including the Financial Business Act of 2009, allows banks to apply to join mortgage banks in issuing Danish mortgage bonds. Another recent change, based on EU requirements, is that collateral must be added to mortgage bonds when an individual mortgage's loan-to-value ratio exceeds 80%.

Key differences between the mortgage finance systems in the United States and Denmark are as follows:

- In Denmark, borrowers have two options to refinance: they can refinance as in the United States or they can purchase their mortgage at the current market price. When interests decrease, they will use the refinancing option. When interest rates increase, bond prices decrease, and Danish homeowners can buy back their mortgages out of the bonds. This second option is not available in the United States.
- The Danish system uses mortgage bonds. In the United States, Federal Deposit Insurance Corporation (FDIC) regulations protect the government's claim on the assets of an insolvent insured depository by limiting the use of mortgage bonds.[43]
- Danish mortgage bonds are issued at market rates, and, except for a small processing fee, the corresponding interest rate is passed directly on to the homeowners. All borrowers with the same kind of mortgage will pay the same interest rate.
- The Danish mortgage bond system does not have risk-based tranches with different repayment priorities. The United States' MBS issued by the GSEs commonly have risk-based tranches.
- Denmark has statutory underwriting standards that would disqualify some homeowners in the United States.
- Foreclosure and deficiency judgments in Denmark are based on national law and typically take six months. In the United States, foreclosure and deficiency judgments vary by state and generally provide greater protection for homeowners.

Danish mortgage banks retain credit (default) risk and pass onto investors prepayment and interest rate risk. In the United States, most mortgage originators pass on all risk to the secondary mortgage market. The housing GSEs and the federal government retain credit risk, but investment banks in the secondary mortgage market pass credit risk on to investors. Prepayment and interest rate risk is held by whoever purchases the MBS (sometimes the housing GSEs, and sometimes institutional investors).

Types of Mortgages

The Danish mortgage system offers three types of mortgages: fixed rate, adjustable rate and floating rate.

FRMs typically are for 30 years and have the same interest rate for the life of the mortgage. Interest rates are usually higher than the alternatives, but monthly mortgage payments are fixed.

The interest rate on ARMs changes at predetermined intervals of one, two, three, four, or five years. The amount of the change depends on the interest index rate on mortgage bonds. ARMs generally offer lower initial interest rates (and monthly payments), but future payments and interest rates are not known. Floating-rate mortgages are similar to ARMs, but the interest rate adjusts at shorter intervals such as three to six months. Floating-rate mortgages are set based on a reference rate (not the bond rate) such as the Copenhagen Interbank Offer Rate (Cibor). Interest rate caps are available.

All three types of mortgages can have initial interest-only payments. Mortgages can be payable either in Kroner or Euro, but most are Kroner-denominated.[44]

Mortgage Payments

Most Danish mortgages are for 30 years and are fully amortized over the term of the mortgage.

Prepayment depends, in part, on the type of the mortgage, but all borrowers can prepay their mortgage by purchasing their bond in the market. Mortgage transaction costs (closing costs) are around 0.4% of the amount borrowed compared with 2% in the United States.[45]

Fixed-Rate Mortgages

FRMs can be prepaid by paying the balance owed. If interest rates decrease, which generally raises the price of a bond, the borrower can use this option. If interest rates increase, which generally lowers the price of the bond, the bond repurchase option is used.

Adjustable-Rate Mortgages

ARMs can be prepaid for the amount owed at any interest rate reset, or by purchasing the bond on the market.

Floating-Rate Mortgages

Floating-rate mortgages can be prepaid in three ways:

- first, for the unpaid balance at an interest rate reset, the same as an ARM;
- second, at a previously agreed price, typically 100% of the unpaid balance at any time; and
- third, by purchasing the underlying bonds.

Loan Limits

There are no absolute limits on the size of Danish mortgages, but there are limits on the LTV (80% for prime residences).

Foreclosure and Recourse

A typical residential foreclosure in Denmark takes six months from default to sale of the property. The homeowner is responsible if the proceeds of the sale do not cover the amount owed.[46] Further legal action is possible if no other arrangements have been made to repay the balance owed.

Assumption

Danish mortgages can be assumed by the purchaser of the house.

Taxation

Mortgage interest payments are partly tax-deductible. There is no tax on capital gains from the sale of one's primary residence.

Australia

The U.S. and Australian housing finance systems exhibit both similarities and differences. Differences include the following:

- Australians appear to be more likely to select ARMs over FRMs. From July 2008 through February 2010 (the most recent available data), fewer than 10% of new mortgages have been "fixed rate," which in Australia means fixed for the first five years or less.[47] The reason for this might be that interest rates on ARMs have been much lower than on FRMs. Sometimes borrowers respond to price wars on a portion of the mortgage market. In contrast, in the United States, approximately 85% of mortgages outstanding are fixed rate.[48]
- Australians that have made extra payments on their mortgages can withdraw the prepaid funds. Some mortgages tie a credit card to the prepaid funds, but other mortgages charge a fee for redraws. This feature is not available in the United States, although U.S. lenders offer home equity lines of credit (HELOCs) that require a new loan application, approval and fees.
- The Australian government has no equivalent to the U.S. government's guaranteed mortgages.

Homeowners obtain mortgages from banks, credit unions and building societies (CUBS), and mortgage originators, which are similar to U.S. mortgage brokers and bankers.

Types of Mortgages and Features

The Australian mortgage finance system offers fixed- and adjustable-rate mortgages.

Fixed-Rate Mortgages

FRMs are generally limited to 15 years or less. Some FRMs convert after one to five years to ARMs for a total term of 25 years.

Adjustable-Rate Mortgages

ARMs (commonly called floating-rate mortgages in Australia) are more common than FRMs.

Most Australian mortgages are for 20-30 years, with the most typical maturity being 25 years. Monthly payments fully amortize the mortgage. Australian lenders charge most borrowers the same rate. There are, however, discretionary discounts offered to some borrowers, with sources indicating that this discount can be as much as 0.70% (70 basis points).

Low documentation loans are available, but they have higher interest rates. Self-employed borrowers frequently have difficulty providing independent verification and take out low-documentation loans even at this higher cost.

ARMs usually do not contain any prepayment penalties. FRMs frequently have either a fixed penalty or a penalty based on the difference between fixed and adjustable interest rates. Some Australians pay their mortgages off early by making monthly payments in excess of the contractual amount. Some mortgages have "redraw" facilities that allow households to withdraw excess payments and provide tax advantages to the homeowner.

In Australia, the cost of refinancing averages about 1.4% of the mortgage amount.[49] Prepayment fees average over 40% of the refinancing cost.

Assumption

Australian mortgages cannot be assumed.

Mortgage Insurance

Unlike the United States, there is no government mortgage insurance in Australia. Authorized deposit-taking institutions (ADIs) making mortgage loans must meet requirements promulgated under Basel II by the Australian Prudential Regulation Authority (APRA).[50] Mortgages are classified as standard eligible or non-standard eligible. To be considered standard, income must be documented and verified, property offered as collateral must be appraised, and the property offered as collateral must be readily marketable. All other mortgages are non-standard. Capital to offset potential losses is reduced for low LTV mortgages, when there is lender insurance covering at least 40% of the mortgage, and for standard mortgages. In the United States, capital requirements are reduced for mortgages packaged by the GSEs into mortgage-backed securities and for government guaranteed mortgages.

In the United States, private mortgage insurance is usually required for mortgages with LTVs above 80%.

Loan Limits

In Australia, there are no loan limits.

Foreclosure and Recourse

In addition to foreclosing on delinquent borrowers, lenders can use the legal process of sequestration to force borrowers into bankruptcy if the proceeds of foreclosure do not satisfy the debt. In the United States, state law determines if a borrower's other assets can be seized.[51]

Table 2. Selected Mortgage Characteristics

Country	Fixed Interest Rate	Adjustable Interest Rate	Pre-payment Allowed?	Owner Occupied Interest Tax Deductable?	Owner Occupied Capital Gains Taxation	Maximum Term
United States	Yes	Yes	Prime—yes, subprime—mostly no	Yes	Exempt if principal residence for two of last five years with maximum of $250-$500,000	30 years
Canada	Yes	Yes	Yes	No	Exempt	35 years
Denmark	Yes	Yes	Yes	Yes	Exempt	30 years
Australia	Limited duration	Yes	Fixed rate— yes, adjustable rate—during teaser (if any)	Yes	Exempt	30 years
Germany	Limited duration	Yes	With penalty	No	Exempt after 10 years	30 years
Italy	Limited duration	Yes		Yes	Exempt after five years	20 years (sometimes more)
Spain	Yes, but not common	Yes	Yes	Yes at 15% on a maximum of Euro 9,015	Exempt with age and holding requirements	60 years
Switzerland	No	Yes	Sometimes with penalty	Yes	Taxed mostly by cantons	Frequently non-amortizing
United Kingdom	Limited duration	Yes	Yes	No	Yes	30 years

Sources: Bank for International Settlements, *Housing Finance in the Global Financial Market,* Committee on the Global Financial System Paper 26, 2004, http://www.bis.org/publ/cgfs26.pdf; Royal Institution of Chartered Surveyors, *RICS European Housing Review 2009*; Martin Brown, *Country Note: Housing Finance in Switzerland*, Bank for International Settlements, 2005, http://www.bis.org/publ/wgpapers/cgfs26brown.pdf.

Taxation

Australia's tax system does not provide for any special treatment of mortgage interest. To the extent that a home is one's principal residence and not used to produce income, gains from selling the home are not taxed. When taxed, capital gains on a home are adjusted for inflation.

First Time Homebuyers

In July 2000, Australia adopted a First Home Owners Grant (FHOG) of AU$ 7,000 (approximately $5,600).[52] Since 2000, there have been a few first homeowners' assistance programs, augmenting the original AU $7,000. Most recently, this has included the "First Home Owners Boost Scheme" between October 2008 and December 2009. However, these temporary programs have expired and only the $7,000 FHOG remains.

Since October 2008, Australia has reduced the tax rate on savings dedicated to purchasing a first home.

Subprime

In the past, subprime (credit-impaired or non-conforming) borrowers have been able to obtain mortgages, but at a higher interest rate than prime borrowers. It is estimated that less than 1% of outstanding loans in 2009 were subprime.[53]

Secondary Mortgage Markets: Funding Mortgages

United States

Mortgages are designed to allow households to purchase homes that cost many times their annual incomes without waiting many years to accumulate sufficient savings to pay the full price. Funding long-term, fixed-rate mortgages, such as the 30-year mortgage, that is most common in the United States and Denmark challenges lenders because most funds directly available to financial intermediaries, such as banks, are for relatively short terms (less than five or 10 years), whereas mortgages are paid off over longer time periods. The United States and the rest of the world have developed different solutions to this mismatch of the duration of funding and mortgages.

The prevalence of 30-year self-amortizing, fixed-rate mortgages in the United States makes mortgage funding more difficult than in countries with shorter-term or adjustable mortgages. A bank can minimize its interest rate risk—the risk that its profit margins will be reduced because of rising interest rates—by matching the term of its mortgages to the term of its deposits. As a practical matter, the longest-term insured bank deposits (certificates of deposit) are for five years. When a bank makes a mortgage loan for more than five years, it knows that it will have to obtain new funds or persuade the depositor to roll over the funds when the deposit term expires.[54] The result is that while funding mortgages with federally insured deposits can be profitable, there are certain risks that lenders need to consider.

One solution to the long-term funding challenges is ARMs, which are more popular in many other countries, because they shift the lender's interest rate risk to the borrower. In the United States, ARMs have been popular only in times of high fixed interest rates, such as the 1970s.

In the United States, a secondary mortgage market has developed in which Fannie Mae, Freddie Mac, Ginnie Mae, and others purchase existing mortgages.[55] The mortgages are pooled into mortgage-backed securities (MBS), which are sold to institutional investors. MBS represent a claim on the monthly payments of the underlying mortgages. Fannie Mae, Freddie Mac, and Ginnie Mae add their guarantee of timely payment of principal and interest to the investor; other MBS issuers do not add any guarantee to the MBS that they create.[56] The MBS are normally liquid and can be resold later to other investors.

Between 2001 and 2009, the GSEs share of the MBS market ranged between a low of 40% (2006) and a high of 73% (2008). Since 2008, the GSEs and Ginnie Mae together have issued 95% or more of the MBS issued.

Table 3 reports covered bonds and MBS issues as a percentage of all residential mortgages outstanding. In the United States, new MBS volume was 10.1% of mortgages outstanding. In Canada, new MBS volume was 3.6%. In Denmark, new MBS were 0.1%, and new covered bonds were 58.5%. In Australia new MBS were 15.6%. New covered bond issues were negligible or zero in the United States, Canada, and Australia.

In many other nations, mortgage funds are frequently raised in financial markets using covered bonds. This financial product, uncommon in the United States, provides the issuer's legal commitment to pay interest and principal, and the pledge of specific mortgages as collateral to guarantee this payment.[57]

The mortgages used as cover remain on the issuer's balance sheet. Covered-bond issuers make the payments regardless of the borrower's actions. As required by law or contract, a mortgage in default must be replaced, and if the value of the mortgages declines, additional mortgages (or other specified high-quality assets) must be added to the collateral pool. Like MBS, mortgage bonds are normally liquid and can be resold. Unlike MBS, Danish mortgage bonds are usually not divided into tranches.[58]

Canada

As a practical matter, the only MBS in Canada are NHA loans pooled by and guaranteed by the government corporation, CMHC. Sometimes lenders will pay for CMHC insurance to allow the mortgages to be pooled. These MBS are pass throughs, have no risk-based tranches, and carry a Canadian government (CMHC) guarantee. In addition to the MBS, the government assumes prepayment and credit risk on Canadian Mortgage Bonds (CMBs). CMHC or a private insurer guarantees the underlying mortgages and CMHC guarantees timely payment of principal and interest on the MBS. This is similar to the roles played by the FHA and Ginnie Mae in the United States. Most non-NHA loans are held and serviced by the original lender.

In the CMB program, the Canada Housing Trust purchases NHA MBS and issues the mortgage bonds, which pay interest semi-annually and return the principal at maturity. These mortgage bonds have a payment stream similar to corporate and government bonds, which usually pay interest semi-annually or quarterly and return the principal at maturity. The bonds are issued in sizes as small as C$ 1,000 and can be issued for any term, but usually are for five years.

In Canada, depositories hold 69% of residential mortgage debt. Of this 69%, chartered banks, which are depositories, hold 56%.[59]

Denmark

To raise funds for mortgages, a Danish mortgage bank sells mortgage bonds to investors. By Danish law, the term and interest rate of the mortgages and bonds must match. This is called the "balance principle." The Danish bonds use "tap" funding, that is, mortgages are added to a bond for two or three years. Bond rates are reported in Danish media. The interest rate on a specific mortgage depends on the specific bond used to fund it. Every qualifying applicant for a given mortgage type gets the same interest rate. The mortgage bank passes through homeowner payments to the investor holding the bond funding the specific mortgage, and the bank charges a margin (typically 0.5% of the loan balance) for operating costs including any losses. Until it is paid off, the mortgage remains on the bank's books. There are currently seven Danish mortgage banks and one other bank issuing Danish mortgage bonds.

Australia

Unlike in the United States, most Australian MBS have adjustable rates. Mortgage originators (brokers) largely sell their mortgages in MBS. The four largest Australian banks, which provide approximately 70% of the mortgage market, generally retain mortgages in portfolio. The CUBS (credit unions and building societies) securitize approximately 22% of their mortgages. The Australian Prudential Regulatory Authority (APRA), which regulates all financial services firms in the country, prohibits covered bonds.

Table 3 reports the extent that various countries issue covered bonds and MBS.

Table 3. Covered Bonds and Mortgage-Backed Securities as a Percentage of Residential Loans Outstanding (2008)

Country	Covered Bond Issues (Percentage of Residential Loans Outstanding)	Mortgage-Backed Security Issues (Percentage of Residential Loans Outstanding)
United States	—	20.1
Canada	—	3.6
Denmark	58.5	0.1
Australia	—	15.6
Austria	2.2	—
Belgium	—	1.9
Finland	2.6	—
France	1.6	1
Germany	3.6	0.2
Greece	—	6.2
Ireland	4	6.6
Italy	—	4.7

Table 3. (Continued)

Country	Covered Bond Issues (Percentage of Residential Loans Outstanding)	Mortgage-Backed Security Issues (Percentage of Residential Loans Outstanding)
Japan	—	4.7
Netherlands	0.7	4.6
Norway	—	—
Spain	11.1	5.7
Sweden	10.1	0.9
United Kingdom	0.9	6.4

Source: International Monetary Fund, "Chapter 3. The Changing Housing Cycle and the Implications for Monetary Policy, "*World Economic Outlook* April 2008, http://www.imf.org/external/pubs/ft/weo/2008/01/pdf/ c3.pdf.

CONCLUSION

The mortgage markets in all four nations—the United States, Canada, Denmark, and Australia— seem to have more differences than features in common. Yet except for Denmark, they have similar homeownership rates. Some possible reasons for this similar outcome are as follows:

- Demographic similarities could be more important than institutional details.
- Some differences in mortgage underwriting, such as minimum downpayment requirements, could delay homeownership on average for relatively short periods of time.
- Some features, such as the mortgage interest deduction and the treatment of capital gains on owner-occupied homes, could be built into the price of housing, reducing or eliminating the advantages given to homeownership.

BIBLIOGRAPHY

General

Green, Richard K. and Susan M. Wachter. "The American Mortgage in Historical and International Context." *Journal of Economic Perspectives*, vol. 19, no. 4 (Autumn 2005), pp. 93-114.

Lehnert, Andreas. "Overview of US Mortgage Markets." Bank for International Settlements. Housing Finance in the Global Financial Market. CGFS Publications no. 26 (2005). At http://www.bis.org/publ/cgfs26cbpapers.htm.

Canada

Canada Mortgage and Housing Corporation. *The Newcomer's Guide to Canadian Housing.* 2007. At http://www.cmhc-schl.gc.ca/en/co/buho/upload/TheNewcomersGuide_E.pdf.

Kiff, John, Steve Mennill, and Graydon Paulin. "How the Canadian Housing Finance System Performed through the Credit Crisis: Lessons for Other Markets." *Journal of Structured Finance* (Fall 2010), pp. 1-21.

Kiff, John. *Canadian Residential Mortgage Markets: Boring but Effective.* International Monetary Fund, Working Paper WP/09/130. June 2009. At http://www.imf.org/external/pubs/ft/ wp/2009/wp09130.pdf.

Klyuev, Vladimir. *Show Me the Money: Access to Finance.* International Monetary Fund, Working Paper WP/08/22. January 2008. At http://www.imf.org/external/pubs/ft/wp/2008/ wp0822.pdf.

Denmark

Frankel, Allen, Jacob Gyntelberg, Kristian Kjeldsen, and Mattias Persson. "The Danish Mortgage Market." *BIS Quarterly Review* (March 2004), pp. 95-109. At http://www.bis.org/publ/qtrpdf/r_qt0403h.pdf?noframes=1.

Realkreditradet, *The Traditional Danish Mortgage Model.* At http://www.realkreditraadet.dk/Files/Filer/Engelsk/2010/Publikation_engelsk.PDF.

Australia

Ellis, Luci, Sue Black, and Liz Dixon Smith. *Housing Finance in Australia: 2005.* Bank for International Settlements. At http://www.bis.org/publ/wgpapers/cgfs26ellis.pdf.

End Notes

[1] The information in this report comes from national and international organizations, and from national housing experts in each of the countries examined. Published information was confirmed with these experts to ascertain that it is current at the time this report was written. Where multiple sources provided differing information, preference was given to the most authoritative and current information.

[2] The home price levels are discussed in more detail later in "House Price Changes." See also http://www.housepriceindex.ca.

[3] In most other nations, a long-term "fixed-rate" mortgage is fixed for only part of the mortgage's life.

[4] United States: U.S. Census Bureau, "Residential Vacancies and Homeownership in the Second Quarter 2010," press release, July 27, 2010, http://www.census.gov/hhes/www/housing

[5] Different nations collect and report this information on different schedules.

[6] Douglas B. Diamond, Jr. and Michael J. Lea, "Housing Finance in Developed Countries: An International Comparison of Efficiency, Chapter 4: Germany," *Journal of Housing Research*, 1992.

[7] Before gaining independence in 1991, Lithuania had been incorporated into the USSR. See Jose Palacin and Robert C. Shelburne, *The Private Housing Market in Eastern Europe and the CIS*, United Nations Economic Commission for Europe, Discussion Paper Series 2005.5, December 2005.

[8] Soula Proxenos, "Homeownership Rates: A Global Perspective," *Housing Finance International*, December 2002, pp. 3-7.

[9] Organization for Economic Cooperation and Development, "Annex Table 59. House Prices," *OECD Economic Outlook*, http://www.oecd.org/dataoecd/26/40/45801547.html.

[10] If there are only a few lenders, they could take advantage of market power to raise interest rates. These four factors would still determine differences in the rates paid by different borrowers.

[11] This can be because the homeowner refinances, moves, or decides to use other assets to eliminate the mortgage.

[12] These reference rates include the monthly weighted average cost of funds for 11th District savings institutions computed monthly by the Federal Home Loan Bank of San Francisco, the weekly average of secondary market interest rates on six-month negotiable certificates of deposit by the Board of Governors of the Federal Reserve System, the weekly average yield on United States Treasury Securities adjusted to a constant maturity of one year (as published by the Board of Governors of the Federal Reserve System), and the average of the London Interbank Offered Rates, also known as "LIBOR," for six-month U.S. dollar denominated deposits, as published in *The Wall Street Journal*.

[13] Financial analysts frequently consider default as an option. There is considerable research on this topic. For example, see Michael J. Brennan and Eduardo S. Schwartz, "Determinants of GNMA Mortgage Prices," *AREUEA Journal*, vol. 13, no. 3 (Fall 1985), pp. 209-228.

[14] Karen M. Pence, "Foreclosing on Opportunity: State Laws and Mortgage Credit," *Review of Economics and Statistics*, vol. 88 (February 2006), pp. 177-182. Also available as a working paper at http://www.federalreserve.gov/ pubs/feds/2003/200316/200316pap.pdf. Hereafter cited as Pence, "Foreclosing on Opportunity."

[15] For more details on how one large company in the secondary mortgage market (Fannie Mae) adjusts interest rates on mortgages, see Fannie Mae, *Loan Level Pricing Adjustment*, https://www.efanniemae.com/sf/refmaterials/llpa/pdf/llpamatrix.pdf. This website works only with Internet Explorer. See, also, Freddie Mac, *Exhibit 19 – Postsettlement Delivery Fees*, http://www.freddiemac.com/singlefamily/pdf/ex19.pdf.

[16] Will Dunning, *Annual State of the Residential Mortgage Market in Canada*, Canadian Association of Accredited Mortgage Professionals, November 2009, p. 26, http://www.caamp.org/meloncms/media Fall%20Report%20FINAL%20ENG.pdf.

[17] The servicer of a pass through bond collects payments and forwards them to the bondholders. There is only one class of bondholder.

[18] European Mortgage Federation, *Quarterly Review of European Mortgage Markets*, 1st Quarter 2010, p. 8, http://www.hypo.org/Content/default.asp?PageID=422. The Federation did not list comparable rates for the United States, Canada, Denmark, or Australia.

[19] Some researchers also refer to mortgages without government insurance as "conventional" mortgages. Conforming mortgages are a subset of conventional mortgages.

[20] GSEs have congressional charters and are stockholder owned; but they are restricted to certain specified businesses such as purchasing existing mortgages. These charters give them advantages over purely privately owned companies including an implied federal guarantee. Fannie Mae and Freddie Mac, two housing GSEs, are currently in conservatorship and managed by the federal government. For more information see CRS Report RL34661, *Fannie Mae's and Freddie Mac's Financial Problems*, by N. Eric Weiss. The Federal Home Loan Bank System is the third housing GSE and is solvent. For more information see CRS Report RL32815, *Federal Home Loan Bank System: Policy Issues*, by Edward V. Murphy.

[21] Technically, FHA insures mortgages, and VA and USDA guarantee them. Mortgage insurance pays the balance of the mortgage if the borrower defaults. A mortgage guarantee is a promise for the government to make specified payments if the borrower defaults.

[22] CRS Report R40937, *The Federal Housing Administration (FHA) and Risky Lending*, by Darryl E. Getter.

[23] Wayne Passmore, Roger Sparks, and Jamie Ingpen, "GSEs, Mortgage Rates, and the Long-Run Effects of Mortgage," *Journal of Real Estate Finance and Economics*, vol. 2-3, no. 25 (2002), pp. 215-244.

[24] Federal Housing Finance Agency, *Conservator's Report on the Enterprises' Financial Performance*, Second Quarter 2010, p. 5, http://www.fhfa.gov/webfiles/16592/ConservatorsRpt82610.pdf. Hereafter cited as FHFA, *Conservator's Report.*

[25] CRS Report RS22172, *The Conforming Loan Limit*, by N. Eric Weiss and Mark Jickling.

[26] Department of Housing and Urban Development, *FHA Mortgage* Limits, https://entp.hud.gov/idapp/html/hicostlook.cfm.

[27] Pence, "Foreclosing on Opportunity."

[28] CRS Report R40955, *An Economic Analysis of the Homebuyer Tax Credit*, by Mark P. Keightley.

[29] Ben S. Bernanke, "Fostering Sustainable Homeownership," Speech to National Community Reinvestment Coalition Annual Meeting, Washington, DC, March 14, 2008, http://www.federalreserve.gov/newsevents/speech bernanke20080314a.htm.

[30] CRS Report RS22934, *Treatment of Seller-Funded Downpayment Assistance in FHA-Insured Home Loans*, by Bruce E. Foote, and CRS Report RS22841, *Mortgage Revenue Bonds: Analysis of Sections 3021 and 3022 of the Housing and Economic Recovery Act of 2008*, by Mark P. Keightley and Erika K. Lunder.

[31] Michael Lea, *International Comparison of Mortgage Product Offerings*, Research Institute for Housing America and Mortgage Bankers Association, Special Report, September 2010, p. 8, http://www.housingamerica.org/Publications/ InternationalComparisonofMortgageProductOfferings.htm.

[32] Patricia Apps, "Home Ownership—The Australian Dream," *The Australian Quarterly*, vol. 48, no. 4 (December 1976), pp. 64-75, http://www.jstor.org/stable/pdfplus/20634876.pdf.

[33] Also known as Société canadienne d'hypothèques et de l'habitation (SCHL).

[34] Arguably, the GSEs have made homeownership more affordable to middle-income households, and the government-mandated GSE housing goals provided homeownership and rental support for low- and moderate-income households.

[35] Canada Mortgage and Housing Corporation, *Canadian Housing Observer 2009*, Chapter 2, pp. 15-35, http://www.cmhc-schl.gc.ca/en/corp/about/cahoob/upload/chapter_2_EN_2009.pdf.

[36] John Kiff, Canadian Residential Mortgage Markets: Boring but Effective, International Monetary Fund Working Paper WP/09/130, June 2009, http://www.imf.org/external/pubs/ft/wp/2009/wp09130.pdf.

[37] Canadian Mortgage and Housing Corporation, *Ready to Buy?*, http://www.cmhc-schl.gc.ca/en/co/buho/hostst/hostst_007.cfm.

[38] Canadian mortgage insurance covers the entire amount of the loan, whereas U.S. mortgage insurance covers only the amount above the 80% LTV level, i.e., it covers 20% of the mortgage.

[39] The Canadian government provides a backstop guarantee for private mortgage insurers. In the event a private mortgage insurer were to fail, the government would replace the company and guarantee 90% of loan. The fee structure is negotiated between the government and the insurer.

[40] CAAMP, p. 22.

[41] In the early 1980s, the rollovers and very large interest rate increases (due to high rates of inflation) caused some Canadian homeowners to default. See, John C. Given, "Loan Renewals Stun Canadian Homeowners," *Washington Post*, February 13, 1982, p. E6.

[42] Canada Mortgage and Housing Corporation, "Housing Finance," *Canadian Housing Observer 2009*, pp. 59-67.

[43] Federal Deposit Insurance Corporation, *FDIC Policy Statement on Covered Bonds*, Financial Institutions Letter FIL73-2008, August 24, 2008, http://www.fdic.gov/news/news/financial

[44] Denmark has not adopted the Euro and uses the Kroner, though the exchange rate is fixed.

[45] European Mortgage Federation, *Study on the Cost of Housing in Europe*, Brussels, Belgium, 2010, p. 13, http://intranet.hypo.org/Common/GetFile.asp?DocID=3379&logonname=guest&mfd=off and Glenn Canner, Karen Dynan, and Wayne Passmore, "Mortgage Refinancing in 2001 and Early 2002," *Federal Reserve Bulletin*, December 2002, p. 476.

[46] International Monetary Fund, *Denmark: Financial Sector Assessment Program—Technical Note—The Danish Market—A Comparative Analysis*, IMF Country Report No. 07/123, March 2007, p. 7, http://www.imf.org/external/pubs/ft/scr/2007/cr07123.pdf.

[47] Australian Bureau of Statistics, "Housing Finance Australia," press release, February 2010, http://www.abs.gov.au/ausstats/meisubs.NSF/log?openagent&560909a.xls&5609.0&Time%20Series%20Spreadsheet&0F9F61B78B418B48CA2577000014BC50&0&Feb%202010&12.04.2010&Latest.

[48] Federal Housing Finance Agency, "Single-Family Mortgages Outstanding, 1990 - 2009Q1," press release, 2010, http://www.fhfa.gov/webfiles/14597/SFMOutstanding1990to2009Q1.xls.

[49] Australian Securities & Investment Commission, *Review of Mortgage Entry and Exit Fees*, Report 125, April 2008, p. 7, http://www.fido.gov.au/asic/pdflib.nsf/LookupByFileName/ REP_125_Review_of_mortgage_entry_and_exit_fees.pdf/ $file/REP_125_Review_of_mortgage_entry_and_exit_fees.pdf.

[50] Australian Prudential Regulation Authority, *Capital Adequacy: Standardised Approach to Credit Risk*, Prudential Standard APS 112, January 2008, pp. 19-22, http://www.apra.gov.au/ADI/upload/Final-APS-112-November-2007.pdf.

[51] Pence, "Foreclosing on Opportunity."

[52] Federal Reserve Bank of New York, *Historical Foreign Exchange XML Data*, July 3, 2000, http://www.newyorkfed.org/xml/fx.html.

[53] Guy Debelle, Assistant Governor of the Reserve Bank of Australia, "The State of the Mortgage Market," Mortgage Innovation Conference, Sydney, March 30, 2010, p. 6, http://www.bis.org/review/r100401e.pdf?noframes=1.

[54] Insured depositories can borrow money by selling bonds, but they pay a higher interest rate than they pay on insured deposits. This higher rate makes bonds a less profitable way to fund mortgages.

[55] Many lenders find it more profitable to keep ARMs as investments and to sell FRMs.

[56] Payments from MBS are frequently divided into tranches that give different investors different amounts of risk, interest, and different timing of payments. In one relatively simple approach to tranches, some investors receive the interest from the mortgages, and other investors receive the repayment of principal.

[57] See CRS Report RS22925, *Covered Bonds: An Alternative to Securitization for Funding Mortgages*, by Edward V. Murphy.

[58] Likewise, European covered bonds are not normally divided into tranches.

[59] John Kiff, *Canadian Residential Mortgage Markets: Boring but Effective?*, International Monetary Fund, IMF Working Paper WP/09/130, June 2009, http://www.imf.org/external/pubs/ft/wp/2009/wp09130.pdf.

In: Select Foreign Markets and Industries
Editor: Peter M. Luján

ISBN: 978-1-62100-133-1

Chapter 2

TAX ADMINISTRATION: INFORMATION ON SELECTED FOREIGN PRACTICES THAT MAY PROVIDE USEFUL INSIGHTS*

United States Government Accountability Office

WHY GAO DID THIS STUDY

The Internal Revenue Service (IRS) and foreign tax administrators face similar issues regardless of the particular provisions of their laws. These issues include, for example, helping taxpayers prepare and file returns, and assuring tax compliance. Understanding how other tax administrators have used certain practices to address common issues can provide insights to help inform deliberations about tax reform and about possible administrative changes in the U.S. existing system to improve compliance, better serve taxpayers, reduce burdens, and increase efficiencies.

GAO was asked to describe (1) how foreign tax administrators have approached issues that are similar to those in the U.S. tax system and (2) whether and how the IRS identifies and adopts tax administration practices used elsewhere.

To do this, GAO reviewed documents and interviewed six foreign tax administrators. In some cases, GAO also interviewed tax experts, tax practitioners, taxpayers, and trade-group representatives who were selected based on their expertise or involvement in developing or using the foreign systems. GAO also examined documents and met with IRS officials.

WHAT GAO RECOMMENDS

GAO makes no recommendations in this report.

The IRS provided technical comments that are included in this report.

* This is an edited, reformatted and augmented version of the United States Government Accountability Office publication, Report to Congressional Requesters GAO-11-439, dated May 2011.

WHAT GAO FOUND

Foreign and U.S. tax administrators use many of the same practices such as information reporting, tax withholding, providing Web-based services, and finding new approaches for tax compliance. These practices, although common to each system, have important differences. This report describes the following six foreign tax administration practices that address common issues in tax administration.

Selected Foreign Tax Administration Practices	
Foreign administrator	Practice
New Zealand	Does integrated evaluations of tax expenditures and discretionary spending programs to analyze their effects and improve program delivery
Finland	Uses the Internet to calculate individual tax withholding rates and revise preprepared tax returns to improve service at lower costs
European Union	Uses multilateral treaty information exchange on interest payments to member nations' citizens to spur compliance by individual taxpayers
United Kingdom	Uses information reporting and withholding so most wage earners do not need to file a tax return
Australia	Uses a compliance program for high-net-wealth individuals that focuses on theirfull set of business interests to improve compliance
Hong Kong	Uses semiannual payments instead of periodic withholding for the Salaries Tax

Source: GAO.

Although differences in laws, culture, or other factors likely would affect the transferability of foreign tax practices to the United States, these practices may provide useful insights for policymakers and the IRS. For example, New Zealand integrates evaluations of its tax and discretionary spending programs. The evaluation of its Working For Families tax benefits and discretionary spending, which together financially assist low- and middle-income families to promote employment, found that its programs aided the transition to employment but that it still had an underserved population; these findings likely would not have emerged from separate evaluations.

GAO previously has reported that the United States lacks clarity on evaluating tax expenditures and related discretionary spending programs and does not generally undertake integrated evaluations. In Finland, electronic tax administration is part of a government policy to use electronic services to lower the cost of government and encourage private-sector growth. Overall, according to Finnish officials, electronic services have helped to reduce Tax Administration staff by over 11 percent from 2003 to 2009 while improving taxpayer service.

IRS officials learn about these practices based on interactions with other tax administrators and participation in international organizations, such as the Organisation for Economic Co-operation and Development.

In turn, the IRS may adopt new practices based on the needs of the U.S. tax system. For example, in 2009, the IRS formed the Global High Wealth Industry program. The IRS consulted with Australia about its approach and operational practices.

ABBREVIATIONS

ATO	Australian Taxation Office
CIAT	Center for Inter-American Tax Administration
EU	European Union
FTA	Forum on Tax Administration
HMRC	Her Majesty's Revenue and Customs
HNWI	High Net Wealth Individuals
IRD	Inland Revenue Department
IRS	Internal Revenue Service
JITSIC	Joint International Tax Shelter Information Centre
MOU	Memorandum of Understanding
MSD	Ministry of Social Development
OECD	Organisation for Economic Co-operation and Development
OMB	Office of Management and Budget
PAYE	Pay As You Earn
RDF	Risk Differentiation Framework
TIN	Taxpayer Identification Number
UK	United Kingdom
VAT	Value Added Tax
WFF	Working For Families

May 24, 2011
The Honorable Max Baucus
Chairman
The Honorable Orrin G. Hatch
Ranking Member
Committee on Finance
United States Senate

The Honorable Charles E. Grassley
Ranking Member
Committee on the Judiciary
United States Senate

Tax administrators around the world all strive to address similar issues regardless of the specific provisions of their laws. These issues include helping taxpayers prepare and file tax returns, keeping track of taxes owed and paid by various types of taxpayers, and assuring tax compliance. Understanding how other tax administrators have used certain practices to address these common issues can provide insights to help inform deliberations about tax reform and about possible administrative changes in our existing system to improve compliance, better serve taxpayers, reduce burden, and increase efficiencies. To assist you in considering the potential applicability of foreign tax administration practices for U.S. policy and practices, we will describe (1) how foreign tax administrators have approached issues that are similar to those in the U.S. tax system and (2) whether and how the Internal Revenue Service (IRS) identifies and adopts tax administration practices used elsewhere.

We selected six foreign tax administrators' approaches to practices that were different than the approach to a similar practice in the United States as shown in table 1.

Table 1. Selected Foreign Tax Administration Practices

Foreign tax administrators	Practice
New Zealand	Does integrated evaluations of tax expenditures and discretionary spending programs to analyze their effects and improve program delivery
Finland	Uses the Internet to calculate individual tax withholding rates and revise preprepared tax returns to improve service at lower costs
European Union	Uses multilateral treaty information exchange on interest payments to member nations' citizens to spur compliance by individual taxpayers
United Kingdom	Uses information reporting and withholding so most wage earners do not need to file a tax return
Australia	Uses a compliance program for high-net-wealth individuals thatfocuses on their full set of business interests to improve compliance
Hong Kong	Uses semiannual payments instead of periodic withholding for the Salaries Tax

Source: GAO.

We based our selection of these practices on several factors, including whether the tax administrators had advanced economies and tax systems, tax information was available in English, and the foreign tax administrator's approach differed, at least in part, from how the United States approaches similar issues. We primarily used documentation from each government's reports that are publicly available. When possible, we confirmed additional information provided to us by officials. To identify taxpayers' attitudes toward Hong Kong's semiannual payment system, we interviewed experts who were either university professors, were the authors of publications on Hong Kong's tax system, or were practitioners in well-known law or accounting firms. To understand the development of Finland's Internet-based withholding estimation and prepared returns system, we met with the public interest and trade groups that provided assistance to Finland's Parliament during the system's development.

To describe whether and how the IRS identifies and adopts tax administration practices used elsewhere, we reviewed related documents and interviewed IRS officials. To help ensure the accuracy of the information we present, we shared a summary of our descriptions with representatives of the six foreign tax administrators and incorporated their comments as appropriate. The IRS provided technical comments that are included in this report.

The descriptive information on the practices of foreign administrators presented in this report may provide useful insights for Congress and others on enhancements to current U.S. tax policies and practices. However, it was beyond the scope of this report to identify and assess the factors that might affect the transferability of the practices to the United States. For example, nations have differing cultures and differing attitudes toward government, sometimes called "tax morale." Generally, higher tax morale has been found to be positively related to high levels of voluntary tax compliance. To the extent that taxpayers in some countries are more willing to fully comply with tax rules, voluntary tax compliance is higher and less enforcement action is needed by the tax administrator. Thus, those nations' tax enforcement practices may not be as appropriate in other nations where citizens have lower tax morale. Measurements of tax morale generally are not well defined or uniform; nor are measurements of voluntary tax compliance.

We conducted our work from October 2009 to May 2011 in accordance with all sections of GAO's Quality Assurance Framework that are relevant to our objectives. The framework requires that we plan and perform the engagement to obtain sufficient and appropriate evidence to meet our stated objectives and to discuss any limitations in our work. We believe that the information and data obtained, and the analysis conducted, provide a reasonable basis for any findings and conclusions in this report. A more detailed discussion of our methodology for each objective is in appendix I.

BACKGROUND

The IRS and tax administrators worldwide generally use similar administrative practices.

Information Reporting

Information reporting is a widely accepted practice for increasing taxpayer compliance. Under U.S. law, some types of transactions are required to be reported to the IRS by third parties who make payments to, or sometimes receive payments from, individual taxpayers. Typically, information returns represent income paid to the taxpayer, such as wages or bank account interest.[1]

After tax returns are filed, the IRS then matches the amounts reported on information returns to the amounts reported on the taxpayer's return. For any differences, the IRS may send a notice to the taxpayer requesting an explanation. If the taxpayer does not respond to the notice, the IRS may make an additional assessment. For fiscal year 2010, the IRS received over 2.7 billion information returns, sent 5.5 million notices on differences between information returns and tax returns, and assessed an additional $20.7 billion in taxes, interest, and penalties.

Withholding

Withholding is a widely accepted practice to increase taxpayer compliance. Under U.S. law, employers must withhold income tax from the wages paid to employees.[2] Withholding from salaries requires wage earners to pay enough tax during the tax year to assure that they will not face a large payment at year end. Also, withholding can be required as a backup to information reporting if a payee fails to furnish a correct taxpayer identification number (TIN).

If the payee refuses to furnish a TIN, the payer generally withholds 28 percent of the amount of the payment— for example, interest payments on a bank account—and remits that amount to the IRS.

Electronic Tax Administration

Many tax administrators in the United States and worldwide have increasingly used electronic tax administration to improve services and reduce costs. The IRS has focused its electronic tax administration on filing tax returns over the Internet, providing taxpayer assistance through its Web site, and providing telephone assistance.

To accept electronically filed tax returns, IRS has authorized preapproved e-file providers to submit the returns. IRS cannot accept electronically filed returns directly from taxpayers. Through its Web site, IRS provides taxpayers with publications explaining tax law and IRS administrative procedure.

The Web site also provides automated services such as "Where's My Refund?" During the 2010 filing season, the IRS Web site had 239 million total visits and 277 million searches. IRS also received 77 million telephone calls of which IRS phone assistors answered about 24 million calls.[3]

Tax Enforcement

The U.S. tax system, as well as many other tax systems worldwide, is based on some degree of self-reporting and voluntary compliance by taxpayers. Tax administrations worldwide have enforcement programs to ensure that tax returns are accurate and complete and taxes are paid. Among others, IRS uses two principal enforcement programs. After tax returns have been filed, the Automated Underreporter Program matches data on information returns (usually on income) provided by employers, banks, and other payers of income to data reported on taxpayers' tax returns.

IRS may contact taxpayers about any differences. The Examination Program relies on IRS auditors to check compliance in reporting income, deductions, credits, and other issues on tax returns by reviewing the documents taxpayers provided to support their tax return.

IRS, like revenue agencies in many countries, administers tax expenditures. Tax expenditures are tax provisions that grant special tax relief for certain kinds of behavior by taxpayers or for taxpayers in special circumstances.

Tax expenditures reduce the amount of taxes owed and therefore are seen as resulting in the government forgoing revenues. These provisions are viewed by many analysts as spending channeled through the tax system. For fiscal year 2010, the U.S. Department of the Treasury reported 173 tax expenditures costing, in aggregate, more than $1 trillion.[4]

Tax expenditures are often aimed at policy goals similar to those of federal spending programs, such encouraging economic development in disadvantaged areas and financing postsecondary education. In 2005, we reported that all U.S. federal spending and tax policy tools, including tax expenditures, should be reexamined to ensure that they are achieving their intended purposes and designed in the most efficient and effective manner.[5]

Examples of Selected Tax Administration Practices to Address Known Tax Administration Issues

The following examples illustrate how New Zealand, Finland, the European Union (EU), the United Kingdom (UK), Australia, and Hong Kong have addressed well-known tax administration issues.[6] Our work does not suggest that these practices should or should not be adopted by the United States.

New Zealand Does Integrated Evaluations of Tax Expenditures and Discretionary Spending Programs to Analyze Their Effects and Improve Program Delivery

New Zealand, like the United States, addresses various national objectives through a combination of tax expenditures and discretionary spending programs. In New Zealand, tax expenditures are known as tax credits. New Zealand has overcome obstacles to evaluating these related programs at the same time to better judge whether they are working effectively.

Rather than doing separate evaluations, New Zealand completes integrated evaluations of tax expenditures and discretionary spending programs to analyze their combined effects. Using this approach, New Zealand can determine, in part, whether tax expenditures and discretionary spending programs work together to accomplish government goals.

One example is the Working For Families (WFF) Tax Credits program, which is an entitlement for families with dependent children to promote employment. Prior to the introduction of WFF in 2004, New Zealand's Parliament discovered that many low-income families were not better off from holding a low-paying job, and those who needed to pay for childcare to work were generally worse off in low-paid work compared to receiving government benefits absent having a job. This prompted Parliament to change its in-work incentives and financial support including tax expenditures.

The WFF Tax Credits program differs from tax credit programs in the United States in that it is an umbrella program that spans certain tax credits administered by the Inland Revenue Department (IRD) as well as discretionary spending programs administered by the Ministry of Social Development (MSD). IRD collects most of the revenue and administers the tax expenditures for the government. Being responsible for collecting sensitive taxpayer information, IRD must maintain tax privacy and protect the integrity of the New Zealand tax system. MSD administers the WFF's program funds and is responsible for collecting data that include monthly income received by its beneficiaries. Given different responsibilities, IRD and MSD keep separate datasets, making it difficult to assess the cumulative effect of the WFF program.

Therefore, to understand the cumulative effect of changes made to the WFF program and ensure that eligible participants were using it, New Zealand created a joint research program between IRD and MSD that ran from October 2004 to April 2010. The joint research program created linked datasets between IRD and MSD. Access to sensitive taxpayer information was restricted to IRD employees on the joint research program and to authorized MSD employees only after they were sworn in as IRD employees.

The research provided information on key outcomes that could only be tracked through the linked datasets. The research found that the WFF program aided the transition from relying on government benefits to employment, as intended. It also found that a disproportionate number of those not participating in the program faced barriers to taking advantage of the WFF. Barriers included the perceived stigma from receiving government aid, the transaction costs of too many rules and regulations, and the small amounts of aid for some participants. On the basis of these findings, Parliament made changes to WFF that provided an additional NZ$1.6 billion (US$1.2 billion) per year in increased financial entitlements and in-work support to low- to middle-income families.[7]

Appendix II provides more details on New Zealand's evaluation of tax expenditures as well as similarities and differences to the U.S. system.

Finland Uses the Internet to Calculate Individual Tax Withholding Rates and Revise Preprepared Tax Returns to Improve Service at Lower Costs

Finland encourages accurate withholding of taxes from taxpayers' income, lowers its costs, and reduces taxpayers' filing burdens through Internet-based electronic services. In 2006, Finland established a system, called the Tax Card, to help taxpayers estimate a withholding rate for the individual income tax. The Tax Card, based in the Internet, covers Finland's national tax, municipality tax, social security tax, and church tax.[8] The Tax Card is accessed through secured systems in the taxpayer's Web bank or an access card issued by Finland's government. The Tax Card system enables taxpayers to update their withholding rate as many times as needed throughout the year, adjusting for events that increase or decrease their income tax liability. When completed, the employer is notified of the changed withholding tax rate through the mail or by the employee providing a copy to the employer. According to the Tax Administration, about a third of all taxpayers using the Tax Card—about 1.6 million people—change their withholding percentages at least annually. Finland generally refunds a small amount of the withheld funds to taxpayers (e.g., it refunded about 8 percent of the withheld money in 2007).

Finland also has been preparing income tax returns for individuals since 2006. The Tax Administration prepares the return for the tax year ending on December 31st based on third-party information returns, such as reporting by employers on wages paid or by banks on interest paid to taxpayers. During April, the Tax Administration mails the preprepared return for the taxpayer's review. Taxpayers can revise the paper form and return it to the Tax Administration in the mail or revise the return electronically online. According to Tax Administration officials, about 3.5 million people do not ask to change their tax return and about 1.5 million will request a tax change.

Electronic tax administration is part of a governmentwide policy to use electronic services to lower the cost of government and encourage growth in the private sector. According to Tax Administration staff, increasing electronic services to taxpayers helps to lower costs. Overall, the growth of electronic services, according to Finnish officials, has helped to reduce Tax Administration staff by over 11 percent from 2003 to 2009 while improving taxpayer service.

According to officials of the Finnish government as well as public-interest and trade groups, the Tax Card and preprepared return systems were established under a strong culture of national cooperation. For the preprepared return system to work properly, Finland's business and other organizations that prepare information returns had to accept the burden to comply in filing accurate returns promptly following the end of the tax year.

Finland's tax system is positively viewed by taxpayers and industry groups, according to our discussions with several industry and taxpayer groups. They stated that Finland has a simple, stable tax system which makes compliance easier to achieve. As a result, few individuals use a tax advisor to help prepare and file their annual income tax return.

Appendix III provides more details on Finland's electronic tax administration system as well as a discussion of similarities to and differences from the U.S. system.

EU's Multilateral Treaty Information Exchange on Interest Payments to Member Nations' Citizens to Spur Compliance by Individual Taxpayers

The EU seeks to improve tax compliance through a multilateral agreement on the exchange of information on interest earned by each nation's individual taxpayers. This agreement addresses common issues with the accuracy and usefulness of information exchanged among nations that have differing technical, language, and formatting approaches for recording and transmitting such information. Under the treaty, called the Savings Taxation Directive, adopted in June 2003, the 27 EU members and 10 other participants agreed to share information about income from interest payments made to individuals who are citizens in another member nation. With this information, the tax authorities are able to verify whether their citizens properly reported and paid tax on the interest income. The directive provides the basic framework for the information exchange, defining essential terms and establishing automatic information exchange among members.[9]

As part of the directive, 3 EU member nations as well as the 5 European nonmember nations agreed to apply a withholding tax with revenue sharing (described below) during a transition period through 2011, rather than automatically exchanging information.[10] Under this provision, a 15 percent withholding tax gradually increases to 35 percent by July 1, 2011. The withholding provision included a revenue-sharing provision, which authorizes the withholding nation to retain 25 percent of the tax collected and transfer the other 75 percent to the nation of the account owner. The directive also requires the account owner's home nation to ensure that withholding does not result in double taxation. The directive does this by granting a tax credit equal to the amount of tax paid to the nation in which the account is located.

A September 2008 report to the EU Council described the status of the directive's implementation. During the first 18 months of information exchange and withholding, data limitations such as incomplete information on the data exchanged and tax withheld created major difficulties for evaluating the directive's effectiveness. Further, no benchmark was available to measure the effect of the changes.

According to EU officials, the most common administrative issues, especially during the first years of implementation of the directive, have been the identification of the owner reported in the computerized format. It is generally recognized that a Taxpayer Identification Number (TIN) provides the best means of identifying the owner. However, the current directive does not require paying agents to record a TIN. Using names has caused problems when other EU member states tried to access the data. For example, a name that is misspelled cannot be matched. In addition, how some member states format their mailing address may have led to data-access problems.

Other problems with implementing the directive include identifying whether investors moved their assets into categories not covered by the directive (e.g., shifting to equity investments), and concerns that tax withholding provisions may not be effective because withholding rates were low until 2011 when the rate became 35 percent. The EU also identified problems with the definition of terms, making uniform application of the directive difficult. Generally these terms identify which payments are covered by the directive, who must report under the directive, and who owns the interest for tax purposes.

Nevertheless, EU officials stated that the quality of data has improved over the years. The EU officials have worked with EU member nations to resolve specific data issues, which has contributed to the effective use of the information exchanged under the directive. EU officials told us that the monitoring role by the EU Commission, the data-corrections process, and frequent contacts to resolve specific issues have contributed to effective use of the data received by EU member states.

Appendix IV provides more details on the EU Saving Taxation Directive and related issues such as avoiding double taxation as well as a discussion of similarities to and differences from the U.S. system.

UK Uses Information Reporting and Withholding So Most Wage Earners Do Not Need to File a Tax Return

The UK promotes accurate tax withholding and reduces taxpayers' filing burdens by calculating withholding rates for taxpayers and requiring that payers of certain types of income withhold taxes at standard rates. The UK uses information reporting and withholding to simplify tax reporting and tax payments for individual tax returns. Both the individual taxpayer and Her Majesty's Revenue and Customs (HMRC)—the tax administrator—are to receive information returns from third parties that make payments to a taxpayer such as for bank account interest.

A key element is the UK's Pay As You Earn (PAYE) system. Under the PAYE system, HMRC calculates an amount of withholding from wages to meet a taxpayer's liability for the current tax year based on information reporting from the employer and other income information employees may provide. According to HMRC officials, the individual tax system in the UK is simple for most taxpayers who are subject to PAYE. PAYE makes it unnecessary for wage earners to file a yearly tax return, unless special circumstances apply. For example, wage earners do not need to file a return unless income from interest, dividends, or capital gains exceeds certain thresholds or if deductions need to be reported. Therefore, a tax return may not be required because most individuals do not earn enough of these income types to trigger self-reporting. For example, the first £10,100 (US$16,239) of capital gains income is exempt from being reported on tax returns.[11]

PAYE also facilitates the reconciliation of tax liabilities for prior tax years through the use of withholding at source for wages. The withheld amount may be adjusted by HMRC to collect any unpaid taxes from previous years or refund overpayments. HMRC annually notifies the taxpayer and employer of the amount to withhold.

HMRC also may adjust the withheld amount through information provided by taxpayers. If taxpayers provide the information on their other income such as self-employment earnings, rental income, or investment income, HMRC can adjust the PAYE withholding. Individuals not under the PAYE system are required to file a tax return after the end of the tax year based on their records.

In addition, HMRC uses information reporting and tax withholding as part of its two-step process to assess the compliance risks on filed returns. In the first step, individual tax returns are reviewed for inherent compliance risks because of the taxpayers' income level and complexity of the tax return. For example, wealthy taxpayers with complex business income are considered to have a higher compliance risk than a wage earner. In the second step, information compiled from various sources—including information returns and public sources—is analyzed to identify returns with a high compliance risk. According to HMRC officials, these assessments have allowed HMRC to look at national and regional trends. HMRC is also attempting to uncover emerging compliance problems by combining and analyzing data from the above sources as well as others.

Appendix V provides more details on the UK's information reporting and withholding system as well as a discussion of similarities to and differences from the U.S. system.

Australia Uses a Compliance Program for High-Net-Wealth Individuals that Focuses on Their Full Set of Business Interests to Improve Compliance

The Australian High Net Wealth Individuals (HNWI) program focuses on the characteristics of wealthy taxpayers that affect their tax compliance. High-wealth individuals often have complex business relationships involving many entities they may directly control or indirectly influence and these relationships may be used to reduce taxes illegally or in a manner that policymakers may not have intended. The HNWI program requires these taxpayers to provide information on these relationships and provides such taxpayers additional guidance on proper tax reporting.

According to the Australian Taxation Office (ATO), in the mid-1990s, ATO was perceived as enforcing strict sanctions on the average taxpayers but not the wealthy. By 2008, ATO found that high-wealth taxpayers, those with a net worth of more than A$30 million (US$20.9 million), had substantial income from complex arrangements,[12] which made it difficult for ATO to identify and assure compliance. ATO concluded that the wealthy required a different tax administration approach.

ATO set up a special task force to improve its understanding of wealthy taxpayers, identify their tax planning techniques, and improve voluntary compliance. Due to some wealthy taxpayers' aggressive tax planning, which ATO defines as investment schemes and legal structures that do not comply with the law, ATO quickly realized that it could not reach its goals for voluntary compliance for this group by examining taxpayers as individual entities. To tackle the problem, ATO began to view wealthy taxpayers as part of a group of related business and other entities. Focusing on control over related entities rather than on just individual tax obligations provided a better understanding of wealthy individuals' compliance issues.

The HNWI approach followed ATO's general compliance model. The model's premise is that tax administrators can influence tax compliance behavior through their responses and interventions. For compliant wealthy taxpayers, ATO developed a detailed questionnaire and expanded the information on business relationships that these taxpayers must report on their tax return. For noncompliant wealthy taxpayers, ATO is to assess the tax risk and then determine the intensity of ATO's compliance interventions.

According to 2008 ATO data, the HNWI program has produced financial benefits. From the establishment of the program in 1996 until 2007, ATO had collected A$1.9 billion (US$1.67 billion) in additional revenue and reduced revenue losses by A$1.75 billion (US$1.5 billion) through compliance activities focused on highly wealthy individuals and their associated entities.[13] ATO's program focus on high-wealth individuals and their related entities has been adopted by other tax administrators. By 2009, nine other countries, including the United States, had formed groups to focus resources on high-wealth individuals.

Appendix VI provides more details on Australia's high-wealth program as well as similarities and differences to the U.S. system.

Hong Kong Uses Semiannual Payments Instead of Periodic Employer Withholding for the Salaries Tax

Although withholding of taxes by payers of income is a common practice to ensure high levels of taxpayer compliance, Hong Kong's Salaries Tax does not require withholding by employers. Instead, tax administrators and taxpayers appear to find a semiannual payment approach effective. Hong Kong's Salaries Tax is a tax on wages and salaries with a small number of deductions (e.g., charitable donations and mortgage interest). The Salaries Tax is paid by about 40 percent of the estimated 3.4 million wage earners in Hong Kong, while the other 60 percent are exempt from Salaries Tax.

Rather than using periodic (e.g., biweekly or monthly) tax withholding by employers, Hong Kong collects the Salaries Tax through two payments by taxpayers for a tax year. Since the tax year runs for April 1st through March 31st, a substantial portion of income for the tax year is earned by January (i.e., income for April to December), and the taxpayer is to pay 75 percent of the tax for that tax year in January (as well as pay any unpaid tax from the previous year). The remaining 25 percent of the estimated tax is to be paid 3 months later in April.

By early May, the Inland Revenue Department (IRD)—the tax administrator—annually prepares individual tax returns for taxpayers based on information returns filed by employers. Taxpayers review the prepared return, make any revisions such as including deductions (e.g., charitable contributions), and file it with IRD. IRD then will review the returns and determine if any additional tax is due. If the final Salaries Tax assessment turns out to be higher than the estimated tax previously assessed, IRD is to notify the taxpayer, who is to pay the additional tax concurrently with the January payment of estimated tax for the next tax year.

Hong Kong's tax system is positively viewed by tax experts, practitioners, and a public opinion expert based on our discussions with them. They generally believe that low tax rates, a simple system, and cultural values contribute to Hong Kong's collection of the Salaries Tax through the two payments rather than periodic withholding. Tax rates are fairly low, starting at 2 percent of the adjusted salary earned and not exceeding 15 percent. Further, tax experts told us that the Salaries Tax system is simple. Few taxpayers use a tax preparer because the tax form is very straightforward and the tax system is described as "stable." Further, an expert on public opinion in Hong Kong told us that taxpayers fear a loss of face if recognized as not complying with tax law. This cultural attitude helps promote compliance.

Appendix VII provides more details on Hong Kong's Salaries Tax system as well as a discussion of similarities to and differences from the U.S. system.

IRS CONSIDERS FOREIGN TAX PRACTICES THAT MIGHT MERIT ADOPTION

IRS officials learn about foreign tax practices by participating in international organizations of tax administrators. IRS is actively involved in two international tax organizations and one jointly run program that addresses common tax administration issues. First, the IRS participates with the Center for Inter-American Tax Administration (CIAT), a forum made up of 38 member countries and associate members, which exchange experiences with the aim of improving tax administration. CIAT, formed in 1967, is to promote integrity, increase tax compliance, and fight tax fraud. The IRS participates with CIAT in designing and developing tax administration products and with CIAT's International Tax Planning Control committee.[14] Second, the IRS participates with the Organisation for Economic Co-operation and Development (OECD) Forum on Tax Administration (FTA), which is chaired by the IRS Commissioner during 2011. The FTA was created in July 2002 to promote dialogue between tax administrations and identify good tax administration practices. Since 2002, the forum has issued over 50 comparative analyses on tax administration issues to assist member and selected nonmember countries.

IRS and OECD officials exchange tax administration knowledge. For example, the IRS is participating in the OECD's first peer review of information exchanged under tax treaties and tax information exchange agreements. Under the peer-review process, senior tax officials from several OECD countries examine each selected member's legal and regulatory framework and evaluate members' implementation of OECD tax standards. The peer-review report on IRS information exchange practices is expected to be published in mid-2011.

As for the jointly run program, the Joint International Tax Shelter Information Centre (JITSIC) attempts to supplement ongoing work in each country to identify and curb abusive tax schemes by exchanging information on these schemes. JITSIC was formed in 2004 and now includes tax agencies of Australia, Canada, China, Japan, South Korea, the United Kingdom, and the United States. According to the IRS, JITSIC members have identified and challenged the following highly artificial arrangements:

- a cross-border scheme involving millions of dollars in improper deductions and unreported income on tax returns from retirement account withdrawals;
- highly structured financing transactions created by financial institutions that taxpayers used to generate inappropriate foreign tax credit benefits;[15] and
- made-to-order losses on futures and options transactions for individuals in other JITSIC jurisdictions, leading to more than $100 million in evaded taxes.

To date, the IRS has implemented one foreign tax administration practice. As presented earlier, Australia's HNWI program examines sophisticated legal structures that wealthy taxpayers may use to mask aggressive tax strategies. In 2009, the OECD issued a report for a project on the tax compliance problems of wealthy individuals and concluded that "high net worth individuals pose significant challenges to tax administrations" due to their complex business dealings across different business entities, higher tax rates, and higher likelihood of using aggressive tax planning or tax evasion.[16] According to an IRS official, during IRS's participation in 2008 in the OECD Project, IRS staff began to realize the value of Australia's program to the U.S. tax system. The IRS now has a program focused on wealthy individuals and their networks.[17]

Agency Comments

The IRS provided technical comments that are included in this report.

As agreed with your offices, unless you publicly announce the contents of this report earlier, we plan no further distribution until 30 days after the report date. At that time, we will send copies to the Commissioner of Internal Revenue and other interested parties. This report also will be available at no charge on GAO's Web site at http://www.gao.gov.

If you or your staff has any questions about this report, please contact me at (202) 512-9110 or brostekm@gao.gov. Contact points for our Offices of Congressional Relations and Public Affairs may be found on the last page of this report. Key contributors to this report are listed in appendix IX.

Michael Brostek
Director, Tax Issues Strategic Issues

Appendix I: Scope and Methodology

For our objective to describe how other countries have approached tax administration issues that are similar to those in the U.S. tax system, we selected six foreign tax administrators. We based our selection of these practices on several factors, including whether the tax administrators had advanced economies and tax systems and the foreign tax administrator's approach differed, at least in part, from how the United States approaches similar issues. These tax systems also needed to have enough information available in English on their Web site for us to preliminarily understand their tax system and practices. In addition, we considered practices of interest to the requesters.

To describe each of the practices, we reviewed documents and held telephone conferences with officials from each tax administrator. We also met with officials of Finland's government in Helsinki. When possible, we confirmed additional information provided to us by officials to assure that we had a reasonable basis for the data presented. We used official reports published by the tax administrators, such as their annual reports, that are made available to the public on their Internet Web site. To identify taxpayers' attitudes toward Hong Kong's semiannual payment system, we interviewed experts who were either university professors, were the authors of publications on Hong Kong's tax system, or were practitioners in well-known law or accounting firms. To understand the development of

Finland's Internet-based withholding estimation and prepared returns system, we met with the public interest and trade groups that provided assistance to Finland's Parliament during the system's development.

To describe whether and how the Internal Revenue Service (IRS) identifies and integrates tax administration practices used in other countries, we interviewed IRS officials and reviewed related documents. We also followed up with IRS officials based on any information we found independently about practices that relate to issues in the U.S. tax system and our comparison of U.S. and other administrator's practices. The descriptive information on the practices of foreign administrators presented in this report may provide useful insights for Congress and others on alternatives to current U.S. tax policies and practices. However, our work did not include the separate analytic step of identifying and assessing the factors that might affect the transferability of the practices to the United States.[1]

To adjust foreign currencies to U.S. dollars, we used the Federal Reserve Board's database on foreign exchange rates. We used rates that matched the time period cited for the foreign amount. For current amounts, we used the exchange rates published for February 25, 2011. If the amounts were for a previous year, we used the exchange rate published for the last business day of that year. For example, if foreign amounts were cited as of 2006, we used exchange rates for December 29, 2006. We did not adjust amounts from previous years for inflation.

To help ensure the accuracy of the information we present, we shared a summary of our descriptions with representatives of the six foreign tax administrators and incorporated their comments as appropriate. The IRS provided technical comments that are included in this report.

We conducted our work from October 2009 to May 2011 in accordance with all sections of GAO's Quality Assurance Framework that are relevant to our objectives. The framework requires that we plan and perform the engagement to obtain sufficient and appropriate evidence to meet our stated objectives and to discuss any limitations in our work. We believe that the information and data obtained, and the analysis conducted, provide a reasonable basis for any findings and conclusions in this report.

APPENDIX II: NEW ZEALAND DOES INTEGRATED EVALUATIONS OF TAX EXPENDITURES AND DISCRETIONARY SPENDING PROGRAMS

Overview of the New Zealand Tax System

The New Zealand tax system is centralized through the Inland Revenue Department (IRD). Most of New Zealand's NZ$49 billion (US$35.5 billion) in revenue for fiscal year 2009 was raised by direct taxation that includes PAYE (Pay As You Earn), Company Tax, and Schedular Payments.[1] In addition, tax expenditures (tax credits in New Zealand) for social programs that were administered by IRD in 2009 include KiwiSaver and Working For Families (WFF) Tax Credits programs.[2]

What Is New Zealand's Working for Families Tax Credits Program?

The WFF Tax Credits program, started in 2004, seeks to assist low- to middle-income families with the goal of promoting employment and ensuring income adequacy. Prior to 2004, New Zealand had another program intended to assist families. However, the New Zealand government discovered that many low-income families were no better off from holding a low-paying job and that those who needed to pay for childcare to work generally were worse off in low-paid work compared to only receiving government benefits. This prompted the government to change in-work incentives and financial support for families with dependent children. These changes were incorporated into the WFF program in 2004. It was estimated that program costs would increase by NZ$1.6 billion (US$1.2 billion) per year.

The WFF Tax Credits program is an umbrella program that spans certain tax credits[3] administered by the IRD as well as discretionary spending programs[4] administered by the Ministry of Social Development (MSD).

Table 2 shows the tax and discretionary spending components of the WFF tax credits program and the agency responsible for them.

Table 2. Joint Administration of New Zealand's WFF Tax Credits Program

	Administered by:	
Expenditures/outlays	IRD	MSD
Family tax credit	X	X
In-work tax credit	X	
Minimum family tax credit	X	
Parental tax credit	X	
Accommodation supplements		X
Childcare subsidies		X
Temporary additional support		X

Source: GAO analysis of New Zealand data.

Under the program IRD makes payments to the majority of eligible recipients during the tax year.[5] The IRD and MSD portions of the WFF tax credit program are intended to work together to assist low- to middle-income families and promote employment.

Information that IRD collects and uses in administering the tax credits is subject to New Zealand's protections for the privacy of sensitive taxpayer information contained in the Tax Administration Act. The information that MSD collects and uses is not subject to the same restrictions. To meet their separate needs, IRD and MSD keep separate datasets.

WHY NEW ZEALAND USED JOINT RESEARCH TO EVALUATE WFF DIRECT BENEFIT PAYMENTS AND TAX EXPENDITURES

New Zealand's joint research projects integrated research between IRD and other governmental agencies with related programs. The projects were designed to ensure that all disbursements of revenue through either direct program outlays or tax expenditures were administered effectively to meet the goals for social programs, making sure people get the assistance to which they are entitled.

One example of joint research was the study of the WFF tax credits program. To overcome the problem of the separate datasets and still protect sensitive tax data, the New Zealand government approved a joint research program that created interagency linked datasets between IRD and MSD. Parliament intended that these linked datasets be used to evaluate the tax expenditures and discretionary spending programs, to ensure that the benefits of the overall program were being fully used by its participants.

These linked datasets, known as the "WFF Research Datasets," were constructed from the combined records of the MSD and IRD. They contained several years of data, and included information about all families who had received a WFF payment during these years. The data included monthly amounts of income received from salary and wages from employment and from the main benefit payments. The linked dataset information was to be used solely to analyze the results of WFF. It could not be used to take any action, whether adverse or favorable, against a particular individual.

In 2004, MSD and IRD developed a Memorandum of Understanding (MOU) for the WFF program. The MOU included processes to share information while ensuring that all sensitive data were protected from unauthorized disclosure. The MOU permitted IRD to provide MSD with aggregate taxpayer information needed to conduct evaluations with a restriction that only allows IRD employees direct access to sensitive taxpayer information. However, IRD was authorized to distribute sensitive taxpayer information to authorized MSD employees if they were part of the joint research team and were sworn in as IRD employees. Swearing in MSD agents as IRD agents permitted IRD to apply the same sanctions to IRD and MSD agents who did not adhere to IRD's data-protection policies.

WHAT ARE THE KNOWN RESULTS AND EFFECTS OF THE JOINT RESEARCH PROJECT?

The WFF joint research revealed social and cultural barriers that prevented targeted participants from taking full advantage of the WFF program. These barriers included the

- perceived stigma from receiving government aid if the person could work or felt that the aid infringed on independence or self-sufficiency;
- transaction costs from accepting government aid such as taking time off from work, arranging childcare, or following many rules and regulations;
- low value of applying for the program when the person was close to the maximum eligibility threshold; and
- geographic barriers when the person lived in areas that were remote or had no transportation, telephone, or Internet.

The WFF joint research provided information needed to identify the population that benefited from the program and reduce some of the barriers that kept recipients, particularly an indigenous population, from participating in the target program. Since the inception of the

WFF program in 2004, the joint research documented the following benefits from reducing barriers to the targeted population:

- The percentage of single parents working 20 hours or more increased from 48 percent in June 2004 to 58 percent in June 2007. This represents 8,100 additional single parents in the workforce.
- The number of single parents receiving benefits from MSD fell by 12 percent from March 2004 to March 2008. Those that received the benefits did so for a shorter time and stayed off the benefit programs longer.

Similarities to and Differences from the U.S. Tax System

While structural differences exist between the New Zealand and U.S. tax systems, both systems use tax expenditures (i.e., tax credits in New Zealand). Unlike the United States, New Zealand has developed a method to evaluate the effectiveness of tax expenditures and discretionary spending programs through joint research that created interagency linked datasets. New Zealand did so while protecting confidential tax data from unauthorized disclosure.

In 2005, we reported that the United States had substantial tax expenditures but lacked clarity on the roles of the Office of Management and Budget (OMB), Department of the Treasury, IRS, and federal agencies with discretionary spending programs to evaluate the tax expenditures.[6]

Consequently, the United States lacked information on how effective tax expenditures were in achieving their intended objectives, how cost-effectively benefits were achieved, and whether tax expenditures or discretionary spending programs worked well together to accomplish federal objectives.[7] At that time, OMB disagreed with our recommendations to incorporate tax expenditures into federal performance management and budget review processes, citing methodological and conceptual issues. However, in its fiscal year 2012 budget guidance, OMB instructed agencies, where appropriate, to analyze how to better integrate tax and spending policies that have similar objectives and goals.[8]

Appendix III: Finland Uses the Internet to Calculate Individual Tax Withholding Rates and Revise Preprepared Tax Returns

Overview of the Finland Tax System

Finland's national and municipal governments as well as local church councils levy taxes. Nationally, 39 percent of all taxes are paid under individual and corporate income taxes and a capital gains tax. Taxes on goods, services, and property total about 33 percent of revenue; most of this revenue is from the Value Added Tax (VAT). The final 28 percent comes from social security taxes (e.g., national health insurance system and employment pension insurance). Finland's individual income tax is levied on a graduated rate schedule with four tax brackets, ranging from 7.0 percent to 30.5 percent for incomes over €64,500 (US$92,441) with the tax on investment income levied at a flat rate of 28 percent in 2009. Finland's corporate income tax is levied at a flat rate of 26 percent.

Under the municipal tax, each municipal council sets its tax rate annually. For 2009, municipal taxes are levied at flat rates ranging from 16.5 percent to 21.0 percent of earned income and averaging 18.6 percent. Individuals who are members of the Evangelical-Lutheran Church or the Orthodox Church pay a church tax. For 2009, local church communities determine the rate of tax, which is levied at a flat rate between 1 and 2 percent.

How Do Withholding Estimation and Preprepared Returns Improve Service?

Using electronic means, Finland helps taxpayers in estimating their tax withholding and by preparing an income tax return for each individual taxpayer based on third-party information returns. The on-line Tax Card system, established in 2006, is an Internet-based system to help Finnish taxpayers estimate the withholding rate for individual income tax. The Tax Card covers national taxes, municipality tax, social security tax, and church tax. Taxpayers access the Tax Card through the Web sites of their bank or the Finland Tax Administration.

Using the Tax Card system, taxpayers can update their withholding rate as many times as needed throughout the year to adjust for events that increase or decrease their potential tax liability. For example, if the taxpayer takes a job with a higher salary, the taxpayer can estimate the change on his or her income tax liability by using the Tax Card system. Taxpayers enter information provided by the employer, based on payroll information, to estimate their adjusted withholding. Annually, 1.6 million taxpayers, about a third of those using the Tax Card, change their tax withholding rate.

When the Tax Card has been completed, employees provide the withholding tax rate to their employer through regular mail or in person. If the employer is not notified of any withholding rate, the employer must withhold at the top marginal rate in Finland for all types of taxes—which is 60 percent of gross pay. Employers manually enter the withholding rate into their payroll systems.

According to Tax Administration officials, some social benefits can complicate the estimation of the tax due and may not be accurately estimated during the tax year. For example, Finland has a deduction for the cost of travel between a residence and work. If the taxpayer does not accurately estimate the deductions or make changes as the year progresses, the Tax Card withholding rate will be inaccurate.

Finland Tax Administration Prepares Returns for Taxpayers

Finland has been operating a tax-return preparation system since 2006. The Finnish Tax Administration prepares an income tax return for each individual taxpayer based on third-party information returns. According to Tax Administration officials, Finland uses information from over 30 types of information-return filers (e.g., employers, banks, and securities brokers). Tax Administration officials said that they have found very little misreporting on the information returns used to prepare the tax returns. They use many ways to try to verify the information. Some taxpayers will correct information returns when reviewing their prepared tax returns. Third parties can be penalized for inaccurate information and Finnish tax officials said those penalties are regularly assessed.

The system prepares the return each tax year, which ends on December 31. According to Tax Administration officials, the individual tax returns are mailed for review during April. The taxpayer has until May to make changes to the paper return.[1] Taxpayers can mark up the paper return for revisions and mail it to the Tax Administration whose staff keys in or electronically scans in the changes. Also, taxpayers can choose to make the changes to the return online, using the taxpayer's account with the Tax Administration.

According to Tax Administration officials, typically about 3.5 million people do not ask to change their tax return and about 1.5 million request a tax change. About 400,000 taxpayers will revise their return using the Tax Administration's Internet portal. Typically, the average taxpayer takes about half an hour to do the adjustments online. One deduction, the commuting adjustment, is not reported on an information return. This adjustment accounts for changes to about 800,000 prepared returns.

Overall, taxpayers need to show some proof to support the change to the prepared return, including any changes they make to the information returns the Tax Administration used to prepare the returns. For example, taxpayers showing deductions for mortgage interest that were not reported on information returns would need to show they own a house and the mortgage interest was paid. Or, if an information return reports interest as income, but taxpayers deduct the interest as paid on a loan, the taxpayers need to document the reason for their deduction claims.

Finland does not prepare tax returns if individual taxpayers have business income. Rather, these taxpayers must file tax returns based on the data or business records that they maintained. However, some of these taxpayers with business income may get a partially prepared return on personal income and deductions based on third party information on their wages and other personal income in Finland's prepared return system. All businesses operating in Finland must register with the government.[2]

Why Did Finland Increase Its Use of Electronic Tax Administration?

Providing enhanced electronic services has been widely recognized in Finland as an approach for improving taxpayer service while reducing costs. Electronic services provide taxpayers with constant access to assistance regardless of the time of day or distance from the tax administration office. According to Tax Administration officials, electronic systems that provide routine taxpayer assistance allows Tax Administration staff to respond to more complex taxpayer problems.

Finland also moved to electronic tax administration to support national policies. As a national policy to encourage economic growth, Finland seeks to have a large private-sector workforce. According to an official of the Finland's government, a large number of citizens are nearing retirement.[3] Thus, the government is seeking to reduce its workforce so that more workers are available for the private sector. To achieve this goal, Finland focused on making the delivery of government programs more efficient by using more electronic transactions.

Another reason for electronic tax administration was to provide equal access to government services. Finnish law requires all e-services to be accessible to all Finnish citizens. With a significant segment of its population living in remote regions, according to officials, improving e-government provides more equal access to government services. To encourage equal access and use of the Internet for delivering services, Finland established standard speeds of Internet access in July 2009.[4]

What Are the Known Results and Effects of Electronic Tax Administration?

Finland's tax system is viewed positively by taxpayers and industry groups. Members of several industry and taxpayer groups told us that Finland has a simple, stable tax system, which makes compliance relatively easy. They also commented that the Tax Card and preprepared annual return system work well and are easy to use. As a result, few individuals use a tax advisor to help prepare and file the annual income tax return. We were told that individuals using a tax advisor have complex tax issues, such as from owning a businesses or having complex investments.

Electronic tax administration has advantages for the government and Finnish taxpayers. According to tax officials, cost savings result from spending less time to prepare and process tax returns. These officials said that electronic tax administration has helped to reduce their full-time-equivalent positions over 11 percent from 2003 to 2009. Further, the tax withholding system results in a small amount of individual income tax withheld that needs to be refunded after final returns are filed. For tax year 2007, 8 percent of the tax withheld was refunded to taxpayers as compared to 26 percent refunded in the United States.

Finland's culture of cooperation and the resulting cooperative arrangements between government, banks, businesses, and taxpayers have led to acceptance of the new Tax Card Online service.

According to public interest and trade groups in Finland, the Finnish society has a great deal of confidence in the banking system and its secure access. This confidence influenced the decision to place the Tax Card online service on bank Web sites. With taxpayers having regular access to a banking Web site,[5] the banks offer a channel for delivering government services, according to government officials. Public interest and trade groups agreed, noting that the banking industry's willingness to support the Tax Card enhanced its development. Representatives of a Finnish banking trade group said that placing the Tax Card system on their Web sites helped banks. That is, the more time customers spend on banks' Web sites, the more opportunities the banks had to offer other services, helping to offset the cost of implementing the system.

According to Finnish trade and public interest groups, Finland's cooperative culture also supports the preprepared individual income tax return system. For this system to work properly, business and other organizations must file accurate information returns within 1 month after the end of the tax year. This short period for filing information returns creates some burden. The burden includes costs to purchase and install special software for collecting the information as well as preparing and filing the returns. According to a professional accounting organization in Finland, buying the yearly software updates can be expensive. Any update has to be available well before the start of the tax year so that transactions can be correctly recorded at the start of the year and not revised at the end of the year.

What Are the Similarities to and Differences from the U.S. System?

In contrast to Finland's self-described "simple" system, the U.S. tax system is complex and changing annually. Regarding withholding estimation, Finland's Tax Card system provides taxpayers an online return system for regularly updating the tax amount withheld. For employees in the United States, the IRS's Web site offers a withholding calculator to help employees determine whether to contact their employer about revising their tax withholding. Finland's system prepares a notice to the employer that can be sent through the mail or delivered in person, whereas in the United States the taxpayers must file a form with the employer on the amount to be withheld based on the taxpayers' estimation.

In the United States, individual income tax returns are completed by taxpayers—not IRS—using information returns mailed to their homes and their own records.[6] Taxpayers are to file an accurate income tax return by its due date. Unlike in Finland, U.S. individual taxpayers heavily rely on tax advisors and tax software to prepare their annual return. In the United States, about 90 percent of individual income tax returns are prepared by paid preparers or by the taxpayer using commercial software.

APPENDIX IV: EU'S MULTILATERAL TREATY INFORMATION EXCHANGE ON INTEREST PAYMENTS TO MEMBER NATIONS' CITIZENS

Overview of the EU Directive

In June 2003, the European Union (EU) adopted the Savings Taxation Directive to encourage tax compliance by exchanging information and in some cases using withholding. The directive is a multilateral agreement that establishes uniform procedures and definitions for exchanging information and facilitating the resolution of common technical problems. Under the directive, the 27 EU members[1] and 10 dependent and associated territories agreed to participate in the directive.[2] With this information, tax authorities in the citizen's nation are able to verify whether the citizen properly reported and paid tax on the interest income. Each of the 27 member nations has a separate tax system, and varies in the tax rates imposed on personal income, as shown in table 3.

Table 3. Range of Highest Personal Income Tax Rate for EU Countries, 2010

Highest personal income tax rate	Number of EU countries
50 percent or greater	6
40 percent or greater and less than 50 percent	10
30 percent or greater and less than 40 percent	4
20 percent or greater and less than 30 percent	2
10 percent or greater and less than 20 percent	5

Source: GAO analysis of EU data.

The highest personal income tax rates range from 10 percent in Bulgaria to over 56 percent in Sweden. This range of tax rates is an important reason for the need for the exchange of information on income. Residents in higher-tax countries could be motivated to move capital outside of the country of residence to potentially avoid reporting income earned on investments of the capital.

How Does the EU Savings Taxation Directive Strive to Encourage Tax Compliance?

The directive provided a basic framework for information exchanges, defining essential terms such as beneficial owner of the asset paying interest, identity and residence of the owner, paying agents,[3] interest payments, and information to be reported, and establishing automatic information exchange among members. The directive also states that five other nonmember nations agreed to information exchange upon request for information defined under the Savings Taxation Directive.[4]

During a transition period from 2005 through 2011, Belgium, Luxembourg, and Austria as well as the five nonmember nations, and six associated territories, agreed to a withholding tax.[5] Under these agreements, a withholding tax was to be remitted at the rate of 15 percent during the first 3 years, 20 percent for the next 3 years, and 35 percent thereafter. The directive authorizes the withholding nations to retain 25 percent of the tax collected and transfer 75 percent of the revenue to the account owner's home nation. The withholding nations may develop procedures so that the owners can request that no tax be withheld. These procedures generally require that the owner provide identification information to the paying agent or to the account owner's home nation.

The directive also requires the account owner's home nation to ensure that the withholding does not result in double taxation. The home nation is to grant a tax credit equal to the amount of tax paid to the nation in which the account is located. If the tax paid exceeds the amount due to the home nation, the home nation is to refund to the account owner the excess amount that was withheld.

The role of the EU Commission is to coordinate among the participants in the directive. The commission sets up and maintains contact points for communications among members. All information to be exchanged must be submitted no later than June 13 each year to the commission and follow the standardized Organisation for Economic Co-operation and Development (OECD) format. The information exchange is completely electronic and automatic. All information is sent and received through a secure network that only member countries can access. As of 2010, all member countries are using this standard format except for Switzerland which is working with the EU on plans for information exchange. The commission is to keep the format updated and periodically review compliance by member countries. The commission is to gather statistics to measure overall performance and success of the directive. Member countries have agreed to provide the commission with the statistics necessary to gauge performance. Every 2 years the commission hosts a conference to receive feedback from member nations on its performance and to gauge the directive's success. Additionally, every 3 years the commission reports to the European Parliament and Commission of the European Communities. The first report on the operation of the directive was issued in September 2008.[6]

Why Does the EU Use the Multilateral Treaty Information Exchange?

The EU adopted the Savings Taxation Directive to encourage tax compliance by exchanging information and using withholding. Using a multilateral agreement provided a way to uniformly establish procedures and definitions for exchanging information as well as for resolving any common technical problems to information exchange across the entire EU.

What Are the Known Results and Effects of the Information Exchange on Savings?

The September 2008 report to the EU described the status of the directive. The report found that 25 members started applying the rules as required in July 2005. In 2006, the first full year in which data were available, 17 members provided information to the exchange. Bulgaria and Romania began implementation in January 2007. The report concluded that the largest economies and financial centers reported the highest amounts of interest paid to other EU citizens. For 2006, Germany, France, Ireland, and the Netherlands accounted for over 98 percent of the dollar value of interest paid by all EU nations to citizens of other EU countries.[7] The report concluded that data limitations created major difficulties for evaluating the effectiveness of the directive. The EU did not have information on withholding results or time-series information from before the directive began. Without this information, the EU had no benchmark to measure the effect of the changes.

According to EU officials, the most common administrative difficulties have been information-technology system problems. Some members have not had the data formatted correctly, which caused problems when other member nations tried to access the data. For example, how member countries format their mailing address has led to data access problems. To overcome this problem, most member countries insert the taxpayer's mailing address in the free text field, but this makes the data difficult to efficiently analyze by other nations. Another example has been accessing data from languages that have special diacritical marks or characters. When information exchanged included these special characters, an error was created during the data importation process. The directive has suffered from other implementation problems, as follows.

Investor Behavior

EU staff said the commission tried to measure changes in the different types of investments before and after implementation of the directive. The commission had difficulty in identifying the overall effect the directive has had on individual investment choices because the data used are generally limited to interest-bearing investments. On the basis of decreases in some investor's total interest savings, the report noted that investors appeared to change their investments before implementation to investments that were not covered by the directive.

Withholding

The effectiveness of the withholding system under the Saving Tax Directive is unclear. The report found that the 14 countries and dependent and associated territories applying the withholding provisions in 2006 shared €559.12 million (US$738 million) withheld on income earned in their nation with the account owner's home nation.[8] Some articles have commented that given the low withholding rates in the early years, taxpayers with higher tax rates in their home nation may have chosen not to report the income.

Definitions

The EU identified problems with the definition of terms, making uniform application of the directive difficult. First, the commission's report raised questions about consistency of coverage of payments made from life insurance contracts where investments were made in securities or funds. Second, confusion existed over whether some paying agents were covered by EU rules on investment managers or by the definition established under the directive for noncovered paying agents.[9] Third, identifying the account owners was another problem.

In general, the EU report suggests that improved monitoring and follow-up by the home nation can help locate paying agents in third counties and ensure accurate information on the citizen who owns the account. The EU is considering several solutions such as enforcing existing customer due diligence rules that are to be used by domestic paying agents, who would transmit interest payments to the owners. These rules require that the paying agents must know who they are paying and should not facilitate transactions to mask the owner(s) and avoid taxes or other legal requirements.

Nevertheless, EU officials stated that the quality of data has improved over the years. The EU officials have worked with EU member nations to resolve specific data issues, which has contributed to the effective use of the information exchanged under the directive.

What Are the Similarities to and Differences from the U.S. System for Sharing Tax Information?

Generally, unlike the EU multilateral directive, the United States establishes bilateral information-sharing agreements. Those agreements allow for automatic information exchange, but definitions of terms, technical standards, and other matters are not worked out and adopted multilaterally. Resolution of some of those issues may be facilitated by the United States' participation in the Convention on Multilateral Administrative Assistance in Tax Matters, which includes exchange of information agreement provisions and has been ratified by 15 nations and the United States.[10]

Appendix V: The UK Uses Information Reporting and Withholding So Most Wage Earners Do Not Need to File a Tax Return

Overview of the UK Tax System

The United Kingdom's (UK) main sources of tax revenue are income tax, national insurance contributions, value added tax, and corporate tax. Her Majesty's Revenue and Customs (HMRC) also administers taxes assessed for capital gains, inheritance, various stamp duties, insurance premium tax, petroleum revenue, and excise duties.[1] The income tax system— where the tax year runs from April 6 through April 5 —taxes individuals on their income from various sources, for example, employment earnings, self-employment earnings, and property income.

Taxable individuals under 65 years of age receive a tax-free personal allowance (£6,475, or US$10,410 for the 2010-11 tax year).[2] If their total income is below the allowance amount, no tax is payable. The three main individual income tax rates for income above the personal allowance are 20 percent (£0-£37,400 or up to US$60,132), 40 percent (£37,401-£150,000 or up to US$241,170), and 50 percent (over £150,000 or over US$241,170).[3] HMRC uses 3 payment systems to collect income tax from individual taxpayers, depending on the type of income and whether the individual is employed, self-employed, or retired.[4]

- Pay As You Earn (PAYE) is used to withhold tax on wages and salaries paid to individuals by employers. Employers are required to notify HMRC every time an employee starts or stops working for them. Then, HMRC determines a tax withholding code for each individual and employers use the tax codes, in conjunction with tax tables, to calculate the amount of tax to be deducted.
- Self-assessment tax returns are used by some employees with higher rates of income or complicated tax affairs and by self-employed individuals with different kinds of business income.
- At-source collection is when the tax, such as on interest and dividend income, is withheld at source when the income is paid. For example, tax is deducted from bank interest as it is credited to an individual.

According to HMRC officials, the majority (68 percent) of taxpayers pay their tax solely through the PAYE system without having to submit a return to HMRC. Other actions have helped remove a large number of taxpayers from submitting a return. For example, the UK requires that tax on some income paid to individuals (such as bank interest) be withheld at a 20 percent rate and remitted to HMRC by the payer, and capital gains income up to the first £10,100 (US$16,239) is exempted from tax.

The UK also is working towards burden reduction for the average taxpayer by simplifying the tax return. For example, according to HMRC officials, information that is not necessary has been removed from the return to reduce the return filing burden, and those taxpayers who are required to file a return find it straight-forward.

How Do Information Reporting and Withholding Facilitate Tax Reporting and Risk Assessment?

HMRC uses data from information reporting and withholding under the PAYE system to simplify the reporting of tax liability on income tax returns for individuals. PAYE adjusts income tax withheld so that the individual's tax liability is generally met by the end of the tax year.

Information reporting helps HMRC and the individual taxpayer determine the total income tax liability, according to HMRC officials. Information returns are to report tax-related transactions by the taxpayer. They are to be supplied by banks and local governments to the taxpayer and HMRC at the end of the tax year. For example, banks are to provide interest payment information. Over 400 local government organizations are to report information on payments made to small businesses. Local government as both an employer and contractor must report information on payments made to others.

The information provided by employers enables HMRC to update the employee's tax record and issue a tax code to the new employer to start the withholding against employee earnings. HMRC calculates the PAYE code using information about the previous year's income or other employment in the current tax year.[5] Employers are to match the PAYE code to a tax table, which shows how much tax to withhold each pay period. The employer has to remit the withheld tax to HMRC on a monthly or quarterly basis to fulfill the taxpayer's tax liability. HMRC annually reviews taxpayer records and issues updated PAYE codes before the start of the tax year for employers to operate at the start of the tax year. The individual will receive a notice showing how the tax code has been calculated. To maintain taxpayer confidentiality, the employer will only receive the tax code itself.

HMRC can refund income tax overpayments or collect underpayments for previous tax years through adjustments to the PAYE code. HMRC reported in 2010 that around 5 million individuals overpaid or underpaid these taxes. HMRC officials said that they use information returns to help determine these adjustments under PAYE.[6] In lieu of having their PAYE codes adjusted, taxpayers may receive a onetime refund of the overpayment or pay the underpaid amount in one lump sum. Taxes owed usually are collected through code adjustments as long as the taxpayer stays within the PAYE system.

HMRC also uses information reporting and withholding to assess the compliance risks on filed returns. In assessing compliance risks, HMRC is attempting to identify underpaid and overpaid tax. The majority of the information for risk assessment is collected centrally from information returns, tax withholdings, filed tax returns, and public sources. This information is mined for risks by special risk-assessment teams. According to HMRC officials, the outcomes of such mining are to be used to verify tax compliance. If low compliance is found, risk specialists are to develop programs to increase compliance.

The data mining uses electronic warehouse "Data Marts" that HMRC has had for about 10 years.[7] They have been configured with subsets of data and have been supplemented by sophisticated analysis tools for doing risk assessments. For example, an analyst can create reports to assess the risk for all self-assessment income tax returns where the legal expense is above a specified amount. HMRC officials told us that Data Marts had recently been revamped and a strategic capability was added that links related information such as a business that files a corporate tax return for its business profits, pays value added tax, and has directors who submit self-assessment returns.

According to HMRC officials, the use of Data Marts combined with their more recent Strategic Risking Capability has allowed them to assess risks at the national and regional levels. HMRC officials said that they have moved towards national risk assessments because risk has not proven to be geographically based at regional levels. HMRC officials noted that while a return is being assessed for one type of risk, another type of risk can be found. HMRC is attempting to uncover emerging compliance risks by combining and reviewing data from the various sources in the Data Marts and elsewhere.

The risk assessment process has two steps, resulting in identifying tax returns for examination. The first step is to identify tax returns that have an inherent risk because of the taxpayers' size, complexity of the tax return, and past tendency for noncompliance. For example, returns filed by high-wealth individuals are viewed as risky returns that are sent to a related specialty office. The second step assesses risk on returns that are not sent to a specialty office. HMRC officials said that a relatively large proportion of the risk-assessment effort focuses on the self-employed, who are seen as having the greatest risk for tax noncompliance since they usually are not under the PAYE system (unless they have some wage income) and instead are to file a self-assessment return. HMRC has separate risk-assessment approaches, depending on the type of individual taxpayer, as discussed below.

- For individuals under the PAYE system, HMRC's computers capture most of the necessary data and the system carries out routine checks to verify data and link it to the taxpayer record. A risk to the PAYE system arises when employees receive benefits from their employers that are not provided to HMRC at the time it determines the annual tax code. Employer benefits may include a car, health insurance, or professional association fees that employers report on information returns after the tax year and that may be subject to income tax. If these benefits received are not included in the tax code then an underpayment of tax is likely to arise. The unpaid tax can be recovered by an annual reconciliation or when the employee reports the benefits on the employee's self-assessment tax return.
- Individuals not under the PAYE system are required to file a self-assessment tax return. To assess risk, HMRC checks some self-assessment tax returns for consistency by comparing them to returns from previous years, focusing on small businesses. For example, if the legal expense jumped from £5,000 to £100,000 (US$8,039 to US$160,780) over 2 years, HMRC may decide to review the reason. HMRC permits any self-employed small business with gross receipts of less than £68,000 (US$109,330) to file a simple three-line tax return to report business income, expenses, and profit. HMRC officials said that the threshold allows over 85 percent of all self-employed businesses to file simplified returns with less burden.

Why Did the UK Use Information Reporting and Withholding for Tax Reporting and Risk Assessment?

According to HMRC officials, their policy is to collect as much data as possible up front through information returns, and correct the amounts of tax due with the PAYE system, facilitating the payment of tax liabilities. Since information is shared with HMRC, taxpayers are likely to voluntarily comply if they have to file a tax return. Further, data from information reporting and withholding are to help simplify or eliminate tax reporting at the end of a tax year. According to HMRC officials, the PAYE system makes it unnecessary for most wage earners to file an annual self-assessment tax return.

HMRC conducts risk assessments because staff cannot check every tax return in depth due to the large number of taxpayers and the need to lower the costs of administering the tax system. Data from information reporting and withholding provide consistent sources for doing risk assessments.

What Are the Known Results and Effects from Using Information Reporting and Withholding to Facilitate Tax Reporting and Risk Assessment?

HMRC officials said the income tax system has been simplified because most individual taxpayers fall under the PAYE system, which generally relieves them of the burden of filing a tax return. Even so, some implementation problems have occurred. The House of Commons identified problems with an upgrade to the PAYE information system in 2009-10.[8] The upgrade was to combine information on individuals' employment and pension income into a single record to support more accurate tax withholding codes and reduce the likelihood of over- and underpayments of tax. However, software problems delayed processing 2008-09 PAYE returns for a year. In addition, data-quality problems from the upgraded PAYE system for 2010-11 generated about 13 million more annual tax coding notices than HMRC had anticipated and some were incorrect or duplicates. With these problems, of the 45 million PAYE records to be reconciled, 10 million cases needed to be reconciled manually.

The House of Commons reported a backlog of cases before the PAYE system was upgraded. Limitations of the previous PAYE system and increasingly complex working patterns have made it difficult to reconcile discrepancies without manual intervention. As of March 2010, a backlog of PAYE cases affected an estimated 15 million taxpayers from 2007-08 and earlier; the backlog included an estimated £1.4 billion (US$2.25 billion) of tax underpaid and £3 billion (US$4.82 billion) of tax overpaid.

HMRC has reported that risk assessment has provided three benefits: (1) improved examination decisions to ensure that they are necessary and reduce the burden on compliant taxpayers; (2) tailored examinations to the risk in question; and (3) deterred taxpayers from concealing income. HMRC's risk-assessment approach has increasingly focused on providing help and support to individuals and smaller businesses to voluntarily comply up front. To minimize the need for examinations, HMRC aims to help larger businesses achieve greater and earlier certainty on their tax liabilities. HMRC's sharper focus on risk assessment means that businesses with reliable track records of managing their own tax risks and being open in their dealings with HMRC benefit from fewer HMRC examinations while those with the highest risks can expect a more robust challenge from dedicated teams of specialists.

What Are the Similarities to and Differences from the U.S. System?

The UK and United States both have individual income tax returns and use information reporting and tax withholding to help ensure the correct tax is reported and paid. However, differences exist between the countries' systems.

- The United States has six tax rates that differ among five filing statuses for individuals (i.e., single, married, married filing separately, surviving spouse, or head of household) and covering all types of taxable income. In general, the UK system has three tax rates, one tax status (individuals), and a different tax return depending on the taxable income (e.g., self-employed or employed individuals).
- U.S. income tax withholding applies to wages paid but not interest and dividend income as it does in the UK.

- U.S. wage earners, rather than the Internal Revenue Service, are responsible for informing employers of how much income tax to withhold, if any, and must annually self-assess and file their tax returns, unlike most UK wage earners.

Another major difference is that the United States automatically matches data from information returns and the withholding system to data from the income tax return to identify individuals who underreported income or failed to file required returns. Matching is done using a unique identifier taxpayer identification number (TIN). HMRC officials told us that they have no automated document-matching process and the UK does not use TINs as a universal identifier, which is needed for wide-scale document matching. The closest form of unique identifier in the UK is the national insurance number. HMRC officials said they are barred from using the national insurance number for widespread document matching. Instead, HMRC officials said that they may do limited manual document matching in risk assessments and compliance checks. For example, HMRC manually matches some taxpayer data—such as name, address, date of birth—from bank records to data on tax returns.

Appendix VI: Australia Uses a Compliance Program for High-Net-Wealth Individuals

Overview of the Australian Tax System

Australia has a federal system of government with revenue collected at the federal, state, and local levels. For 2009-2010, about 92 percent of federal revenue was collected from taxes rather than nontax sources, like fees. The principal source of federal revenue for Australia is the income tax, which accounted for about 71 percent. Australia's state and local governments rely on grants from the national government and have limited powers to raise taxes. The states receive significant financial support from the federal government. In 2009-10, total payments to the states were 28 percent of all federal expenditures. Individuals accounted for about 65 percent of the 2009-2010 income tax revenue. The system is progressive with tax rates up to 45 percent for taxable income in excess of A$180,000 (US$161,622). In 2007-2008, a small proportion of Australian taxpayers paid a large proportion of Australian taxes, as shown in figure 1.

What Is the Australian High Net Wealth Individuals Program?

The Australian High Net Wealth Individuals (HNWI) program focuses on the characteristics of wealthy taxpayers that affect their tax compliance. According to the Australian Taxation Office (ATO), in the mid 1990s, it was perceived as enforcing strict sanctions on the average taxpayers but not the wealthy. ATO found that high-wealth taxpayers, those with a net worth of more than A$30 million (US$20.9 million), tend to have complex business arrangements, which made it difficult for ATO to identify and assure compliance. ATO concluded that the wealthy required a different tax administration approach.

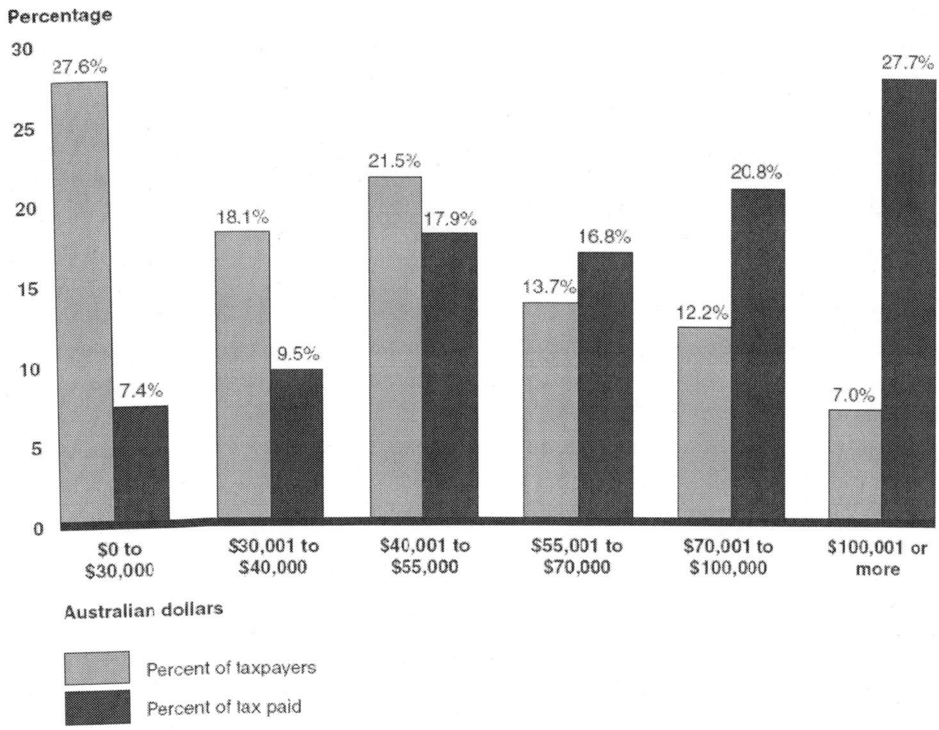

Source: GAO analysis of government of Australia data.

Figure 1. Australian Individual Income Tax Paid and Number of Taxpayers by Taxable Income for 2007-2008.

ATO set up a special task force to improve its understanding of wealthy taxpayers, identify their tax planning techniques, and improve voluntary compliance. Initially, the program focused on the tax return filed by a wealthy individual. Due to some wealthy taxpayers' aggressive tax planning, which ATO defines as investment schemes and legal structures that do not comply with the law, ATO quickly realized that it could not reach its goals for voluntary compliance for this group by examining taxpayers as individual entities.

To tackle the problem, ATO began to view wealthy taxpayers as part of a group of related business and other entities. Focusing on control over related entities rather than on just individual tax obligations provided a different understanding of wealthy individuals' compliance issues. To address the special needs of the wealthy, ATO developed publications that included a separate high-wealth income tax return form, a questionnaire on the wealthy as an entity and a tax guide, Wealthy and wise—A tax guide for Australia's wealthiest people.

Why Australia Developed the High Net Wealth Program

According to ATO, a number of factors led to the HNWI program. First, ATO was dealing with a perceived public image that it showed preference to the wealthy while enforcing strict sanctions on average taxpayers during the 1990s. Second, ATO was perceived as losing revenue from noncompliant taxpayers. Third, high-wealth individuals used special techniques to create and preserve their income and wealth through a "business life cycle." The cycle includes creating, maintaining, and passing on wealth through complex tax shelters. For example, businesses owned or controlled by wealthy individuals are more likely to have more diverse businesses arrangements, which tend to spread wealth across a group of companies and trusts. Each of these groups controlled by wealthy individuals was classified as a separate taxpayer entity, which made understanding the tax implications of these networks of entities difficult for the ATO.

The HNWI approach followed ATO's general compliance model. The model's premise is that tax administrators can influence tax compliance behavior through their responses and interventions. Since taxpayers have different attitudes on compliance, ATO used varied responses and interventions tailored to promote voluntary tax compliance across different taxpayer groups.

The first part of the standard model is to understand five factors that influence taxpayer compliance. The factors are Business, Industry, Social, Economic, and Psychological. For example, the Business factor included the size, location, nature, and capital structure of the business as well as its financial performance—all of which help ATO understand why compliance or noncompliance occurs.[1]

The second part of the model involves taxpayers' attitudes on compliance. It refers to one of four attitudes that a taxpayer may adopt when interacting with tax regulatory authorities. These attitudes are

- willing to do the right thing,
- try to do the right thing,
- do not want to comply, and
- decided not to comply.

The third part of the model aligns four compliance strategies with the four taxpayer attitudes on compliance[2] and refers to the degree of ATO enforcement under the concept of responsive regulation. ATO prefers to simplify the tax system and promote voluntary compliance through self-regulation. If the taxpayer tries to comply, ATO should respond by helping the taxpayer be compliant. If the taxpayer is not motivated to comply, ATO should respond to the level of noncompliance with some degree of enforcement, ending with harsh sanctions for the truly noncompliant.

ATO created a High Wealth Individual (HWI) taskforce to assess wealthy individuals on their probability of compliance and place them into one of four broad risk categories using its Risk Differentiation Framework (RDF). RDF is similar to the compliance model in that it is to assess the tax risk and determine the intensity of the response for those with high net wealth, ranging from minimizing burden on compliant wealthy taxpayers to aggressively pursuing the noncompliant. The four broad categories of the RDF are as follows:

- Higher Risk Taxpayers—ATO performs continuous risk reviews of them with the focus on enforcement.
- Medium Risk Taxpayers—ATO periodically reviews certain transactions from them or where there is a declining trend in effective tax performance with a focus on enforcement.

- Key Taxpayers—ATO continuously monitors them with the focus on service.
- Low Risk Taxpayers—ATO periodically monitors them with the focus on service.

What Are the Known Results and Effects of the Australian High Net Wealth Program?

The HNWI program has produced financial benefits since its establishment in 1996. ATO 2008 data showed that the program had collected A$1.9 billion (US$1.67 billion) in additional revenue and reduced revenue losses by A$1.75 billion (US$1.5 billion) through compliance activities focused on highly wealthy individuals and their associated entities. ATO's approach also has been adopted by other tax administrators. According to a 2009 Organisation for Economic Co-operation and Development (OECD) study, nine other OECD countries, including the United States, had adopted some aspect of Australia's HNWI program.[3]

Similarities to and Differences from the U.S. Tax System

Like ATO, the IRS is taking a close look at high-income and high-wealth individuals and their related entities. In 2009, IRS formed the Global High Wealth Industry (GHWI) program to take a holistic approach to high-wealth individuals. IRS consulted with the ATO to discuss ATO's approach to the high-wealth population as well as its operational best practices. As of February 2011, GHW field groups had a number of high-wealth individuals and several of their related entities under examination.

One difference is that Australia has a separate income tax return for high-wealth taxpayers to report information on assets owned or controlled by HNWIs. In contrast, the United States has no separate tax return for high-wealth individuals and generally does not seek asset information from individuals. According to IRS officials, the IRS traditionally scores the risk of individual tax returns based on individual reporting characteristics rather than a network of related entities.[4] However, IRS has been examining how to do risk assessments of networks through its GHWI program since 2009. Another difference is that ATO requires HNWIs to report their business networks, and IRS currently does not.

Appendix VII: Hong Kong Uses Semiannual Payments Instead of Periodic Employer Withholding for the Salaries Tax

Overview of the Hong Kong Tax System

Hong Kong's Inland Revenue Department (IRD) assesses and collects the "earnings and profits tax," which includes a Profits Tax,[1] Salaries Tax, and Property Tax. IRD also assesses and collects certain "duties and fees" including a stamp duty, business registration fees, betting duty, and estate duty. Hong Kong only taxes income from sources within Hong Kong. Principle revenue sources for tax year 2009-10 are shown in figure 2.

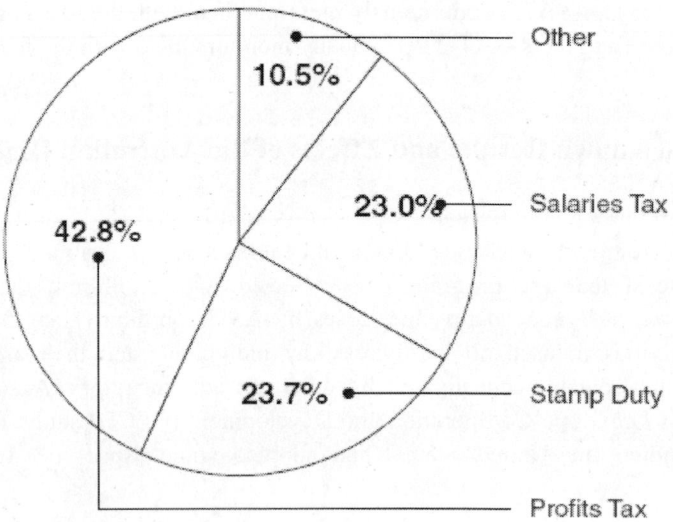

Source: GAO analysis of Hong Kong data.

Figure 2. Hong Kong Tax Year 2009 to 2010 Revenue Sources.

According to a Hong Kong tax expert, Hong Kong created the Salaries Tax at the start of World War II without using periodic tax withholding. The lack of withholding was not then, and is not now, considered to be a significant problem.[2] The Salaries Tax is paid by about 40 percent of the estimated 3.4 million wage earners in Hong Kong, while the 60 percent are exempt from the Salaries Tax.

Taxpayers whose salary income is lower than their entitlement to deductions (i.e., basic allowance, child allowance, dependent parent, etc.) are exempt from paying Salaries Tax and neither they nor IRD prepare a tax return for this income. However, exempt taxpayers may receive a tax return from IRD once every few years to verify their tax-exempt status. If these exempt taxpayers receive a tax return from IRD, they are required to complete and submit it within 1 month.[3]

The Salaries Tax rates are fairly low, according to Hong Kong tax experts. The Salaries Tax has progressive rates starting at 2 percent of the adjusted salary earned and may not exceed the standard rate of 15 percent. In comparison, the highest personal income tax rates in the EU range from about 10 percent to over 56 percent as described in appendix IV.[4]

How Does Hong Kong Collect Salaries Tax?

Hong Kong does not use periodic tax withholding (e.g., biweekly or monthly) by employers to collect Salaries Taxes. Rather, IRD collects the Salaries Tax through two payments from taxpayers for a tax year, which runs from April 1 to March 31. The first payment is due in January (9 months into the tax year) and is to be 75 percent of the estimated tax for the whole year. The second payment is for the remaining 25 percent, which is due 3 months later in April—immediately after the end of the tax year.

In May, IRD is to mail the tax return to the individual for the just-completed tax year based on information provided by employers and other sources. Information reporting to IRD has four parts. First, employers must report when each employee is hired and the expected annual salary amount. Second, at the end of the tax year, employers must report the salary paid to each employee. Third, the employers must report when the employee ceases employment. Fourth, employers must report and temporarily withhold payments to an employee they know intends to leave Hong Kong. If the employer fails to comply with these requirements without a reasonable excuse, penalties may be imposed.

Individuals have 1 month to file the return.[5] For those who elect to file their returns electronically, IRD will prefill the return based on information provided in their past returns and by their employers. They have a month and a half to review the prepared tax return, make any revisions such as changes to deductions, and file it with IRD.

IRD reviews the filed tax returns to determine the final Salaries Tax. IRD electronically screens all returns to check for consistency between the information provided by the employer and taxpayer. Assessments will normally be made based on the higher amount reported, and taxpayers have the right to object within 1 month. IRD also can cross-check reported salary amounts with salary deductions claimed by businesses on Profit Tax returns, which should normally be supported by information returns on employee salary amounts. If the final Salaries Tax for the tax year turns out to be higher than the estimated tax assessment, taxpayers are to pay the additional tax along with the first payment of the estimated tax for the next tax year during the following January, as shown in figure 3.

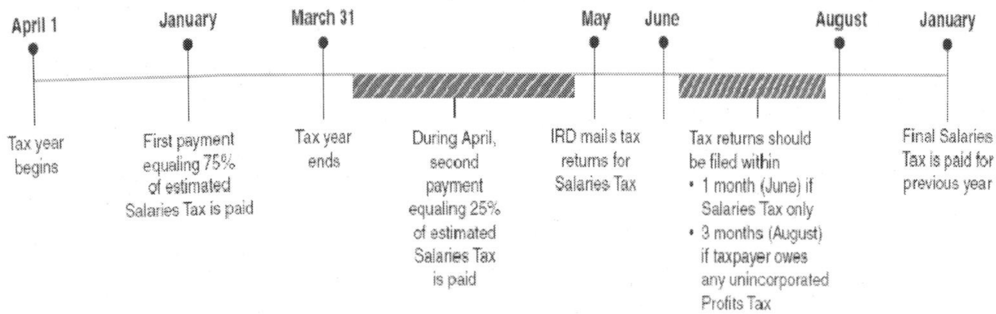

Source: GAO analysis of IRD data.

Figure 3. Hong Kong's Salaries Tax Process Timeline.

Why Does Hong Kong Collect Salaries Tax through Two Yearly Payments?

Several factors contribute to Hong Kong's collection of the Salaries Tax through two payments for a tax year without resorting to periodic withholding by employers.

- The tax only affects about 40 percent of the wage earners who have the highest salaries and uses relatively low tax rates, making it more likely that the taxpayers will have the funds necessary to make the two payments when due.
- The simplicity of Hong Kong's tax system, according to Hong Kong tax experts, makes it easier to compute tax liability and to manage the payments.
- IRD uses a combination of controls to assure that tax payments are made, according to a senior IRD official. In addition to information reporting, island geography

contributes to the controls. Hong Kong entry/departure points are limited and tax evaders are likely to be identified. Hong Kong government can detain a tax evader from leaving or entering Hong Kong until the tax is paid. IRD has varied processes to trace the assets of delinquent taxpayers as part of collecting any unpaid tax.

- Culture encourages taxpayers to pay their taxes. Hong Kong experts said taxpayers fear a loss of face if they are recognized as noncompliant, which could reflect negatively on the family. A Hong Kong official told us that residents try to avoid being taken to court.

An expert on public opinion in Hong Kong told us that this cultural attitude generates high tax morale. The expert told us that Hong Kong residents have high regard for Hong Kong's government as being "cleanly" run and as putting tax revenues to good use. IRD is viewed as having fair and equal treatment of all taxpayers.

What Are the Known Results and Effects from Collecting the Salaries Tax through Two Yearly Payments?

A senior official of Hong Kong's IRD believes that the Salaries Tax collection system leads to high tax compliance. Low tax rates in concert with a simple tax system that offers generous deductions and effective enforcement mean that taxpayers are fairly compliant, according to the Hong Kong official. It also means that few taxpayers use a tax preparer because the tax forms are very straightforward and the tax system is "stable."

The official also said that taxpayers comply because the cost of noncompliance is high. If a taxpayer does not pay by the due date, the costs include paying the tax liability, interest surcharges on the debt, and legal costs. Further, submitting an incorrect tax return without reasonable excuse may carry a fine of HK$10,000 (US$1,283) plus three times the amount of tax underpaid and imprisonment.

What Are the Similarities to and Differences from the U.S. System?

Unlike Hong Kong's twice-a-year payments for the Salaries Tax, the U.S. income tax on wages relies on periodic tax withholding. IRS provides guidance (e.g., Publication 15) on how and when employers should withhold income tax (e.g., every other week) and deposit the withheld income taxes (e.g., monthly). Further, the U.S. individual tax rates are higher and the system is more complex. These tax rates begin at 10 percent and progress to 35 percent. Further, the United States taxes many forms of income beyond salary income on the individual tax return.

Appendix VIII: Overview of Tax Systems for Five Nations

Nations have many choices on how to structure their tax systems across the federal, as well as state and local, government levels. The proportion of revenue collected at each governmental level can widely vary. Finland, New Zealand, and the United Kingdom (UK) have a unitary system in which government, including tax administration, is generally centralized at the national level with limited state and local government. For example, in New Zealand, the national government assessed about 90 percent of all the revenue collected across the nation. In contrast, the United States has a federal system in which the national level shares governmental authority with state and local governments. In the United States about half of all tax revenue is collected by the national government and about half is collected by the 50 states and tens of thousands of local governments.

The revenue data in table 4 below were provided by each nation and compiled by the Organisation for Economic Co-operation and Development (OECD) for consistent presentation.[1] These data cover all taxes in each nation including federal and state/local levels. Using these data, we computed the percent that each type of tax represents of the nation's total revenue. OECD provided the following definition for each of the major categories of tax in the table:

- Taxes are compulsory unrequited payments to general government and are not for benefits provided by government to taxpayers in proportion to their payments. Governments include national governments and agencies whose operations are under their effective control, state and local governments and their administrations, certain social security schemes and autonomous governmental entities, excluding public enterprises.
- Taxes on income, profits, and capital gains cover taxes levied on the net income or profits (i.e., gross income minus allowable tax deductions) of individuals and businesses (including corporations). Also covered are taxes levied on the capital gains of individuals and enterprises, and gains from gambling.
- Social security contributions are classified as all compulsory payments that confer an entitlement to receive a (contingent) future social benefit. Such payments are usually earmarked to finance social benefits and are often paid to institutions of general government that provide such benefits. These social security benefits would include unemployment insurance benefits and supplements, accident, injury and sickness benefits, old-age, disability and survivors' pensions, family allowances, reimbursements for medical and hospital expenses or provision of hospital or medical services. Contributions may be levied on both employees and employers.
- Taxes on payroll and workforce cover taxes paid by employers, employees, or the self-employed either as a proportion of payroll or as a fixed amount per person, and which do not confer entitlement to social benefits.
- Taxes on property, goods, and services cover recurrent and nonrecurrent taxes on the use, ownership, or transfer of property. These include taxes on immovable property or net wealth, taxes on the change of ownership of property through inheritance or gift, and taxes on financial and capital transactions. Taxes on goods and services include all taxes and duties levied on the production, sale, and lease of goods or services. This category covers multistage cumulative taxes; general sales taxes, value added taxes, excise taxes, or taxes levied on imports and exports of goods.

Table 4 shows that the largest source of revenue for 4 of 5 countries is the tax on individuals' and corporations' income, profits, and capital gains.

Table 4. Revenue, Governmental Structure, and Population Data for Five Nations, 2008

Source of revenue	United States	United Kingdom	Finland	New Zealand	Australia
Taxes on income, profits and capital gains (percent)	45	40	39	60	59
Individuals (percent)	38	30	31	41	38
Corporate (percent)	7	10	8	13	22
Unallocable between individual and corporate (percent)	0	0	0	7	0
Social security contributions (percent)	25	19	28	0	0
Taxes on payroll and workforce (percent)	0	0	0	0	5
Taxes on propery, goods, and services (percent)	30	41	33	40	36
Value added and sales taxes (percent)	14	28	29	31	25
Total tax revenue, excluding customs duties (percent)	100	100	100	100	100
Other data					
Total tax revenue as a percentage of GDP (2008)	26.1	35.7	43.1	33.7	27.1
Structure of government	federal	unitary	unitary	unitary	federal
2008population in millions	304.4	61.4	5.3	4.3	21.4

Sources: GAO analysis of OECD and World Bank data.

Note: Data are from OECD, *Revenue Statistics 2010 – Special feature: Environmental Related Taxation* (OECD Publishing, 2010), and World Bank Population data set, 2000 to 2009 by Country, www.worldbank.org (downloaded Dec. 23, 2010).

Also, the tax paid by individuals is a larger percentage of revenue than the corporation tax in each country. The tax on property, goods, and services is the next most important tax except in the UK where the income tax is the second largest source. A large component of the taxes on property, goods, and services is the value added tax and sales tax. In Australia, New Zealand, the UK, and Finland, value added tax and sales tax ranged from 25 percent to 31 percent of the taxes collected in the nation. The United States does not have a value added tax, but sales taxes alone totaled about 14 percent of all U.S. revenue.

End Notes

[1] See 26 U.S.C. § 6041-6050W.

[2] 26 U.S.C. § 3402.

[3] GAO, *2010 Tax Filing Season: IRS's Performance Improved in Key Areas, but Efficiency Gains are Possible in Others*, GAO-11-111 (Washington, D.C.: Dec. 16, 2010). The Web site data are from January 1 to July 31, 2010, and the telephone call data are from January 1 to June 30, 2010.

[4] Revenue loss estimates are intended to provide information about the value of tax expenditures. However, separate tax expenditure estimates do not incorporate any behavioral responses and thus do not necessarily represent the exact amount of revenue to be gained by repealing a specific tax expenditure.

[5] For a discussion of the issues related to tax expenditures, see GAO, *Government Performance and Accountability: Tax Expenditures Represent a Substantial Federal Commitment and Need to Be Reexamined*, GAO-05-690 (Washington, D.C.: Sept. 23, 2005), and Office of Management and Budget, *Analytical Perspectives, Budget of the United States Government, Fiscal Year 2012* (Washington, D.C.: 2010).

[6] Details on these practices are provided in the appendixes. In addition, The Hong Kong Special Administrative Region is part of the People's Republic of China. Throughout this report, we will use Hong Kong as the abbreviation for this region.

[7] To adjust foreign currencies to U.S. dollars, we used the Federal Reserve Board's foreign exchange rates. New Zealand dollars converted to U.S. dollars as of December 31, 2004.

[8] Individuals who are members of the Evangelical-Lutheran Church or the Orthodox Church pay a flat-rate church tax. Local church communities determine the tax rate, which varies between 1 and 2 percent of taxable income. Individuals who are not members of either church do not pay the tax.

[9] Under automatic information exchange, countries agree to routinely provide information about tax-related transactions. Under another information exchange practice, information exchange upon request, the exchange generally requires a specific justification for the information needed by the requesting tax authority.

[10] These nations are the Swiss Confederation, the Principality of Liechtenstein, the Republic of San Marino, the Principality of Monaco, and the Principality of Andorra.

[11] We used rates that matched the time period cited for the foreign amount. The currency conversion for the capital gains amount is as of February 25, 2011.

[12] Australian dollars converted to U.S. dollars as of December 31, 2008.

[13] Australian dollars converted to U.S. dollars as of December 31, 2007.

[14] Center for Inter-American Tax Administration, http://www.ciat.org.

[15] When JITSIC uncovered transactions used by large corporations to generate inappropriate foreign tax credit benefits, the information was shared among members. The IRS made the generator a compliance concern for large corporations and has been pursuing these cases.

[16] OECD, *Engaging with High Net Worth Individuals on Tax Compliance* (2009).

[17] For more information on IRS's related entities program, see GAO, *IRS Can Improve Efforts to Address Tax Evasion by Networks of Businesses and Related Entities*, GAO-10-968 (Washington, D.C.: Sept. 24, 2010).

End Notes for Appendix I

[1] For more information about factors that limit the comparability of tax administration systems, see Organisation for Economic Co-operation and Development (OECD), *Tax Administration in OECD and Selected Non-OECD Countries: Comparative Information Series* (2008).

End Notes for Appendix II

[1] PAYE is an amount an employer deducts from an employee's salary and wages to satisfy income tax and other obligations. Company Tax is income taxed at the company rate. Schedular Payments are paid by self-employed contractors and companies often in the agricultural, horticultural, and viticulture industries. The business or person paying the contractor is required to deduct a pre-determined percentage of income and remit this to IRD.

[2] KiwiSaver is a voluntary, work-based retirement savings initiative.

[3] The Family tax credit provides payments to families with dependent children age 18 or younger earning less than specified minimum income levels and varying depending on the number of children. The In-work tax credit provides payments for parents based on the number of hours of weekly paid employment. The Minimum family tax credit provides payments to parents with dependent children based on the number of hours of weekly paid employment. The Parental tax credit provides payments for a newborn baby for the first 8 weeks and is an alternative to Paid Parental Leave, which is administered on behalf of the Department of Labour.

[4] Accommodation supplements assist families with rent, board, or costs of owning a home. Childcare subsidies assist families with childcare costs for children under 14. Temporary additional support is a weekly payment to help families meet essential living costs.

[5] Generally, IRD makes WFF tax credit payments (weekly, biweekly or annually). MSD may make the Family tax credit payment instead of IRD, such as when recipients are receiving welfare benefits. MSD makes its WFF tax credit payments mainly through the benefit system.

[6] GAO, *Opportunities to Reduce Potential Duplication in Government Programs, Save Tax Dollars, and Enhance Revenue*, GAO-11-318SP (Washington, D.C.: Mar. 1, 2011).

[7] GAO, *Government Performance And Accountability: Tax Expenditures Represent a Substantial Federal Commitment and Need to Be Reexamined*, GAO-05-690 (Washington, D.C.: Sept. 23, 2005).

[8] A similar approach is now required under the recently enacted GPRA Modernization Act of 2010, Pub. L. No. 111-352, 124 Stat. 3866 (2011). The act requires OMB, in coordination with agencies, to develop federal government priority goals including a limited number of crosscutting goals, and assess the contributions made toward those goals by various agencies and federal activities—including spending programs and tax expenditures.

End Notes for Appendix III

[1] All returns are final at October 31. The taxpayer must appeal before the end of the 5th year following the assessment year.

[2] Finland has about 500,000 businesses, of which about half were solely owned by individual taxpayers as of 2010.

[3] Based on 2011 estimates, the population median age in Finland is 42.5 years as compared to the U.S. median age of 36.9 years.

[4] A Decree of the Ministry of Transport and Communications specifies the minimum rate of functional Internet access as a universal service and requires a functional rate for downstream traffic as 1 megabit per second.

[5] About three-quarters of Finnish citizens use an Internet bank.

[6] If the taxpayer fails to file a return and enough information returns reporting income have been filed, the IRS can create a return, based on that information, and mails it to the taxpayer for acceptance or adjustment. IRS prepares these returns under a compliance program and the taxpayer may be assessed penalties.

End Notes for Appendix IV

[1] EU members include Austria, Belgium, Bulgaria, Cyprus, the Czech Republic, Denmark, Estonia, Finland, France, Germany, Greece, Hungary, Ireland, Italy, Latvia, Lithuania, Luxembourg, Malta, the Netherlands, Poland, Portugal, Romania, Slovakia, Slovenia, Spain, Sweden, and the United Kingdom.

[2] In addition to EU members, certain dependent and associated territories of member countries have agreed to participate with the directive. These territories include the Cayman Islands, Anguilla, Turks and Caicos Islands, Montserrat, Aruba, Jersey, Guernsey, the Isle of Man, the British Virgin Islands, and the Netherlands Antilles. Four of the territories (Anguilla, Aruba, Cayman Islands, and Montserrat) have agreed to information exchange. As of October 2010, the Netherlands Antilles became an independent nation.

[3] Paying agents are defined as intermediaries responsible for paying interest income received from debtors to owners of the debt. For example, a bank can be considered a paying agent.

[4] These nations are the Swiss Confederation, the Principality of Liechtenstein, the Republic of San Marino, the Principality of Monaco, and the Principality of Andorra. The information upon request exchange generally requires a more detailed justification for the information needed by the requesting tax authority.

[5] Six dependent and associated territories (Turks and Caicos Islands, Jersey, Guernsey, the Isle of Man, the British Virgin Islands, and the Netherlands Antilles) have agreed to the withholding provisions.

[6] See Commission of the European Communities, Commission Staff Working Document, *Presenting an economic evaluation of the effects of the Council Directive 2003/48/EC on the basis of the available data*; SEC(2008) 2420 (Brussels: Sept. 15, 2008).

[7] The United Kingdom reported information from July 1, 2005, to April 5, 2006.

[8] The amount corresponds with 75 percent of the total withholding tax or about €745.47 million (about US$984 million). The British Virgin Islands and the Netherlands Antilles did not share withholding.

[9] An example would be Liechtenstein foundations where payments made are covered by the directive, but in practice the payments rarely were reported as interest payments.

[10] The convention is in force among Azerbaijan, Belgium, Denmark, Finland, France, Iceland, Italy, the Netherlands, Norway, Poland, Slovenia, Spain, Sweden, Ukraine, and the United Kingdom.

End Notes for Appendix V

[1] Excise duties are levied on items such as alcohol products, tobacco products, and mineral oils.

[2] After April 2011, the personal allowance will be reduced for those with income above £100,000 (US$160,780).

[3] The UK has additional tax rates for interest savings and dividend income. The rates for both savings and dividend income start at 10 percent, and higher rates may apply depending on the amount of the related income.

[4] Retired individuals receiving a pension will pay income tax through the Pay As You Earn (PAYE) or self-assessment systems.

[5] The employees can also ask HMRC to include other income such as some self-employment, rental, or savings income in determining their PAYE code.

[6] HMRC officials said that only HMRC can adjust PAYE codes because only HMRC knows a taxpayer's total income. A taxpayer can provide HMRC with additional information that can be used to adjust the PAYE code.

[7] Data mining is a technique for extracting knowledge from large volumes of data. See GAO, *Data Mining: Federal Efforts Cover a Wide Range of Uses*, GAO-04-548 (Washington, D.C.: May 4, 2004).

[8] House of Commons Committee of Public Accounts, *HM Revenue and Customs' 2009-10 Accounts* (January 2011).

End Notes for Appendix VI

[1] For the list of all factors and their elements, see the ATO publication on *Large Business and Tax Compliance,* Australian Taxation Office (June 2010).

[2] Kristina Murphy, *Moving forward towards a more effective model of regulatory enforcement in the Australian Taxation Office*, Centre for Tax System Integrity, Research School of Social Sciences, Australian National University (2004).

[3] OECD, Engaging with High Net Worth Individuals on Tax Compliance (2009).

[4] GAO, *IRS Can Improve Efforts to Address Tax Evasion by Networks of Businesses and Related Entities*, GAO-10-968 (Washington, D.C.: Sept. 24, 2010).

End Notes for Appendix VII

[1] Profits tax is paid on all profits arising in or derived from Hong Kong from a trade, profession, or business carried on in Hong Kong.

[2] Michael Littlewood, *Taxation Without Representation: The History of Hong Kong's Troublingly Successful Tax System,* University of Hong Kong Press, Hong Kong, (2010).

[3] In addition to declaring income and any claimed deductions and allowances, the return includes name and address, and a Hong Kong Identity Card number or passport number.

[4] The Salaries Tax is imposed on income from employment or pension, while income tax generally is imposed on income from many sources beyond salaries, including interest, dividends, and capital gains.

[5] Individuals have 3 months to file if they solely-owned any unincorporated business.

End Notes for Appendix VIII

[1] OECD, *Revenue Statistics 2010—Special feature: Environmental Related Taxation* (2010). More information about these taxes can be obtained from the OECD publication Annex A.

In: Select Foreign Markets and Industries
Editor: Peter M. Luján

ISBN: 978-1-62100-133-1

Chapter 3

U.S. POSTAL SERVICE: FOREIGN POSTS' STRATEGIES COULD INFORM U.S. POSTAL SERVICE'S EFFORTS TO MODERNIZE*

United States Government Accountability Office

WHY GAO DID THIS STUDY

The foreign postal operators (foreign posts) in industrialized countries in GAO's review have been experiencing declining letter mail volumes and have modernized their delivery and retail networks to address this challenge. As requested, GAO reviewed the innovations and initiatives that foreign posts are using and the lessons the U.S. Postal Service (USPS) might learn to help it address plummeting mail volumes and record financial losses.

This report examines initiatives foreign posts have implemented to improve mail delivery and retail networks and related results, and modernization strategies used by foreign posts that can inform consideration of proposals to improve USPS's financial condition and customer service.

GAO selected foreign posts in Australia, Canada, Finland, Germany, Sweden, and Switzerland as case studies based on characteristics, such as delivery and retail changes and country size and location. GAO reviewed foreign posts' documents, including annual reports and strategic plans related to delivery and retail network changes and innovations. GAO met with foreign post officials, toured their retail facilities, received briefings on their delivery and retail networks and other areas, and met with regulators, labor unions, and mailers to obtain their views on the effects of their posts' modernization efforts. USPS generally agreed with GAO's findings and mentioned both its own modernization efforts and the barriers it faces.

---

* This is an edited, reformatted and augmented version of the United States Government Accountability Office publication, Report to the Ranking Member, Subcommittee on Federal Workforce, U.S. Postal Service and Labor Policy, Committee on Oversight and Government Reform, House of Representatives GAO-11-282, dated February 2011.

WHAT GAO FOUND

The foreign posts GAO reviewed have developed alternative delivery choices for customers that, according to the posts, have reduced costs and improved customer satisfaction and service. All of these posts now offer digital (purely electronic) or hybrid mail (a blend of physical and digital) options. Some posts offer parcel pick up at retail facilities like grocery stores, which are open longer than post offices, and are often owned and operated by businesses that partner with the posts, thus reducing costs.

One post allows customers to pick up parcels from a publicly-located machine, or parcel locker, that is available 24 hours a day.

The selected foreign posts have modernized their legacy brick and mortar retail networks in response to customers' changing use of the mail. For example, they have expanded retail access through alternatives such as Internet sales and partnerships with retail businesses such as grocery stores or pharmacies, while reducing the number of post-owned and -operated facilities (see figure). According to all of the posts, retail modernization has either (1) improved customer service, in some cases because the partner stays open longer, or (2) reduced operating and labor costs, by closing post-owned and -operated facilities, or both.

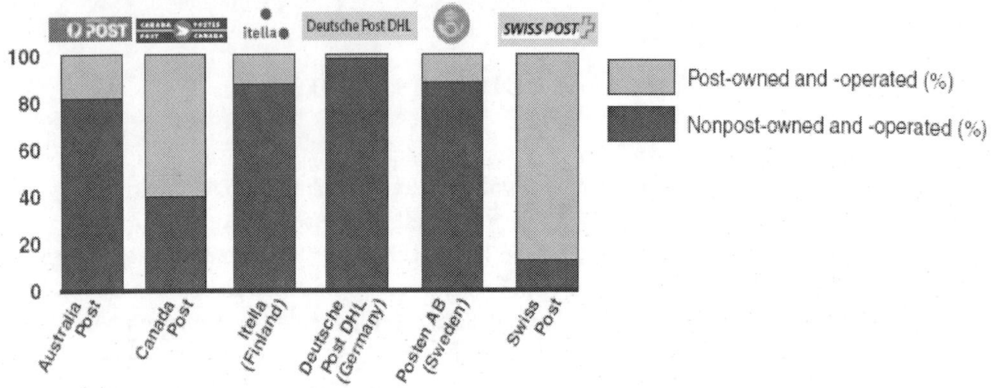

Sources: GAO analysis of foreign posts' data; logos used with permission from Australia Post, Canada Post, Itella, Deutsche Post DHL, Posten AB, and Swiss Post.

Foreign Posts' and Partner Retail Facilities in 2009.

The foreign posts faced resistance to change and challenges similar to those USPS faces, and they have used strategies that could be helpful to USPS as it moves forward with plans to modernize its own delivery and retail networks. In particular, they relied on outreach and communication strategies to inform public officials and customers of increased access to products and services and help gain acceptance for retail network changes.

A few posts also developed labor transition plans or strategies under which they provided training, relocation and job search services, and financial incentives to support employees who were negatively affected by the modernizations.

While USPS has taken steps in the past year to generate ideas for modernizing its retail and delivery networks, the experiences of foreign posts suggest that it will be critically important for USPS to fully develop and implement similar outreach, communication, and labor transition strategies.

View GAO Components

- Video showing Posten AB's (Sweden) public campaign effort.

February 16, 2011
The Honorable Stephen F. Lynch
Ranking Member
Subcommittee on Federal Workforce,
U.S. Postal Service and Labor Policy
Committee on Oversight and Government Reform
House of Representatives

Dear Mr. Lynch:

Foreign postal operators (foreign posts) in industrialized countries have seen mail volumes decline and electronic communication and payment alternatives (referred to as electronic substitution of mail) take the place of traditional mail. In addition, their legacy infrastructure remained larger than necessary to handle declining mail volumes. Over the past 10–20 years, foreign posts have engaged in strategic efforts to modernize their delivery and retail networks to address these challenges. For example, they are taking advantage of technological innovations and partnerships to facilitate new delivery services, such as offering hybrid mail, an electronic service combining physical and digital mail delivery options. Additionally, many foreign posts are planning to make or have already made changes to modernize their delivery and retail networks. For example, some foreign posts have installed parcel pick-up lockers in public locations as an alternative to home parcel delivery, or have transitioned from traditional post offices to partner-owned and -operated facilities. These retail and delivery modernization efforts encompass aspects of "universal service," such as requirements related to delivery of the mail and other access to postal retail services and facilities, among other areas.[1] (See appendix I for more information on universal service.)

Similarly, the U.S. Postal Service (USPS) faces declining mail volumes and changing use of the mail. Mail volume fell from 213 billion pieces in fiscal year 2006 to 171 billion pieces in fiscal year 2010—or about 20 percent. This decline resulted from the recession as well as electronic substitution. However, USPS has not been able to cut costs fast enough or generate sufficient net revenue to offset the lower mail volume and revenue that have occurred as customers have moved to electronic substitution of the mail. USPS has introduced a number of initiatives and efforts to reduce its costs and to try to mitigate expected future losses, but its financial condition and future viability will continue to be a concern as electronic substitution increases and mail volumes continue to drop.

Congress seeks to learn how USPS can effectively address its challenges and return to financial viability. The Postal Accountability and Enhancement Act of 2006 mandated that we report in 2011 to the President and Congress on options and strategies for long-term structural and operational reforms of USPS, including the experiences of other countries.[2] Because of concerns about USPS's deteriorating financial condition and future viability, we completed this work early and reported to Congress in April 2010 with options and strategies for financial viability.[3] In that report, we discussed the challenges to USPS's business model and options to address these challenges, including improvements to its retail, delivery, and mail processing operations. Further, we noted that we planned to address the experiences of foreign posts in a separate review. The subcommittee[4] requested that we review foreign posts in order to learn lessons for USPS related to technological innovations, as well as cost savings and efficiencies achieved through changes in delivery and retail networks. In accordance with this request, we addressed the following objectives:

1) What major initiatives have foreign posts implemented to improve or enhance mail delivery, and what have been the results?
2) What major initiatives have foreign posts implemented to improve or enhance their retail networks and what have been the results?
3) What modernization strategies have foreign posts used that could help inform USPS and Congress as they consider proposals to improve USPS's financial condition and customer service?

To address our three objectives, we employed a case study approach and selected from among industrialized countries six countries based on changes in delivery and retail networks, innovations and technology (from a literature review), rank of broadband usage per 100 inhabitants, nature of business or diversification, convenience and cost of travel, country population, location and size of the country, number of delivery points in 2008 (last year data were available), and 2008 mail volume (last year data were available). We used this information to select countries that have made changes to adapt to the changing use of mail and communication.

For each of the countries we selected—Australia, Canada, Finland, Germany, Sweden, and Switzerland—we reviewed foreign posts' documents, including annual reports and strategic plans related to retail and delivery network changes and innovations. We met with the postal operators and toured their innovation centers, retail facilities, or both. We also received briefings on their retail and delivery networks, strategic planning, and other matters. We observed a number of demonstrations of the foreign posts' innovations. In addition, we met with regulators, labor unions, and private sector mailers to gain their perspectives on the effects of the modernization efforts. Following the in-country interviews, we requested additional data and information on each foreign post's strategies, goals, and results related to its modernization efforts. We also met with USPS officials to discuss innovations and strategies related to USPS's retail and delivery network but we did not compare these innovations to those of foreign posts. We also did not assess whether the foreign posts' operational changes were profitable since that information is either proprietary or not consistently reported. In 2009, we reported on USPS's efforts to reduce costs and improve delivery efficiency.[5] We have another ongoing review that will examine in more detail USPS's use of and plans for retail alternatives and the challenges it faces related to implementing the alternatives. (See appendix II for more details on the scope and methodology for this review.)

We conducted this performance audit from January 2010 to February 2011 in accordance with generally accepted government auditing standards. Those standards require that we plan and perform the audit to obtain sufficient, appropriate evidence to provide a reasonable basis for our findings and conclusions based on our audit objectives. We believe that the evidence obtained provides a reasonable basis for our findings and conclusions based on our audit objectives.

BACKGROUND

Declining letter mail volumes and increasing electronic substitution, which have accelerated with the recent recession, have reduced postal revenues for both the foreign posts and USPS. Additionally, foreign posts told us they, like USPS, faced high infrastructure and workforce costs. Some foreign posts began to modernize their delivery or retail networks, or both, as early as the 1990s. One of the factors precipitating these changes occurred when the European Union began to establish a timetable for the gradual ending of monopolies of letter markets, in its 1997 Council Directive.[6] In 2008, the European Union directed its members to fully "open" their domestic letter markets to competition by 2010 (i.e., remove their monopoly on delivering letter mail).[7] In doing so, the European Union stated that it wanted to "allow sufficient time to put in place the...modernization and restructuring measures required to ensure longterm viability under the new market conditions" of the posts.[8] In all six countries we reviewed, the posts were experiencing challenges related to declining mail volumes or high infrastructure, labor, or operating costs, or both, which necessitated the need for modernization. See figure 1 for a list of the six foreign posts we reviewed, including how we identified them in this report.

Country	Official name of postal operator	Web site (English)	Brand or Logo used in report	Referred to in report
Australia	Australian Postal Corporation[a]	auspost.com/au	AUSTRALIA POST	Australia Post
Canada	Canada Post Corporation	www.canadapost.ca/	CANADA POST POSTES CANADA	Canada Post
Finland	Itella Corporation	www.itella.com	[b] itella	Itella
Germany	Deutsche Post DHL	www.dp-dhl.com	Deutsche Post DHL	DP DHL
Sweden	Posten AB	www.posten.se/m/startpage		Posten AB
Switzerland	Swiss Post	www.swisspost.com	SWISS POST	Swiss Post

Sources: GAO; logos used with permission from Australia Post, Canada Post, Itella, DP DHL, Posten AB, and Swiss Post.

Note: To view each foreign post's Web site, click on the corresponding link. Web sites were accessed on February 11, 2011.

[a] Australia Post and associated trade marks, whether registered or unregistered, are owned by the Australian Postal Corporation. Australia Post reserves the right to take action to stop any unauthorized or infringing use of its trade marks.

[b] The Itella and Posti names and logos are protected symbols and trademarks of the Itella Corporation.

Figure 1. Names of Foreign Posts and Logos Used in Report.

USPS is facing similar challenges as other industrialized nations' posts. For example, USPS has a brick and mortar retail infrastructure it cannot afford to maintain. However, USPS currently manages more retail outlets— approximately 32,500—than all of the foreign posts we reviewed combined. In addition, USPS has twice as many delivery points as any foreign post we studied—USPS delivers to 151 million homes, businesses, and post office boxes. Another challenge that USPS experienced was a record loss of $8.5 billion in fiscal year 2010. Thus, as we have reported, without substantial changes to its business model, USPS's ability to fulfill its mission through self-supporting, businesslike operations is not sustainable.[9]

Foreign Posts Are Offering More Alternatives to Traditional Delivery in an Effort to Increase Customer Service and Convenience and Decrease Costs

All of the foreign posts discussed in this report have implemented various initiatives to complement or enhance traditional delivery by offering customers more alternatives to send and receive letters and packages.[10]

Traditional Mail Delivery and Challenges

Traditional delivery methods for foreign posts of letters, packages or parcels, and advertising mail, can include:

- post office boxes,
- carrier-to-home (to a customer's door or mail box), and
- cluster boxes (grouping of boxes for customers in a particular neighborhood, instead of individual mail boxes at a personal residence, which are often found within a housing development).

Although letter mail volumes have been decreasing, some foreign posts expect parcel volumes to strengthen as economic conditions improve, particularly with the emergence of online shopping and small business growth. According to foreign post officials we spoke with, customers have been increasingly changing the way they use and receive their mail. With increasing Internet and broadband access[11] and related changing use of the mail, use of traditional mail has been declining as customers find more convenient and faster ways to communicate. Several of the posts we met with said that customers were using various electronic means to conduct their daily business, such as paying bills online, sending postcards and greeting cards electronically, or receiving news and other periodicals via the Internet instead of hard copy (all referred to as e-substitution).[12] This changing use of the mail was a primary factor driving changes in the way the posts do business. In addition, foreign post officials told us they have a significant amount of costs associated with delivering traditional letter mail and packages. Some posts have been experiencing increases in the number of delivery points every year, at the same time that mail volumes overall have been declining. Australia Post and Canada Post officials told us the number of addresses has generally grown each year by about 200,000 addresses. A few of the posts attribute a major part of their costs to delivering the mail (also known as the "last mile").

Given all of these factors, the foreign post operators we met with have begun to focus on adjusting or downsizing their delivery networks and providing multi-channel approaches to give their customers more choices in how they send and receive mail.

Foreign Posts Have Introduced a Number of Alternatives to Traditional Mail Delivery

Hybrid and Digital Mail

All six posts we met with offered some form of digital or hybrid means of sending and receiving mail, and several of the posts reported increased customer service and satisfaction as a result of these offerings. Digital mail is communication between a sender and a recipient through completely electronic communication (this could include personal e-mail and electronic bills and other communication with businesses). While postal experts have a variety of definitions for hybrid mail, there is no consensus on the exact definition. In this report, we use the term "hybrid mail" to describe different ways of sending and receiving mail and communication using a blend or combination of electronic or digital mail and physical forms. For example, an item—a bill, letter, card, or other communication—is electronically transmitted, processed and converted into a letter post item for physical delivery to the addressee. Figure 2 illustrates examples of digital and hybrid mail services, and figure 3 shows examples of their availability through the six foreign posts we reviewed.

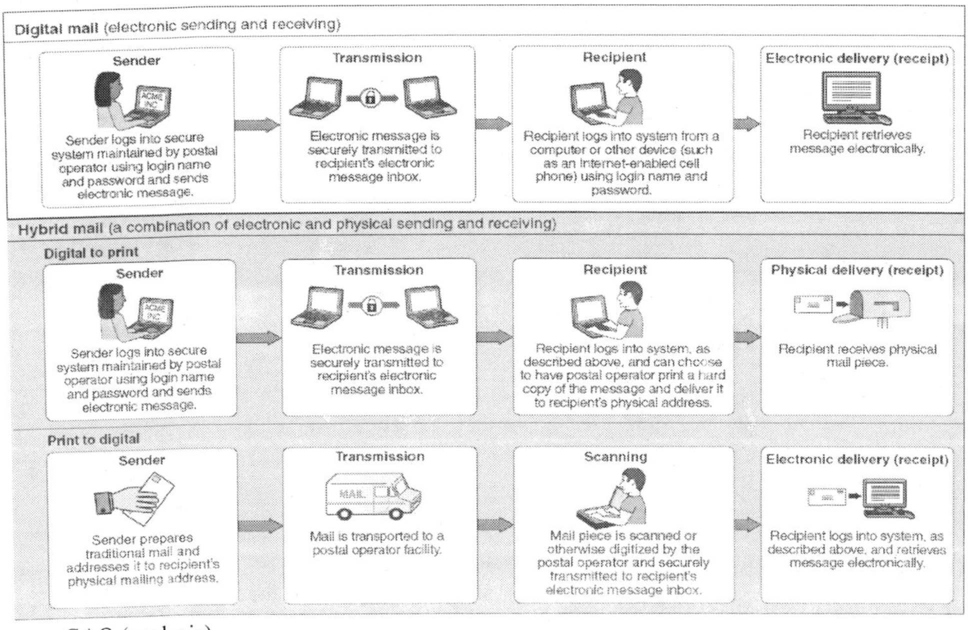

Source: GAO (analysis).

Figure 2. How Digital Mail and Hybrid Mail Services Work.

Postal service	Description of digital and hybrid mail offerings by the six foreign posts
Australia	**eLetter®**–Australia's eLetter business unit includes several subsidiaries that provide logistics and printing services, including hybrid mail, among others. It offers a complete mail solution from design, preparation, and addressing to delivery and archiving. eLetter includes a print and processing network across Australia, which has nationally located sites where mail is sent digitally for printing at locations closest to the final delivery points.
Canada	**epost™**–Canada Post's free (to consumers) online bill presentment service allows customers to view pay, and manage bills and financial documents electronically. Allows archiving for up to 7 years. The epost™ box is a secure, Internet-based service. Customers select mailers to receive bills and other documents from. **epost™2.0**–Currently under development, this service will add to the current epost™ electronic bill presentment services offered by Canada Post, induding adjacent secure online services. government services, and consolidation of documents. In addition, secure delivery boxes mirroring physical mailing addresses will be introduced. Canada Post will require identity authentication before assigning a user account and entitlement to the electronic delivery box.
Finland	**Netposti**–Free service offered to users to receive various types of addressed letter mail through a secure electronic postbox. Each digital mail box is linked to a single person, and letters that otherwise were received physically are now received electronically. In practice, letters are channeled to the electronic postbox in the hybrid mail process, where the print shops match all letters against a Netposti customer preference database. Matching can be done with the physical street address or some other identifier (like a social security number) that is included in the data stream for hybrid mail operators. Letters received through this service look the same in electronic format as they would in physical format, but they can include data elements that help streamline other electronic processes, such as invoice payment. Digital mail is secure since content is not transferred through the public Internet, and user identification is authenticated. Netposti also offers archiving of documents and mail for up to 7 years free of charge, and users can receive various types of letters, such as pay statements, bills, health care sector documents, and digital magazines. Netposti recipients and users can receive mail from only senders they have approved.
Germany	**E-Postbrief™**–Allows customers to communicate securely via the Internet. When customers register for the service, they are required to authenticate their identity by presenting an identification card or passport. All communications sent and received via the E-Postbrief™ secure gateway are end-to-end encrypted. Cost is the same as for a letter. In cases when an E-Postbrief™ is sent to a recipient who is not registered for the service or if the sender choses this option, the E-Postbrief™ will be printed by DP DHL and delivered physically. Documents sent and signed through E-Postbrief™ are legally binding and confidential.
Sweden	**e-Letter**–A hybrid mail delivery service that allows customers to e-mail letters to be delivered physically to non-e-mail recipients. Posten AB prints the letters at dedicated print locations and then delivers them physically via the post.
Switzerland	**SuisseID**–Offers secure identification and digital signature capabilities for its customers. Customers receive an identification card or USB device after presenting proof of identification at a Swiss Post retail office. SuisseID uses high-grade security technology for secure login and legally valid digital signatures. **Swiss Post Box**–Registered customers can have their physical mail received, scanned, and delivered by Swiss Post. Customers can choose how they would like to accept their mail. After receiving an initial scanned image of the front and back of a physical piece of mail (for example, a letter), a customer can request that Swiss Post (1) open the mail, scan the entire contents of the mail, and send the contents electronically to the customer; (2) leave the mail unopened and have the mail sent to the customer's physical address; or (3) shred the mail piece.

Sources: GAO (analysis); logos used with permission from Australia Post, Canada Post, Itella, DP DHL, Posten AB, and Swiss Post.

Figure 3. Digital and Hybrid Mail Services Available through Foreign Posts.

> "We want to change the way people think about the last mile—as no longer physical, but digital."
>
> Source: Swiss Post official.

A video depiction of Swiss Post Box, described previously, is available here. (Accessed on Feb. 9, 2011)

While there is no consensus on a definition of hybrid mail, there does seem to be agreement that the way customers communicate is changing, and moving more toward a digital environment. According to Canada Post officials, in order to stay relevant to customers, the Post began to make a number of revisions to its corporate plans and strategies in 2005, focusing more on electronic and hybrid options. Over the years, Canada Post has been engaged in a number of efforts to reinvent, update, and enhance customer use of the mail through digital alternatives. Canada Post officials observed that some initiatives were successful, while others failed because they may have been ahead of their time. For example, according to a Canada Post official, epost 2.0 will be an improvement on a former digital offering and will be introduced within the next 2 years. Some postal officials see digital and hybrid mail as the "new last mile" and are gearing toward incorporating more digital mail delivery options for their customers.

Foreign postal officials told us that their digital and hybrid mail options offered three benefits. First, some of the officials said these digital and hybrid mail services offer enhanced security and trust. They told us that they use their customers' trust and loyalty in the "brand" of the postal operator to illustrate that digital and hybrid mail communications through the postal operator are secure. According to an Itella official, the biggest advantage of NetPosti was mail security. The official said that a NetPosti account was not as easily accessible as an e-mail account and its contents. The primary concern for Itella was ensuring security of the mail. Swiss Post created its Suisse ID to incorporate security encryption on the actual identification card or Universal Serial Bus (USB)[13] used by customers to sign into their accounts. This encryption provided customers with a secure encryption whenever they logged in. Customers must have their identification verified in person at a post office before receiving the SuisseID.

> "...for those who want the speed of an e-mail but with the security of a letter."
>
> Source: DP DHL 2009 Annual Report, describing E-Post Brief.

Second, officials at three of the six posts we spoke with offered their customers who use digital or hybrid mail solutions the opportunity to archive not only their digitally transmitted mail, but other documents as well. NetPosti offered archiving of all data and documents for 7 years free of charge. Customers could also bring into their NetPosti accounts personal files, such as scanned receipts, for a fee. Swiss Post offered customers the option to archive their documents.

Third, three of the six foreign posts offered hybrid mail options combined with a "platform of services." This platform offered integration between the sending and receipt of mail (letters, bills, cards, etc.) in a mixture of electronic and physical forms, along with other electronic capabilities such as archiving data for the customer (including the mail itself, as mentioned above), and financial services, such as bill presentment or bill pay and bill consolidation. For example, Swiss Post offered its Suisse ID customers a number of options, including bill pay and receipt, marketing services, and electronic archiving.

Posts reported that these digital and hybrid mail initiatives have resulted in increased convenience and customer satisfaction, primarily because they make mail more accessible. A number of the foreign posts mentioned wanting to be where their customers shop or work, a goal that affected posts' decisions about where to locate services. Officials with Swiss Post stated that their products are not only about making money but also about decreasing the cost of delivering the mail, which for Swiss Post they estimated was more than 50 percent of its operating costs.

Pick up at Retail Store Counter

Several of the posts we spoke with have partnered with major retailers as well as individual stores and shops, such as grocery and drug stores, to provide a number of postal products and services to their customers, including parcel pick up. These stores offer more convenient locations and longer hours than traditional post offices. This partnering was part of a major transformation in the foreign posts' retail networks, and part of an approach to provide multiple alternatives and choices for customers. In Sweden, Posten AB customers receive a notice, sent as a text message or a hard copy by the letter carrier, that they have a package available for pick up at a retail store counter convenient to them.[14] They then take the paper notice to show the text to a postal retail partner outlet, such as a grocery store, and pick up the package. Posten AB officials noted that customer service has improved, evidenced by customers' more timely pick up of these packages and parcels (reduced from an average of about 10 days to about 3), longer hours of access to these services, and an increased number of service points.

Canada Post offers a variation on alternative parcel pick up with its community boxes, similar to cluster boxes (see fig. 4). Some community boxes have parcel boxes built in. Carriers leave a note along with a key in the private box of a customer with a parcel delivery, and leave the parcel itself in the parcel section of the community box. If there is no parcel section, the carriers leave the parcel elsewhere for customer pick up (for example, at a convenient retail outlet).

Delivery options	Australia	Canada	Finland	Germany	Sweden	Switzerland
Traditional post office	✓	✓	✓	✓	✓	✓
Home delivery	✓	✓	✓	✓	✓	✓
Cluster boxes		✓	✓		✓	✓
24-hour automated parcel locker				✓		
Pick up at nonpost-owned retail counter	✓	✓	✓	✓	✓	✓
Digital and hybrid mail	✓	✓	✓	✓	✓	✓

Sources: GAO (analysis); logos used with permission from Australia Post, Canada Post, Itella, DP DHL, Posten AB, and Swiss Post.

Figure 4. Delivery Alternatives for Letters or Parcels Available through Foreign Posts.

Swiss Post customers can use Swiss Post's PickPost service at no additional cost. With PickPost, customers can select a time and place most convenient for them to pick up their parcels. Customers register online and receive a personal customer number. When customers place an order, for example, for a parcel delivery, they provide the sender with the address of their chosen PickPost collection point (there are approximately 350 countrywide). The customers are then notified by text or e-mail as soon as the item has been delivered. They have 7 days to retrieve the parcel from the location. Four of the posts we spoke with use partnerships or contracts with private sector businesses and shops to offer their customers parcel pick up. Both Posten AB and Australia Post use retail partners to offer postal products and services in place of traditional post offices. Canada Post has a network of authorized dealers it contracts with to offer postal products and services.

As mentioned previously, foreign post officials told us they improved customer service by offering parcel pick up at more convenient locations with later hours and realized some reduction in costs due to, for example, offering services and products through shops that were nonpost-owned. This helped posts to decrease their infrastructure costs and rightsize their workforces to accommodate changes in their networks.

Parcel Delivery Machines

In 2002, DP DHL introduced its "Packstation," a set of automated, standalone lockers where packages are sent and received, and as of 2010 had 2,500 nationwide. Packstations are typically located in high-traffic, public locations such as train stations. Fig. 5 shows an example of a DP DHL Packstation. Customers can sign up for delivery (free of charge to both the sender and the receiver) and have their identity verified in person by the Post. When customers want to receive parcels at a Packstation, they can give the Packstation as the delivery address (instead of their home address). The parcel is then delivered to the Packstation and the customers are notified via text message or e-mail that they have a package. Delivery to a Packstation eliminates the need for home parcel delivery for the postal operator and allows customers to pick up their parcels more conveniently, according to DP DHL. Packstations can also be used to dispatch small packets and parcels 24 hours a day, 7 days a week. As of the end of January 2011, DP DHL had more than 1 million registered users who could collect or send parcels. According to the DP DHL officials, self-service parcel pick up machines have enhanced customer service and convenience because customers can use them at any hour of the day. We observed a demonstration of DP DHL's Packstation at its Innovation Center. According to DP DHL officials, DP DHL created its Innovation Center in part, for specialists from academic, industrial, and technological fields to exchange information about logistics solutions. The center offers a method for networking and development of solutions from start to finish, and visitors to the center can view DP DHL's developments.

Swiss Post also offered a parcel locker-style delivery option for its customers. Customers could receive their parcels at a parcel box, which is a large, lockable storage box at the entrance to a neighborhood. Both DP DHL and Swiss Post noted that their parcel locker options were aimed at increasing customer service and convenience, and decreasing costs related to delivering packages (the last mile).

Perhaps one of the most dramatic examples of changes to delivery frequency and hybrid mail offerings was Itella's Antilla Living Lab trial. Antilla is a small village in the countryside near Porvoo, Finland, where Itella was testing new ideas for service in remote areas.

Source: Deutsche Post DHL.

Figure 5. Example of DP DHL Parcel Delivery Locker in Germany.

Changes in customers' use of the mail and digitization, among other reasons, motivated Itella to begin this trial, which involved 124 households and 17 small companies. Mail was physically delivered to customers' homes or businesses 2 days a week. On the 3 other days that mail was delivered, it was placed in assigned post lockers located near the Antilla village main shop. Customers received a text message daily letting them know if they had mail, so they could decide whether to travel to the postal locker and retrieve their mail. Any mail not retrieved was delivered to the customer on 1 of the 2 days when mail was delivered to the home or business. First and second class letters were scanned and then delivered electronically to the customer's NetPosti digital account. These letters were then placed back in their envelopes and delivered in paper form. Customers could also receive letters directly to NetPosti from selected senders digitally without having to convert the letter to physical format.

Foreign Posts' Modernized Retail Networks Have Increased Access to Products and Services, Improved Customer Service, and Reduced Costs

All of the foreign posts we met with have modernized their legacy brick and mortar retail networks in response to customers' changing use of the mail.

All Posts Have Increased Access to Alternative Retail Points

All of the foreign posts we met with offer increased access to retail products and services. As communication has changed and broadband usage increased, foreign posts have adapted their offerings to better fit their customers' needs. Alternative retail points are points of service other than traditional postal retail facilities or post offices owned and operated by the postal operator. Examples include postal counters at retail partners such as a grocery store in Sweden or a pharmacy in Canada, as well as the postal operators' Web sites, among others.

Internet Access and New Mobile Applications

All of the posts we met with provided customer access to online services. The six posts offered a range of services on their Web sites, from sales of stamps and other products to online bill payment. Figure 6 shows Swiss Post's online store where a customer can buy stamps and chocolate, create postcards, and perform numerous other transactions, such as subscribe to magazines and register for Swiss Post Box, described previously.

Source: Swiss Post.

Note: To view Swiss Post's virtual online store, click anywhere on the figure. To return to the report close out of the store Web site. Web site was accessed on January 12, 2011.

Figure 6. Swiss Post Virtual Online Store's Web Link.

In addition to online offerings, all six of the foreign post we reviewed have developed postal applications for mobile devices.

Partnerships with Private Firms Offer Posts Increased Access to Postal Products and Services and Decreased Postal Costs

Foreign posts told us they have decreased operating costs (largely facility- and labor-related) by forming partnerships with private-sector entities that own and operate retail sites. As table 1 indicates, the majority of the foreign posts we met with maintained a network with a majority of partner-owned and -operated retail facilities rather than their own traditional post offices. For example, in 2009, about 98 percent of DP DHL's retail network was owned and operated by partners.[15]

Table 1. Foreign Posts Retail Facilities in 2009

	Post-owned facilities	Post-owned (percentage)	Nonpost-owned facilities	Nonpost-owned (percentage)	Total
Australia Post	827	19%	3,606	81%	4,433
Canada Post	3,955	61	2,548	39	6,503
Itella (Finland)	140	13	960	87	1,100
Deutsche Post (Germany)	400	2	16,400	98	16,800
Posten AB (Sweden)[a]	300	12	2,200	88	2,500
Swiss Post[b]	2,065	88	283	12	2,348

Source: Foreign posts.

Note: All percentages are rounded to nearest whole number.

[a] Posten AB told us its figures are approximate.

[b] Swiss Post has a majority of post-owned facilities (per the numbers above) versus nonpost-owned facilities, primarily because Switzerland has a tradition of customers paying bills in person at a post office. Swiss Post officials said they are considering alternatives for about 420 of their post offices by the end of 2011(for example, replacing them with retail partners).

Posten AB in Sweden has dramatically changed its postal retail network since 2001, replacing all traditional brick and mortar post-owned and -operated post offices with partner-owned and -operated retail facilities.[16]

In visiting a postal retail partner outlet at a grocery store in Stockholm, a sign in front clearly displayed the services offered inside (see figure 7). Four or five of the store's 20–25 employees were trained to work at the postal counter.

One employee said he spent about 4 hours a day selling postal services and products and the rest of the time he sold nonpostal items. We witnessed him moving back and forth, like a photo counter clerk at a drugstore. If he had questions, he could call a Posten AB-operated phone assistance service line. He said he liked the work because there was little down time.

Source: GAO.

Figure 7. Posten AB Partner Outlet Showing Services Available at Grocery Store in Stockholm, Sweden.

> "We want to be where the people shop...we do not want to be the last business in town."
>
> Source: Canada Post official.

Figure 8 depicts another example of a partnership between a postal operator and a private business.

All of the posts we interviewed reported positive results as a result of retail modernization in one or both of two key areas: (1) customer service, which has improved because, for example, the retail partner is open for more hours during a day and open on a weekend versus a traditional post office, and (2) savings in operating and labor costs achieved by closing post-owned and -operated facilities.

In Australia, 81 percent of retail facilities were owned and operated by partners and were mostly located in commercial areas. When Australia Post modernized its retail network, some post offices were moved to newer, lower-cost smaller structures, such as facilities in a commercial area "where the shoppers are." For example, we visited an Australia Post partner's retail facility (licensed post office) in Kilmore, Australia that was relocated from the outskirts of town to a strip mall and Australia Post officials said the move saved the Post 20 percent in operating costs.

Source: GAO.

Figure 8. Canada Post Retail Partner Outlet.

Foreign Posts Have Experienced Mixed Results from Nonpostal Retail Products and Services

Some foreign posts have traditionally offered banking or financial services, while others no longer do. Three of the posts that we visited were continuing or seeking to expand these services. For example, Swiss Post and Australia Post, which have traditionally offered financial or banking services, offered in-person bill paying services. Swiss Post also provided some financial services and was seeking a banking license. Australia Post provided banking services as an agent for more than 70 banks and financial institutions. Similarly, DP DHL and its partners offer banking and financial services.[17] Other posts—Itella and Posten AB—have experienced mixed results from offering nonpostal services.

Several foreign posts made government services available. Australia Post and Itella offered government services in their retail facilities, including those in remote or rural areas where citizens may have difficulty traveling to a large city. For example, Itella offered voter registration services as well as fishing licenses. Itella and the Finnish Ministry of Justice first established a framework for the voter registration service under which local government officials could choose whether to make advance voting available in post offices in their municipalities. Itella officials reported that in 2010 Itella offered this service to 127 post offices and its goal was for 93 post offices to provide this service. Australia Post reported its identity verification service was used, for example, when applying for a government service or to open a bank account. This service was a successful revenue-generator, according to Australia Post, leveraging the trusted brand of the Post and provided a needed government service in rural areas. For example, citizens seeking to work with children could fill out an identity verification application in order to initiate a required background check. A senior official noted that services such as assisting a customer with a passport application would generally need to be provided in person, with assistance, rather than online. Figure 9 depicts a retail employee in Australia assisting a customer with questions related to nonpostal services.

> "...the value of our staff...cannot be underesti-mated and will remain a key value proposition well into the future."
>
> Source: Australia Post official.

Figure 9. Australia Post Nonpostal Products and Services.

All foreign posts have traditionally sold postal products, such as stamps and envelopes at their retail facilities. In the past 5 years, several posts began selling other retail products as a means to increase revenue. For example, Itella exclusively partnered with a major Finnish design firm to license merchandise including designed packaging, gift wrapping, postcards, and gift items, resulting in what it reported as a successful partnership.

Itella officials noted that sales of other nonpostal products, such as jewelry and candy, have not been as successful. They said selling luxury items such as jewelry required focused work by the salespeople to make the sale. In addition, they said the market for luxury items was limited. Officials reported that although candy was inexpensive, sales have not been successful because candy was available for purchase in so many other places. Figure 10 depicts nonpostal items for sale.

"The shop of the future [is]...where customers are [and]...develops according to customer needs."

Source: Itella Corporation Presentation, June 2010.

Source: © Itella Corporation 2010.

Figure 10. Nonpostal Products for Sale at Itella Retail Outlet in Helsinki, Finland.

In Australia, officials told us some nonpostal products such as children's books sold well. However, their future plans place less emphasis on selling products and more on selling services, including identity and financial services. Both Posten AB and Canada Post introduced alternative retail products.

Canada Post officials stated they discontinued many of the sales because the products were not making money. However, a number of the services—including the selling of money transfers, wireless prepaid, and long distance services, among other government services—have been maintained and are growing.

In most cases, we were unable to determine the revenue generated from retail products and services because the information was proprietary or it was not reported.

STRATEGIES USED BY FOREIGN POSTS TO MODERNIZE DELIVERY AND RETAIL NETWORKS COULD HELP INFORM USPS MODERNIZATION EFFORTS

Foreign posts have faced resistance to change and challenges similar to those USPS faces, and they have developed communication, outreach, and labor transition strategies to address stakeholder concerns and address resistance to changes.

Key Lessons of Foreign Posts' Modernization Efforts

Lessons to be learned from foreign posts' experiences modernizing their retail and delivery networks include the following:

1) *Strategic outreach and coordination with governments can address political resistance.* Foreign posts have developed public relations campaigns to inform both national and local government officials as well as the public about the need for modernization and the benefits of improved access to services. They have also coordinated with local governments to resolve concerns raised by communities affected by facility closures.

> "We needed to change the mindset of our customers from the Post as a *Place*, to the Post as a *Service*."
>
> Source: Posten AB official.

For example, Sweden's Posten AB developed a comprehensive public campaign and communication effort to inform its stakeholders of what is perhaps one of the most expansive and earliest examples of retail network transformations of any of the posts we met with. (Video of Sweden's national campaign effort, courtesy of Posten AB.) Part of this communication effort was intended to help change the perception of "the post as a place" to "the post as a service." Despite this extensive and planned effort, Posten AB officials said the Post's brand and customer satisfaction ratings suffered, taking 10 years to recover.

2) *Strategic communication and outreach with mailers, small businesses, and retail customers.* Foreign posts communicated with and reached out to customers to increase acceptance of changes and to better meet customers' needs, including providing alternatives before implementing major retail network changes. In some cases, they have established ongoing outreach with their customers to determine how they can best serve them. In addition, when adjustments to the posts' retail networks meant that alternative facilities would be further away for some customers than their traditional post offices, the posts emphasized that the new locations would have extended operating hours.

Posten AB and DP DHL officials, in Sweden and Germany respectively, told us they made efforts to show customers and other stakeholders that although post-owned and -operated retail facilities were closing, the new retail partnerships offered more access points and made postal products and services more convenient to obtain.

If Swiss Post planned to close, replace, or relocate a post office, the Post was required by law to attempt to reach an agreement with the affected community, according to officials. Typically, Swiss Post approached the area officials first and offered a variety of solutions, such as creating an alternative retail access point if a partner could be found. The Post negotiated with the local community on the best way to address closures or moves. Although Swiss Post owned 88 percent of retail facilities at the end of 2009, it reported that it was considering increasing the number of nonpost-owned facilities. In some cases, such as in Australia, when closures or relocation were planned, the affected community first had an opportunity to propose an alternative.

3) *A labor relations strategy can ease transition.* Foreign posts also anticipated employee resistance and developed strategies to address how changes could affect employees and to assist employees in making the necessary transition to changes in operations. For example, for retail network changes—such as closures—strategies were developed to assist employees in making the necessary transition to any downsizing. Foreign postal officials told us that although they viewed the modernization efforts as necessary, some of the labor changes were unpopular; however, they also said that support for affected employees helped alleviate some of the resistance the posts faced. In most cases, either the foreign posts negotiated changes with the labor unions or created industrial relations (labor relations) strategies to help transition the workforce, or both. For example:

- Australia Post created a labor relations policy that was central to how it managed structural change, which involved reducing excess staff. This policy was known as the RRR Agreement:[18]
  - *Redeployment to other areas of the business.* Australia Post sometimes needed to retain and attract more employees in certain areas. To do this, Australia Post could redeploy an employee from one area to another job or facility.
  - *Retraining to provide skills required in new positions.* In some cases, if employees were not redeployed, Australia Post could retrain the employees.
  - *Redundancy.* When Australia Post needed to reduce the number of positions, it tried to obtain them through voluntary means, using incentives to encourage employees to retire.
- Itella reported a number of ways in which it supported its employees through changes in Finland:
  - Career consultants worked with employees to find new placements within Itella when they would lose their jobs.
  - Job-seeking training was provided in collaboration with the Finnish government's employment office, which helped employees fill out job applications and search for jobs.
  - Outplacement services within Itella helped employees find new jobs in other companies or helped employees set up their own business.

  - Monetary support measures helped to alleviate the effects on the individual in case of redundancy, relocation, or a change from full-time to a part-time employment.
- Posten AB officials noted that labor was not as resistant to changes in Sweden as in some other countries, in part, because labor was represented on Posten AB's governing board, which ultimately helped the relationship between management and labor.

Strategies Used by Foreign Posts Could Help USPS Gain Critically Needed Support as It Plans and Implements Network Modernization Efforts

USPS has taken steps to modernize its retail and delivery networks, but, as we have previously reported, it faces ongoing challenges related to legislative restrictions and stakeholder resistance to changes.[19] Some stakeholders have been concerned about how USPS's network changes might affect jobs, services, employees, and communities, particularly in small towns or rural areas. According to some members of Congress, and others, post offices are an important aspect of small towns, providing them with an economic and social anchor. Another concern is that inadequate USPS financial resources could impede efforts to optimize postal mail processing, retail, and delivery networks by limiting available funding for transition costs. In addition, concerns have been raised about whether USPS should be allowed to introduce new products and services that are not directly related to postal activities. Some of the steps USPS has taken to modernize include the following:

1) *Issued an action plan that outlined a general modernization strategy.* USPS issued a plan on March 2, 2010,[20] that identified modernization strategies for addressing financial challenges associated with declining letter mail volumes. Among other changes, USPS requested flexibility to
   - *Change delivery frequency.* Adjust delivery days to better reflect current mail volumes and customer usage.
   - *Expand access.* Modernize customer access by providing services "where the customers are." Increase and enhance customer access through partnerships, kiosks, and improved online offerings, while reducing costs.
   - *Expand products and services.* Permit USPS to evaluate and introduce more new products consistent with its mission, and allowing it to better respond to changing customer needs.
2) *Identified the need for legislative clarification and changes.* After issuing its action plan, USPS developed legislative proposals for changes needed to implement its action plan. In September 2010, Senator Carper introduced a bill that included some of USPS's legislative proposals related to these areas.[21] Senator Collins introduced another bill that included a provision to encourage USPS to enhance its retail presence and consider the impact of any changes to retail facilities on small communities and rural areas.[22]
3) *Conducted initial outreach to stakeholders and is developing a more detailed long-term strategy for modernizing its retail network and services.* Senior USPS officials we met with stated that they are continuing to work on developing strategies for

modernizing their retail and delivery networks. USPS plans to make these details public in early 2011.[23] USPS has held a number of meetings to involve stakeholders in this ongoing discussion, such as a 2010 innovation symposium whose goal was to discuss potential initiatives to help address its financial sustainability. Similarly, USPS has begun a dialogue with its customers, including major mailers, through its previously mentioned innovation efforts.

As USPS moves forward with its modernization efforts, the experiences of foreign posts suggest that outreach and communication strategies will be critically important to help it address concerns raised by the public, Congress, postal unions, and the Postal Regulatory Commission. In recent testimony we discussed some of the public policy questions related to legislative proposals that require congressional decisions to determine how USPS should modernize to achieve sustainable financial viability.[24] For example:

- Should USPS have greater flexibility to rightsize its retail network and workforce, which may involve closing post offices and moving retail services to alternative commercial locations that are often open more days and longer hours?
- Should it retain retail facilities and provide new nonpostal products and services to help it cover costs and generate net revenues?

Foreign posts did not plan and implement changes to their networks, nor realize results, overnight. In many cases they planned for the modernization 10–20 years in advance, and were met with a great deal of stakeholder resistance. Thus, Congress and USPS urgently need to make critical decisions about actions USPS will take to restore its financial viability. In doing so, they can potentially learn from a number of strategies that foreign posts have used to modernize their networks.

AGENCY COMMENTS AND OUR EVALUATION

We provided a draft of this report to USPS for review and comment. USPS provided comments in a letter from the Chief Financial Officer/Executive Vice President dated February 4, 2011. These comments are presented in appendix III and our evaluation of them is summarized below. USPS also provided technical comments, which we incorporated where appropriate.

USPS generally agreed with our conclusion that it must pursue modernization and that modernization could be more quickly and effectively instituted if legal and political barriers are removed. USPS suggested that we use the word "improve," rather than "modernize", when discussing its retail and delivery networks. USPS believes some stakeholders interpret modernize to mean automate. Further, USPS stated that many of its modernization and optimization efforts in the areas of delivery, networks, access, and products and services have been underway for some time and that political barriers have slowed these efforts. We recognize that USPS has made changes to its retail networks by transitioning to alternative retail locations, and we are evaluating these efforts in an ongoing review. However, in this report we focused not only on delivery and retail changes made by foreign posts, but also on the strategies used to address resistance to change. We thus use the term modernization to emphasize much more than automation. USPS also stated that incremental steps are not going to get the USPS where it needs to be to serve its customers in the 21st century. USPS listed some modernization efforts it described as similar to those mentioned in this report. Finally, we share USPS's view that there is an urgent need for actions that will restore its financial viability and modernize it to meet the challenges of the 21st century.

We are sending copies of this report to the appropriate congressional committees, the Postmaster General, the Chairman of the Postal Regulatory Commission, and other interested parties. In addition, the report will be available at no charge on GAO's Web site at http://www.gao.gov.

If you or your staffs have any questions regarding this report, please contact me at (202) 512-2834 or herrp@gao.gov. Contact points for our Offices of Congressional Relations and Public Affairs may be found on the last page of this report. GAO staff who made key contributions to this report are listed in appendix IV.

Sincerely yours,

Phillip Herr
Director, Physical Infrastructure Issues

APPENDIX I: OVERVIEW OF FOREIGN POSTS' UNIVERSAL SERVICE OBLIGATIONS

Retail and delivery modernization efforts of postal operators encompass aspects of "universal service" or "community service," such as requirements related to delivery of the mail and access to postal retail services and facilities, among other areas. In the United States, annual appropriations language mandates mail delivery 6 days a week.[1]

The Postal Reorganization Act of 1970 placed requirements on delivery and retail access standards by mandating that the USPS provide "prompt, reliable, and efficient services to patrons in all areas and shall render postal services to all communities" as well as "...a maximum degree of effective and regular postal services to rural areas, communities, and small towns where post offices are not self-sustaining."[2]

Table 2. Overview of Key Universal Service Standards by Country

Country	Key domestic delivery access standards	Key domestic retail access standards
Australia	• Required to provide delivery 5 days a week for at least 98% of all delivery points. • Delivery address within or adjacent to city must be delivered the next business day after day of posting.	• Required to operate at least 4,000 retail outlets, of which 2,500 must be located in rural or remote areas. • In metropolitan areas, at least 90% of residences shall be located within 2.5 km (1.56 miles) of a retail outlet. • In nonmetropolitan areas, at least 85% of residences shall be located within 7.5 km (4.66 miles) of a retail outlet.

Table 2. (Continued)

Country	Key domestic delivery access standards	Key domestic retail access standards
Canada	• Required to deliver 5 days a week where logistically feasible. • Will deliver letters within a community within 2 business days; within a province within 3 business days; and between provinces within 4 business days.	• Required to provide retail postal outlets, including both corporate post offices and private dealer-operated outlets, which are conveniently located and operated so that • 98% of consumers will have a postal outlet within 15 km (9.32 miles), • 88% of consumers will have a postal outlet within 5 km (3.11 miles), and • 78% of consumers will have a postal outlet within 2.5 km (1.55 miles). • Maintains a federal government moratorium on the closure of rural post offices. Has a community outreach consultation process that addresses unusual cases.
Finland	• Required to provide delivery 5 days a week. • Shall deliver 85 percent of Priority (first class) letters by the following workday and no less than 98 percent of priority letters by the second work day.	• Every Finnish municipality must have at least one postal outlet.
Germany	• Required to provide a minimum of one delivery per working day. • 80% (on average over the year) of letters must be delivered on the first working day after posting. • 95% (on average over the year) of letters must be delivered by the second working day after posting.	• Minimum of 12,000 fixed-location postal facilities nationwide, offering basic postal services as defined by the German Postal Act. • At least one post office in every town of 2,000 or more persons. • In towns with 4,000 or more persons, a post office must be within 2,000 meters (1.24 miles) of every mailer. • In rural areas, there must be at least one post office per 80 sq. km. (49.71 sq. miles).
Sweden	• Required to provide delivery at least 5 days a week. • 85% of first class letters shall be delivered the next working day. • 97% of first class letters shall be delivered within 3 working days.	• Density of access points must take into account the needs of users.
Switzerland	• Required to deliver at least 5 days a week. • Home delivery required to all permanently inhabited settlements (households). • Will deliver 97% of the mail to its end destination in 1 day.	• Must operate a nationwide network of post offices that offer all universal services and are available to all sections of the population within a reasonable distance. • Mandated to take account of regional concerns in the various parts of Switzerland

Source: Foreign postal operators.

Note: Australia Post generally refers to universal service as community service.

APPENDIX II: OBJECTIVES, SCOPE, AND METHODOLOGY

The objectives of our work were to describe (1) what major initiatives foreign postal operators (foreign posts) have implemented to improve or enhance mail delivery, and what have been the results; (2) what key initiatives foreign posts have implemented to improve or enhance their retail network and what have been the results and (3) what strategies used by foreign posts in their modernization efforts can help U.S. Postal Service (USPS) as it tries to improve its financial condition and customer service.

To describe the major initiatives implemented by foreign posts in mail delivery and retail networks, and the results of those initiatives, we initially reviewed documents, presentations, and articles from a variety of postal experts, trade journals, and textbooks, related to postal innovations in the digital, retail and delivery areas.

We also conducted interviews with experts in the international postal field. We then employed a case study approach to select six countries from among industrialized countries, using the following criteria:

- change in delivery frequency,
- change in retail network,
- use of innovations and technology,
- rank of broadband usage per 100 inhabitants, and
- convenience and cost of travel.

In addition to the above criteria, we also considered the following to ensure that our selection of the countries included a range of characteristics:

- country population,
- location and size of the country,
- number of delivery points in 2008 (last year data were available),
- 2008 mail volume (last year data were available), and
- regulatory framework and business model.

After applying these criteria we selected six countries—Australia, Canada, Finland, Germany, Sweden, and Switzerland—and conducted site visits to each, where we met with the foreign posts and a number of postal stakeholders to gain their perspectives on the effects of modernization efforts.

These stakeholders included:

- regulatory agencies,
- private sector companies and businesses with partnerships with foreign posts,
- mailer and marketing associations,
- private sector mailers, and
- labor unions.

In addition, we observed a number of demonstrations of foreign posts' innovations, toured their retail facilities, and received briefings on their retail and delivery networks, strategic planning, innovation strategies, and other areas.

We reviewed foreign post documentation including annual reports from 2006 to 2010, strategic plans related to retail and delivery network changes and innovations, reports on postal services and products, fact sheets on foreign post innovations and initiatives, and sustainability reports and strategic reviews.

In addition, we also reviewed documentation from foreign posts' stakeholders such as foreign post regulator studies; and position papers related to foreign posts' modernization efforts.

We also distributed a request for information to the six foreign posts we reviewed, to gain additional information regarding goals, strategies, and results of the initiatives implemented by the posts. Some of the information we received from the foreign posts in response to our request for information was not complete, and most data we requested was not quantified by the posts.

In addition, the information we received was not consistent across the six foreign posts. We did not assess whether the foreign posts' operational changes were profitable since that information is either proprietary or not consistently reported.

To describe how the strategies used by foreign posts could help USPS, we reviewed USPS's action plan entitled *Ensuring a Viable Postal Service for America: An Action Plan for the Future*, reports from the USPS Office of Inspector General and the Congressional Research Service, relevant congressional testimonies, pending postal reform legislation, and our past work. We also interviewed key officials from USPS to address innovations and strategies related to their retail and delivery network.

We conducted this performance audit from January 2010 to February 2011 in accordance with generally accepted government auditing standards. Those standards require that we plan and perform the audit to obtain sufficient, appropriate evidence to provide a reasonable basis for our findings and conclusions based on our audit objectives.

We believe that the evidence obtained provides a reasonable basis for our findings and conclusions based on our audit objectives.

APPENDIX III: COMMENTS FROM THE UNITED STATES POSTAL SERVICE

JOSEPH CORBETT
CHIEF FINANCIAL OFFICER
EXECUTIVE VICE PRESIDENT

UNITED STATES POSTAL SERVICE

February 4, 2011

Mr. Phillip Herr
Director, Physical Infrastructure Issues
United States Government Accountability Office
Washington, DC 20548-0001

Dear Mr. Herr:

Thank you for the opportunity to review and comment on the draft report titled *U.S. Postal Service: Foreign Posts' Strategies Could Inform U.S. Postal Service's Efforts to Modernize* (GAO-11-282). The Postal Service appreciates the Government Accountability Office's (GAO) evaluation of the strategies used by foreign posts to address mail volume decline, insufficient revenue, and legacy infrastructure challenges. We also agree with the conclusion that there is an urgent need for Congress and the United States Postal Service to make decisions and take actions that will restore the Postal Service's financial viability and allow it to continue to evolve as a profitable, market-responsive 21st Century organization.

This report is informative and forward-looking. It supports our position that regardless of whether legislative changes such as those proposed by Senator Thomas Carper, Senator Susan Collins, and others are made,[1] the Postal Service must tirelessly pursue modernization and adjust its business model in every way currently possible. The report does not include comparisons of the Postal Service in its analysis of the foreign posts' activities. It is important to note that the Postal Service has been engaged for years in numerous modernization efforts. On GAO's Highlights page, when the GAO mentions the Postal Service "modernizing" its retail and delivery networks, we recommend the wording be changed from "modernize" to "improve". This will eliminate confusion over the word "modernize" which some stakeholders interpret to mean "automate". As illustrated by the GAO's earlier report on the Postal Service's financial viability,[2] and by the Postal Service's 2010 Action Plan,[3] many of the Postal Service's modernization and optimization efforts in the areas of delivery networks, access, and products and services, have been underway for some time.

Such efforts at the Postal Service can be found in all aspects of our organization. For example, just as foreign posts have improved their retail networks by transitioning to alternative retail locations and online applications, which provide a combination of increased hours and convenience to customers, so has the Postal Service pursued such changes. The Postal Service has sought to engage its

---

[1] Including, for example, changes to the aggressive retiree health benefits prepayment schedule required by law (the 2010 payment accounted for $5.5 billion of the Postal Service's $8.5 billion net loss) or an adjustment of the Postal Service's overpayment into the Federal Employees Retirement System.

[2] *U.S. Postal Service: Strategies and Options to Facilitate Progress toward Achieving Financial Viability*, GAO-10-455 (April 12, 2010).

[3] www.usps.com/strategicplanning/_pdf/ActionPlanfortheFuture_March2010.pdf

475 L'ENFANT PLAZA SW
WASHINGTON DC 20260-5000
202-268-5272
FAX: 202-268-4364
www.usps.com

stakeholders on altering the frequency of delivery to five days a week, which substantially reduces our highest cost activity and better matches costs with declining volumes. We have expanded product and service offerings to better meet evolving customer needs, such as the successful Priority Mail flat rate products.

Many of the foreign posts' innovations and initiatives highlighted in this report were possible, at least in part, because of actions taken by their governments and regulators.[4] To a great extent, the six foreign posts featured in the report possess the flexibility and authority to rightsize their networks and workforces and introduce new products and services to meet customers' evolving needs and interests. Aspects of the Postal Service's modernization could be more quickly and effectively instituted if legal and political barriers are removed to provide greater flexibility.

As the report correctly notes, the measures taken by these foreign posts did not produce results overnight, and initially many of them were not popular with stakeholders. In most cases, realizing results and gaining stakeholder support has taken years, if not decades. As much as we might hope the experiences of these posts reveal surefire solutions for our specific challenges, they do not, and we appreciate GAO's acknowledgment of that.

Incremental steps and slow processes are not going to get the Postal Service where it needs to be to serve 21st Century customers. That is why we are working hard every day to address the challenges facing us. In fiscal year 2010, we reduced expenses by $3 billion, bringing total cost savings over the last three years to $10 billion. Our workforce today is smaller—by 100,000—than it was three years ago. Closure of all Airport Mail Centers was completed in 2010 and over the next two years we plan to save up to $500 million leveraging our alternative access locations to allow for the closing of more than 2,000 of our current locations. At the same time, within current constraints, we are expanding our partnerships, alternate access (i.e., Internet, contract postal units, retail stores, stamps by mail), and products and services such as Flat Rate boxes, Carrier Pickup, and Click-N-Ship. We will continue to look for—and act on—every available opportunity to control costs and raise revenue.

We appreciate the work that the GAO has done in recent years to help inform the discussion of the Postal Service's challenges and long-term viability. We particularly appreciate the many opportunities afforded us to discuss these issues with you and members of your staff. We are committed to working with Congress and all of our stakeholders to modernize the Postal Service, return to financial viability, and best serve our customers and the United States.

Sincerely,

Joseph Corbett

[4] To assist with modernization of their posts, some foreign governments have, for example: assumed legacy costs; required post competitors to contribute to universal service obligation (USO) costs; or, allowed for broad product and service offerings.

End Notes

[1] For example, according to Deutsche Post DHL officials, the Post must maintain a minimum of 12,000 postal retail outlets, and in terms of delivery, Canada Post officials stated that Canada Post is required to deliver letters and basic parcels 5 days a week to every resident and business, among others.

[2] Pub. L. No. 109-435, § 710 (Dec. 20, 2006).

[3] GAO, *U.S. Postal Service: Strategies and Options to Facilitate Progress toward Achieving Financial Viability*, GAO-10-455 (Washington, D.C.: Apr. 12, 2010).

[4] The Subcommittee on Federal Workforce, Postal Service and the District of Columbia Committee on Oversight and Government Reform, U.S. House of Representatives requested this work during the 111th Congress. In the 112th Congress, its name changed to the Subcommittee on Federal Workforce, U.S. Postal Service and Labor Policy, Committee on Oversight and Government Reform, U.S. House of Representatives.

[5] GAO, *U.S. Postal Service: Mail Delivery Efficiency Has Improved, but Additional Actions Needed to Achieve Further Gains,* GAO-09-696 (Washington, D.C.: July 15, 2009).

[6] Council Directive 97/67/EC, 1997 O.J. (L15/20) 7.

[7] The 2nd European Union Directive adopted steps for the opening of the letters market to competition by January 2009. Council Directive 2002/39/EC, 2002 O.J. (L176/24) 1. The deadline for European Union members to fully open its letter market was extended to December 31, 2010, by the 3rd European Union Directive with the exception of 11 countries. 2008/6/EC, 2008 O.J. (L52/20) Three of the foreign posts we visited—Finland, Germany, and Sweden—are members of the European Union.

[8] 2008/6/EC, 2008 O.J. (L52/4).

[9] GAO-10-455.

[10] In addition to delivery alternatives offered by foreign posts, foreign posts had competition for letter and parcel delivery. For example, in Sweden a private firm delivers mail and competes with Posten AB.

[11] As of September 2010, in 27 of 30 Organization for Economic Co-operation and Development (OECD) countries, broadband access has been deployed to 90 percent or more of households. OECD is a unique forum through which governments of 30 democracies work together to address the economic, social, and environmental challenges of globalization.

[12] E-substitution, according to a number of postal experts, has had one of the most significant impacts on mail volume and demand over the last decade.

[13] USB is a specification established by computer and peripheral (camera, mobile phone, memory, hard disk, etc.) manufacturers that enables high speed communication between the computer and other peripherals. A computer can send and receive data as well and control the operations of the various peripherals that are connected to it via the USB port.

[14] This requires prior registration by the customer to determine where packages will be delivered for that customer, which depends on where the recipient lives.

[15] DP DHL officials told us that during 2011, the remaining DP DHL post offices will be transformed into partner outlets or Postbank finance centers.

[16] Posten AB has retained 300 business centers that it owned and operated, but officials told us they were in the process of changing these business centers into mail acceptance points, with no sales counters.

[17] At 850 PostBank branches, DP DHL partners offer all DP and Postbank products and services as well as customized consulting for Postbank financial services.

[18] The agreement covered Australia Post's primary unions, which included the majority of its workforce.

[19] GAO-10-455.

[20] USPS, *Ensuring a Viable Postal Service for America: An Action Plan for the Future* (Washington, D.C., March 2010). This plan is available at the following Web address: http://www.usps.com/strategicplanning/_pdf/ActionPlanfortheFuture_March2010.pdf (accessed on Jan. 6, 2011).

[21] Postal Operations Sustainment and Transformation Act of 2010 (Post Act), S. 3831, 111th Cong. (2010).

[22] U.S. Postal Service Improvement Act of 2010, S. 4000, 111th Cong. (2010).

[23] USPS officials told us they are updating their retail strategy. We have recently initiated a review that will assess these details when they become available.

[24] GAO, *U.S. Postal Service: Legislation Needed to Address Key Challenges*, GAO-11-244T (Washington, D.C.: Dec. 2, 2010).

End Notes for Appendix I

[1] For example, see Pub. L. No. 111-117, 123 Stat. 3034, 3200 (Dec. 16, 2009).

[2] Pub. L. No. 91-375, § 2, 84 Stat. 719 (Aug. 12, 1970), *codified at* 39 U.S.C. § 101(a), (b).

In: Select Foreign Markets and Industries
Editor: Peter M. Luján

ISBN: 978-1-62100-133-1

Chapter 4

FOOD SAFETY: SELECTED COUNTRIES' SYSTEMS CAN OFFER INSIGHTS INTO ENSURING IMPORT SAFETY AND RESPONDING TO FOODBORNE ILLNESS*

United States Government Accountability Office

WHY GAO DID THIS STUDY

Like other nations, the United States faces growing food safety challenges resulting from at least three major trends. First, imported food makes up a growing share of the food supply. Second, consumers are increasingly eating foods that are raw or have had minimal processing and that are often associated with foodborne illness. Third, changing demographic patterns mean that more of the U.S. population is, and increasingly will be, susceptible to foodborne illness. In 2005, GAO reported on the approaches and challenges seven countries faced in reorganizing and consolidating food safety functions. Since then, the European Union (EU) has taken on a larger role in overseeing food safety within its 27 member states.

GAO was asked to describe how Canada, the EU, Germany, Ireland, Japan, the Netherlands, and the United Kingdom (UK) (1) ensure the safety of imported food, (2) respond to outbreaks of foodborne illness, and (3) measure the effectiveness of their reorganized food safety systems. GAO also asked experts in these countries and the EU to identify emerging food safety challenges that they expect to face over the next decade. In doing this work, GAO did not evaluate the countries' management of their food safety systems or explicitly compare their efforts with those of the United States.

WHAT GAO FOUND

The countries GAO examined have a comprehensive approach to ensuring the safety of imported food. Specifically, they focus on the entire food supply chain, from "farm to table;"

* This is an edited, reformatted and augmented version of the United States Government Accountability Office publication, Report to Congressional Requesters GAO-08-794, dated June 2008.

place primary responsibility for food safety on producers; separate risk assessment and risk management; use a risk-based inspection system; and take steps to ensure that certain food imports meet equivalent safety standards. Under the farm-to-table approach, for example, food safety laws cover every stage of the food production process, starting with how animals are raised and ending when food reaches the consumer. All countries GAO reviewed focus import inspections on the foods likeliest to pose the greatest risk. The EU, for example, requires that all imports of live animals and products of animal origin—which are considered high risk—enter the EU through approved border inspection posts.

Several of the selected countries reported that three elements of their food safety systems are critical in helping them respond to outbreaks of foodborne illness. These elements are traceback procedures, cooperative arrangements between government veterinarians and public health officials, and mandatory recall authority. In EU member states, all food must be traceable "one step forward and one step back" so industry and government can quickly track any food products to minimize harm to public health and reduce the economic impact on industry. Food and feed business operators must be able to document the names and addresses of the supplier and customer, as well as the nature of the product and date of delivery. Officials in several countries told GAO that mandatory recall authority—the legal authority to remove, or require another party to remove, a product from the market—is rarely used but is an important part of the food safety system because it is the last stop in the supply chain.

None of the selected countries had comprehensively evaluated its reorganized food safety system, although several track certain indicators, such as the number of inspections, enforcement actions, and foodborne illness. However, some countries' national audit offices (GAO's counterparts) have evaluated specific aspects of their countries' systems. For example, the UK audit office found that the country's Food Standards Agency had improved public confidence, a stated objective. The EU's Food and Veterinary Office has conducted numerous reviews of aspects of all EU countries' food safety systems and identified areas needing improvement. Most of the selected countries use proxy measures, such as public opinion surveys, to assess their effectiveness. Public opinion in several countries has improved in recent years. Countries' industry and consumer stakeholders also generally had positive views of the reorganized food safety systems.

Experts identified food safety challenges that they expect to face over the next decade. These include climate change; demographic change, with increases in elderly people and immigration; and new types of foods, such as ready-to-eat salads, that may result in more incidents of foodborne illness.

ABBREVIATIONS

BSE	bovine spongiform encephalopathy
BVL	Federal Office of Consumer Protection and Food Safety
CFIA	Canadian Food Inspection Agency
DAFF	Department of Agriculture, Fisheries, and Food
DG-SANCO	Directorate General for Health and Consumer Protection
EC	European Commission
ECDC	European Centre for Disease Prevention and Control

EEA	European Economic Area
EFSA	European Food Safety Authority
EPA	Environmental Protection Agency
EU	European Union
FDA	Food and Drug Administration
FSAI	Food Safety Authority of Ireland
FSC	Food Safety Commission
FVO	Food and Veterinary Office
GDP	gross domestic product
HACCP	Hazard Analysis and Critical Control Point
HC	Health Canada
HPA	Health Protection Agency
HPSC	Health Protection Surveillance Centre
MAFF	Ministry of Agriculture, Forestry, and Fisheries
MHLW	Ministry of Health, Labor, and Welfare
NMFS	National Marine Fisheries Service
RFID	Radio-Frequency Identification
RIVM	National Institute for Public Health and the Environment
SALSA	Safe Food for Local Suppliers Association
SPS	Sanitary and Phytosanitary
TRACES	Trade Control and Expert System
UK	United Kingdom
USDA	U.S. Department of Agriculture
VWA	Food and Consumer Product Safety Authority
WTO	World Trade Organization

June 10, 2008
The Honorable Richard J. Durbin
United States Senate

The Honorable Rosa L. DeLauro
Chair
Subcommittee on Agriculture, Rural Development, Food and
Drug Administration, and Related Agencies
Committee on Appropriations
House of Representatives

Like other nations, the United States faces growing food safety challenges resulting from at least three major trends. First, imported food makes up a growing share of the food supply. According to an analysis by the U.S. Department of Agriculture (USDA), the dollar value of agricultural imports to the United States for consumption increased by about 53 percent in just 4 years, from $46 billion in fiscal year 2003 to $70 billion in fiscal year 2007. The United States also trades with more than 150 countries and territories, with food products coming into more than 300 U.S. ports. USDA estimates that approximately 60 percent of the fresh fruits and vegetables consumed in the United States is imported, as is 75 percent of the seafood. Second, we are increasingly eating foods that are consumed raw or with minimal processing and that are often associated with foodborne illness. For example, according to USDA, leafy greens such as spinach are the category of produce most likely to be associated with an outbreak, and the average consumer ate 2.4 pounds of fresh spinach in 2005—a 180 percent increase over 1992. Third, changing demographic patterns mean that more of the U.S. population is, and increasingly will be, susceptible to foodborne illness. The U.S. population is aging, and older people tend to be more vulnerable to foodborne illness than younger ones. The risk of severe and life-threatening symptoms from infections caused by foodborne pathogens is also higher for young children, pregnant women, and immune-compromised individuals. According to the Food and Drug Administration (FDA), these groups make up about 20 to 25 percent of the U.S. population.

Recent outbreaks of foodborne illness have focused public attention on the increasing potential for widespread dissemination of contaminated products. For example, beginning in September 2006, the United States experienced an outbreak of *E. coli* associated with the consumption of tainted spinach grown in California; this outbreak resulted in confirmed illnesses and deaths. Widespread outbreaks of other foodborne illnesses, such as *Salmonella,* have also occurred from contaminated peanut butter and tomatoes. In addition, there have been problems with certain meat products, resulting in recalls (which in the United States are nonmandatory). Although the number of recalls has declined in recent years, the quantity of meat and poultry recalled has increased sharply. Meat and poultry product recalls declined from 125 in 2002 to 58 in 2007. However, 2 of the 6 biggest meat recalls in U.S. history occurred in a 6- month period, between October 2007 and February 2008.

In the United States, 15 different federal agencies are responsible for food safety. Two agencies, USDA and FDA, have primary responsibility. USDA is responsible for the safety of meat, poultry, and certain egg products, while FDA is responsible for the safety of virtually all other foods, including milk, seafood, and fruits and vegetables. Food safety responsibility is further divided among the 50 states, which may have their own statutes, regulations, and agencies for regulating and inspecting the safety and quality of food products. Over the past 30 years, we have detailed problems with the current fragmented federal food safety system and reported that the system has caused inconsistent oversight, ineffective coordination, and inefficient use of resources. This fragmentation calls into question whether the government can plan more strategically to inspect food production processes, identify and react more quickly to outbreaks of foodborne illness, and focus on promoting the safety and integrity of the nation's food supply. This fragmentation is the key reason that we added federal oversight of food safety to our *High-Risk Series* in January 2007 and called for a governmentwide examination of the food safety system.[1] We recommended, among other things, that Congress enact comprehensive, uniform, and risk-based food safety legislation and commission the National Academy of Sciences or a blue ribbon panel to conduct a detailed analysis of alternative organizational structures for food safety.

In 2005, we reported on the approaches and challenges seven countries faced in consolidating food safety functions.[2] These countries were Canada, Denmark, Germany, Ireland, the Netherlands, New Zealand, and the United Kingdom (UK). Some of these countries reorganized their food safety systems in response to public concern about the safety of the food supply during outbreaks of bovine spongiform encephalopathy (BSE, also known as mad cow disease) and, in the case of the European countries, widespread dioxin contamination in chicken products during the 1990s. Some countries—notably Canada,

Denmark, and New Zealand— reorganized to improve the overall effectiveness of their systems. Since our 2005 report, the food safety system of the European Union (EU) has been fully integrated and is regulated by legislation that applies to all 27 member states. Japan also reorganized part of its food safety system in 2003, creating a new agency, the Food Safety Commission, to assess the health risks associated with food. Even with updated measures in place, however, it is not possible to totally eliminate all foodborne pathogens from the food supply. For example, incidents of *E. coli* have increased slightly in the EU over the past 10 years, and in early 2008, a number of Japanese citizens became seriously ill after eating frozen dumplings imported from China that contained a dangerous level of pesticides.

In this context, you asked us to describe (1) how 6 countries (Canada, Germany, Ireland, Japan, the Netherlands, and the UK) that have reorganized their food safety systems and the EU ensure the safety of imported food, (2) what these countries and the EU consider to be the most critical elements in helping them respond to recent outbreaks of foodborne illness, and (3) how they measure the effectiveness of their reorganized food safety systems, as well as how effective the reorganized systems have been in minimizing harm to public health from outbreaks of foodborne illness. In addition, we asked experts in these 6 countries and the EU to identify what they consider to be some of the most important emerging food safety challenges they expect to face over the next decade.

To address these questions, we collected and reviewed laws and directives, and analyzed agencies' annual reports, performance reports, strategic plans, official brochures, and guidance documents on policies and procedures from these 6 countries and the EU. We also met with food safety officials, industry experts, and consumer advocacy representatives in Belgium (for the EU), Canada, Germany, Ireland, Japan, the Netherlands, and the UK. Canada, Germany, Ireland, the Netherlands, and the UK were selected because we had reviewed those countries in our 2005 report. They were selected then because they had reorganized their food safety systems within the past 10 years and, like the United States, had high per capita income, and their consumers had high expectations for food safety. We added Japan because it also has a high per capita income and recently reorganized part of its food safety system. We added the EU because of its major role in coordinating member countries' food safety activities. In this report, we refer to the changes to their food safety systems that the selected countries have made as reorganization. In describing the changes to systems of Canada, Germany, Ireland, the Netherlands, and the UK, however, we use the countries' term, which is consolidation.

After we collected the information, we prepared appendixes that described each country's and the EU's food safety system. We then sent the draft appendixes to officials in those countries for review and comment. We received comments from at least one agency (food safety or public health) in 6 of the selected countries. Japan did not provide comments. After receiving their feedback and making revisions, where appropriate, we sent the appendixes to representatives of the various countries' national audit offices. We also sent copies of the report to the Department of Agriculture, the Department of State, the Food and Drug Administration, and the Office of the U.S. Trade Representative for their review; we incorporated their comments as appropriate.

The information on countries' food safety systems in this report, including descriptions of laws, is based largely on interviews with and documentation provided by food safety officials as well as food industry or consumer stakeholders from the countries we examined. Most of the information obtained was qualitative. We did not compare any elements of these countries' systems to the United States' system—although in some cases, country officials told us that aspects of their food safety systems were similar to aspects of the U.S. system—and we did not independently evaluate the effectiveness of any of the programs or systems described.

We also did not independently verify the foreign laws and directives discussed. Instead, we relied on our discussions with foreign officials and the documents we collected. We recognize that the selected countries have much smaller populations and also differ from the United States in climate and agricultural production as well as in organizational structure. However, these countries and the United States have at least one important similarity: All are high-income countries where consumers have high expectations for food safety. We conducted our work from July 2007 to June 2008 in accordance with generally accepted government auditing standards. Those standards require that we plan and perform the work to obtain sufficient, appropriate evidence to provide a reasonable basis for our findings and conclusions based on our objectives. We believe that the evidence obtained provides a reasonable basis for our findings and conclusions based on our objectives. Detailed information on each country's and the EU's food safety systems can be found in appendix I. In this report, when we refer to selected countries, we mean the 6 countries named above and the EU. Of the 6 countries, 4—Germany, Ireland, the Netherlands, and the UK—are EU member states.

RESULTS IN BRIEF

The selected countries have a comprehensive, risk-based approach to ensuring the safety of imported food. Specifically, they focus on the entire food supply chain, from "farm to table;" place primary responsibility for food safety on food producers with the government providing oversight; separate risk assessment and risk management; employ a risk-based inspection system; and take steps to ensure that certain food imports meet equivalent food safety standards. More specifically, we found the following:

- *Farm-to-table oversight.* Under this approach, the entire food production process is regulated, starting with how animals are raised on the farm and ending when food reaches the final consumer. For example, according to EU sources, under the EU's integrated farm-to-table approach, food and feed laws cover all stages of production, processing, and distribution. The laws also cover imported products from the primary production of a food, through its storage, transport, sale, or supply to the final consumer and, where relevant, the importation, production, manufacture, storage, transport, distribution, sale, and supply of feed. We were told that this is a comprehensive and integrated approach that focuses on the prevention of problems throughout the food chain.
- *Producer responsibility.* The burden for food safety in most of the selected countries lies primarily with food producers, rather than with inspectors, although inspectors play an active role in overseeing compliance. This principle applies to both domestic and imported products. We were told that like the farm-to-table concept, producer accountability is a proactive approach that focuses on prevention.

- *Separate risk assessment and risk management.* To create independent safeguards, the EU and some countries created separate agencies for (1) risk assessment—scientific evaluation of all known and potential adverse health effects resulting from foodborne hazards—and (2) risk management—the process for weighing policy alternatives to accept or minimize assessed risks and select appropriate responses. In addition, some of the countries also separated their risk management agencies from those that promote industry in order to ensure independence. For example, before they reorganized, risk management in Ireland, Japan, and the UK had been conducted by the same agency that oversaw agricultural production, and consumers perceived that these dual responsibilities presented conflicting priorities.
- *Risk-based inspection systems.* The selected countries focus their inspection of imports on the foods most likely to pose the greatest risk. A risk-based approach is critical in light of the volume of products in the food supply. The EU, for example, requires that all imports of live animals and products of animal origin—which are considered high risk—enter the EU through approved border inspection posts. These shipments cannot clear the port without veterinary approval. Shipments containing products the EU considers lower risk, such as fruits, vegetables, cereals, and spices, must meet less stringent requirements. The EU and Japan require that importers bear the cost of disposing of or reinspecting noncompliant food products.
- *Certain food imports must meet equivalent safety standards.* Each of the selected countries takes steps to ensure that certain types of food— most often, meat or animal products—meet equivalent food safety standards. Japan also has specific arrangements with some governments to certify exports of certain high-risk products. According to Japanese officials, under a Japanese-Chinese agreement, for example, the Chinese government certifies Chinese spinach processors, who in turn oversee the practices of local farmers and test the product at three stages of production. Chinese authorities then conduct preshipment tests on the spinach before exporting, confirming that the exporter has observed the proper procedures on pesticide management. The spinach may be inspected again once it arrives in Japanese ports.

Several of the selected countries generally reported that three elements of their food safety systems are critical in helping them respond to outbreaks of foodborne illnesses. These elements include traceback procedures, cooperative arrangements between government veterinarians and public health officials, and mandatory recall authority.

- *Traceback procedures.* All food and feed must be traceable "one step forward and one step back" in EU member states so industry and governments can quickly track any questionable food or feed products to minimize harm to public health and reduce the economic impact on industry. Food and feed business operators must be able to document the names and addresses of the supplier and customer, as well as the nature of the product and date of delivery. They are also required to have in place systems and procedures that allow for this information to be made available to government officials on demand. Exporters in trading partner (non-EU) countries do not need to meet this requirement, except under certain circumstances, but EU importers should be able to identify their direct supplier in trading partner countries. In addition, the selected countries also have mandatory animal identification programs for certain livestock species.

- *Cooperation between government veterinarians and public health officials.* In light of highly pathogenic avian influenza, BSE, and recognition of the connection between animal and human diseases, such cooperation has been critical in tracking the source of zoonotic (animal-tohuman) diseases in some countries. For example, in the UK, the Veterinary Laboratories Agency has several memorandums of understanding with the Health Protection Agency, the UK agency that monitors outbreaks of infectious diseases, to conduct research. The agencies also support joint efforts to standardize laboratory methods and databases. The Veterinary Laboratories Agency can also assist in cases where a direct or indirect animal source is suspected in outbreaks of zoonotic diseases and where veterinary investigation or intervention could help reduce risks to the public. For example, according to UK officials, during the investigation of a 2004 outbreak of an antibiotic-resistant strain of *Salmonella* among cattle on an English farm, rapid communication of test results and epidemiological information between the Health Protection Agency and the Veterinary Laboratories Agency led to containment of the outbreak before it could spread to humans.
- *Mandatory recall authority.* Officials in several countries told us that mandatory recall authority—the legal authority to remove, or require another party to remove—a product from the market is rarely used. However, according to a Canadian industry representative, this authority is an important part of the food safety system because it is the last stop in the supply chain. Moreover, as Canadian government officials indicated, they rarely need to exercise mandatory recall authority because the threat of such a recall generally prompts food suppliers to remove products from the market.

None of the selected countries had conducted a comprehensive evaluation of its reorganized food safety system, but most countries track certain indicators, such as the number of inspections conducted, the number of enforcement actions taken, and the number of foodborne illness outbreaks. However, most of the selected countries have assessed specific aspects of their food safety systems. For example, some of the countries' national audit offices had evaluated specific aspects of their countries' food safety systems, and Health Canada has assessed some elements of the Canadian system. In the EU, the Food and Veterinary Office has conducted numerous reviews of certain aspects of member countries' food safety systems. For example, in June 2005, the office assessed the import control system and four operating border inspection posts in Germany. It found that import controls were generally applied correctly in the posts visited, with only minor shortcomings. However, the office also found that supervision of imports that do not comply with EU regulations was inadequate, traceability was not reliable, and exit of these noncompliant products from the EU was not ensured. It also found that there were significant deficiencies at some of the border inspection facilities. As a result of the audit, Germany took steps to address the shortcomings. Most of these countries also use proxy measures, such as consumer surveys, to assess their effectiveness, and the public impression of food safety has improved in several countries in recent years. Finally, stakeholders we interviewed cited the benefits of their country's reorganized food safety system.

Experts in the selected countries identified a number of challenges related to food safety that they expect to face over the next decade, with climate change the most frequently identified challenge. Specifically, they indicated that climate change may result in an increase in foodborne pathogens that thrive in warmer conditions, such as the *Vibrio* bacterium in oysters. Furthermore, some officials expressed concern that their populations are aging, and older people are more vulnerable to foodborne illness than younger ones. Additionally, the emergence of new types of foods—for example, ready-to-eat foods, including those that do not require cooking and therefore may retain pathogens—may result in illness.

BACKGROUND

In the United States, USDA and FDA have primary responsibility for ensuring the safety of domestic and imported foods. USDA is responsible for the safety of meat, poultry, and certain egg products and for performing certain food quality inspections and certifications that include food safety elements. FDA is responsible for the safety of all other foods, including milk, seafood, and fruits and vegetables. In addition, the Environmental Protection Agency (EPA) sets limits on the amount of pesticide residues that are allowed in food, and the National Marine Fisheries Service (NMFS) within the Department of Commerce provides fee-for-service inspections of seafood safety and quality. The Department of Homeland Security is responsible for coordinating agencies' food security activities, including at U.S. borders. The U.S. Centers for Disease Control and Prevention is responsible for monitoring, identifying, and investigating foodborne disease problems and for working with FDA, NMFS, USDA, state and local public health departments, universities, and industry to develop control methods.

In January 2007, we added the federal oversight of food safety to our *High-Risk Series*, which is intended to raise the priority and visibility of government programs that are in need of broad-based transformation to achieve greater economy, efficiency, effectiveness, accountability, and sustainability. Over the past 30 years, we have detailed problems with the current fragmented federal food safety system and reported that the system has caused inconsistent oversight, ineffective coordination, and inefficient use of resources, all of which suggest that the federal oversight of food safety should be designated as a high-risk area. The fragmented nature of the federal food oversight system raises the question of whether the government can plan more strategically to inspect food production processes, identify and react more quickly to outbreaks of foodborne illnesses, and focus on promoting the safety and integrity of the nation's food supply.

As in the United States, government agencies in other countries also share responsibility for their nation's food safety. In February 2005, we reported on the experiences of several countries in reorganizing their food safety systems. Food safety officials in the countries we selected said they faced similar divisions of responsibilities and that their countries' reorganizations were intended to address this problem. The countries streamlined and consolidated their food safety functions, establishing a single agency to lead food safety management or enforcement of food safety legislation. Table 1 lists the reasons each country gave for consolidating its food safety responsibilities.

Table 1. Reasons for Consolidating Food Safety Responsibilities

Canada	Canada consolidated its food safety system to (1) improve effectiveness by making inspections and enforcement more consistent, clarifying responsibilities, and enhancing reporting to the Canadian Parliament, (2) improve efficiency by reducing duplication and overlap in food safety activities, and (3) reduce federal spending.
Denmark	Denmark consolidated its food safety system to improve effectiveness (e.g., communication with consumers and consistency of inspections) and to improve efficiency (e.g., move resources to high-risk areas and reduce overlaps in responsibilities).
Germany	Germany consolidated its food safety system in response to public concerns about food safety stemming from the discovery of BSE in 2000 and other food safety problems. An additional objective was improved compliance with EU food safety legislation.
Ireland	Officials stated that Ireland consolidated responsibility for food safety and food law enforcement within a single national agency to address public concern about food safety stemming from food scares and the detection of BSE in Ireland. Also, some consumers perceived that the ministry that was responsible for inspecting farms and meatpacking plants had favored the interests of the food industry over consumer protection.
The Netherlands	The Netherlands consolidated its food safety system out of a need to reduce overlap and improve coordination among the Dutch government's multiple food safety entities, as well as public concern about food safety stemming from the dioxin contamination of animal feed, BSE, and other animal diseases. Officials noted that the need to comply with recently adopted EU legislation also motivated the Netherlands' consolidation.
New Zealand	New Zealand consolidated its food safety system to improve effectiveness in several areas, including coordination within the food safety system, and to eliminate inconsistencies in the country's oversight of domestic food, imports, and exports.
The UK	Officials stated that the UK consolidated its food safety system due to a loss of public confidence in food safety, which largely resulted from the government's perceived mishandling of the BSE outbreak. By early 1999, the human form of BSE, variant Creutzfeldt-Jakob disease, had caused 35 deaths. It was widely perceived that the fragmented and decentralized food safety system allowed this outbreak to occur. According to a consumer organization representative, consumers believed that the Ministry of Agriculture, Fisheries, and Food—which had dual responsibilities to promote the agricultural and food industry as well as to regulate food safety—favored industry over consumers in making decisions related to food safety.

Source: GAO-05-212.

Although the countries whose food safety systems we reviewed are much smaller in population than the United States, they, like the United States, are high-income countries whose consumers have very high expectations for food safety.

Most of the countries we selected for this review are members of the EU and, as such, are subject to applicable requirements of EU food safety legislation. The development and implementation of EU food safety legislation is the responsibility of the Brussels-based Directorate General for Health and Consumer Protection (referred to by its French acronym, DG-SANCO). In 2002 the EU also created a new independent food safety institution, the European Food Safety Authority (EFSA), which is responsible for providing independent scientific advice on all matters related to food and animal feed safety. In April 2004, the EU adopted additional, comprehensive food safety legislation that became effective on January 1,

2006. Together with the earlier regulation establishing EFSA, the legislation was intended to create a single, transparent set of EU food safety rules applicable to both animal and nonanimal products. Since that time, individual EU countries have worked to bring their national food safety laws in line with EU requirements—a process referred to as harmonization.

These selected countries also face the challenge of foodborne illness caused by known hazards as well as new threats. To address these challenges, the United States and other countries have undertaken certain measures to protect human health. These measures include the use of a science-based safety system for certain food products, known as Hazard Analysis and Critical Control Point (HACCP), and the requirement that exporting nations meet food safety standards similar to the importing country's own standards. A HACCP system is designed to improve the safety of food by having industry identify and control biological, chemical, and physical hazards in products before they enter the market. In the United States, USDA established HACCP requirements for meat and poultry establishments in 1996. FDA implemented similar HACCP requirements for seafood in 1997 and for juice in 2002. Under the HACCP system, processing firms must identify hazards that are reasonably likely to occur and must develop and implement plans to control those hazards. HACCP systems, under USDA and FDA regulations, are not required for other stages of production, such as on the farm. In general, the federal food safety regulation begins at the point of processing, rather than on the farm itself.

With regard to equivalent food safety standards between countries, the Agreement on the Application of Sanitary and Phytosanitary Measures— entered into force with the establishment of the World Trade Organization (WTO) on January 1, 1995—affirms that member countries are allowed to adopt and enforce measures necessary to protect human, animal, or plant life or health, provided, among other things, the measures are based and maintained on scientific principles and evidence, do not arbitrarily or unjustifiably discriminate among WTO members, and are not applied in a manner that would constitute a disguised restriction on international trade. In turn, member countries are expected to accept the sanitary or phytosanitary measures of other member countries as equivalent if the exporting member objectively demonstrates that its measures achieve the importing member's appropriate level of sanitary or phytosanitary protection. Members are encouraged to use relevant international standards and work toward harmonization—that is, the adoption of common sanitary or phytosanitary measures—to facilitate trade. Consistent with the principles of the sanitary and phytosanitary agreement, many countries use equivalency agreements to certify that their food safety systems are equivalent to those of the country importing products. All countries in our review are parties to the WTO and to the Agreement on the Application of Sanitary and Phytosanitary Measures.

In response to these increasing challenges, FDA and other U.S. agencies recently released plans that discuss the oversight of food safety. In November 2007, FDA released its *Food Protection Plan*, which sets forth FDA's framework for overseeing the safety of food.[3] Concurrently, a 12- agency working group presented to the President its *Action Plan for Import Safety*, which contains, among other things, recommendations for improving the safety of food imports entering the United States.[4] Both plans spell out numerous actions FDA plans or is requesting authority to take to enhance food safety, including writing new food protection guidelines for industry and helping foreign countries improve their regulatory systems.

Selected Countries Have a Comprehensive, Risk- Based Approach to Import Safety

The selected countries have a comprehensive, risk-based approach to ensuring the safety of imported food that focuses on the entire food supply chain, from "farm to table." The selected countries emphasize prevention, placing primary responsibility for food safety on food producers, with government bodies providing oversight. Some of these countries separate risk analysis and risk management, and some also separate food safety from the promotion of agricultural trade. Each country also employs a risk-based inspection system so that foods with increased risk receive the most attention. The selected countries also take steps to ensure certain food imports meet equivalent food safety standards.

The Selected Countries' Food Safety Systems Are Based on Farm-to-Table Oversight

The selected countries have generally adopted a farm-to-table approach, under which the entire food production process is regulated, starting with how animals are raised on the farm and ending when food reaches the final consumer. Farm-to-table oversight in the selected countries applies to both domestic and imported foods. We were told that farm-to-table is a comprehensive and integrated approach that focuses on prevention of problems throughout the food chain. In the EU, for example, according to EU sources, food and feed laws under this approach (referred to in the EU as "farm to fork") cover all stages of production (including farming), processing, and distribution. According to these sources, EU laws also cover imported products from the primary production of a food, through its storage, transport, sale, or supply to the final consumer and, where relevant, the importation, production, manufacture, storage, transport, distribution, sale, and supply of feed. Individual EU member states, through their bodies charged with food safety oversight (referred to as competent authorities), ensure surveillance and control of food and feed operators, and the European Commission (EC—the administrative, implementing, and enforcement body of the EU) tests the performance of member states' control capacities through audits and inspections. Farms and food producers in non-EU countries that export to the EU must observe the same safety standards that apply in the EU in order to export their products.

Canada also takes a farm-to-table approach to food safety to safeguard not just the food supply but also the plants and animals upon which safe food depends. Products subject to inspection by the Canadian Food Inspection Agency range from agricultural inputs, such as seeds, feeds, and fertilizers; to fresh foods, including meat, fish, eggs, grains, dairy products, fruit and vegetables; and prepared and packaged foods. The government also works with commodity sectors to develop and review food safety plans.

At the consumer end of the spectrum, the food safety agency educates Canadians about safe food-handling practices and various food safety risks through its Web site, food safety fact sheets, and the Canadian Partnership for Consumer Food Safety Education, a group of industry, consumer, and government organizations that jointly develop and implement a national program to educate consumers on how to safely handle food. Moreover, in December 2007, Canada's Prime Minister announced the new Food and Consumer Product Safety

Action Plan aimed at strengthening and modernizing Canada's safety system for health, consumer, and food products. The plan responds to changes in trade, industry supply chains, and consumer buying patterns. Under the plan, the government will implement programs focused on prevention, targeting highest risks, and promoting rapid response. Among other things, the initiative will involve working with industries, provinces, and territories to implement preventive food safety control measures along the food chain.

Like the EU and Canada, Japan takes a farm-to-table approach (referred to there as a "food chain" approach) to food safety. According to the Japanese Food Safety Commission, Japanese law stipulates that food safety be ensured at each stage of the food production process and apportions responsibility for food safety among the national government, the local governments, food operators, and consumers. (Consumers are responsible for improving their knowledge and understanding of food safety and expressing their opinions about policies to ensure food safety.

One of the ways they can educate themselves about food safety is by paying close attention to food labels, and according to USDA's Foreign Agricultural Service, the Japanese government has recently introduced initiatives to strengthen food labeling requirements.) At the national level, the Ministry of Agriculture, Forestry, and Fisheries oversees primary production processes, including animal health and the use of agricultural chemicals, and the Ministry of Health, Labor, and Welfare oversees the processing and distribution stages. Moreover, with regard to imports, the ministry develops a monitoring plan each year for imports that prescribes measures for ensuring food safety in three stages: (1) in the exporting countries, (2) at entry into Japan, and (3) during internal distribution.

Producers in Most of the Selected Countries Are Responsible for Food Safety

The burden for ensuring food safety in most of the selected countries lies primarily with food producers, rather than with inspectors, although inspectors play an active role in overseeing compliance. This principle applies to both domestic and imported products. We were told that like the farm-to-table concept, producer accountability is a proactive approach that focuses on prevention.

According to EU sources, for example, food and feed operators have primary responsibility for food safety, while member states provide oversight over these operators at all stages of production. Business operators are responsible for the food and animal feed (such as cattle fodder or pet food) that they produce, transport, store, or sell. They must (1) be able to rapidly identify any supplier or consignee, (2) immediately inform the competent authorities if they have a reason to believe their food or feed is not safe, (3) immediately withdraw a product from the market if they have reason to believe the product is not safe, (4) apply HACCP principles in their processes and ensure that controls are applied at critical points,[5] and (5) cooperate with the competent authorities in actions taken to reduce risk. The competent authority in each member state is responsible for monitoring producers to ensure that they are meeting these obligations. The EU Food and Veterinary Office then assesses the performance of the member states' competent authorities, countries aspiring to join the EU, and non-EU countries intending to export to the EU to verify the effectiveness of national control systems for enforcing EU requirements in the areas of food safety, animal health and welfare, and plant health.

Producer Responsibility: The Case of EU Feed Suppliers

Feed suppliers in the EU must apply HACCP principles, register with their national competent authorities to help ensure traceability, and comply with specific microbiological criteria, such as for levels of *Salmonella*, molds, and yeast. The competent authorities in each country approve certain feed operators (i.e., those manufacturing and/or selling certain feed additives) by visiting the facility before they start up any activity to ensure that the operators meet the requirements of the legislation, and once the operator is approved, the competent authority provides oversight and imposes penalties for noncompliance. The EU Food and Veterinary Office, in turn, inspects the competent authorities' oversight and provides recommendations when there are shortcomings. It also inspects countries aspiring to join the EU, and non-EU countries intending to export to the EU, to verify the effectiveness of their national control systems to implement EU standards in the areas of food safety, animal health and welfare, and plant health. As for imported feed, importers must ensure that their feed meets EU standards.

In Japan, business operators who produce, import, sell, or conduct other business for fertilizers, agricultural chemicals, feed, feed additives, veterinary medicines, and other agricultural products bear primary responsibility for ensuring food safety when conducting their business activities. These operators are also responsible for providing accurate and appropriate information on their products and for cooperating with policies implemented by the national and local governments. The national government is responsible for formulating and implementing policies to ensure food safety.

With regard to imports, the burden of compliance with Japanese food safety regulation lies with importers, but the Japanese government (specifically, the Ministry of Health, Labor, and Welfare) further ensures compliance through a high level of import monitoring. In 2006, for example, Japan reported that its inspectors examined 11 percent of declared products coming into its ports. Some producers in selected countries have commented that placing responsibility on them is generally positive.

One industry representative, for example, told us that, "farmers and producers can no longer hide behind meat inspectors." An industry representative from another country said that, because producers are concerned with protecting their name brands, greater accountability makes them proactive.

A consumer representative from a third country echoed this view, stating that importers are bearing more responsibility for ensuring the safety of their food imports because they are aware of the damages— financial and image-related—that violations cause to their business.

Some Countries Separate Risk Assessment from Risk Management

To create independent safeguards, some of the selected countries created separate agencies for (1) risk assessment—scientific evaluation of all known and potential adverse health effects resulting from foodborne hazards—and (2) risk management—the process for weighing policy alternatives to accept or minimize assessed risks and to select appropriate responses. The EU, for example, created the European Food Safety Agency to conduct risk assessment, while Japan created the Food Safety Commission for this purpose. Germany created the Federal Institute for Risk Assessment to assess risks and the Federal Office of Consumer Protection and Food Safety to lead food safety risk management.

Table 2. Risk Assessment and Risk Management Bodies in Selected Countries

Country	Risk assessment body	Risk management body
Canada	Health Canada	Canadian Food Inspection Agency
EU	European Food Safety Agency	Risks are managed by individual EU member states
Germany	Federal Institute for Risk Assessment	The Federal Office of Consumer Protection and Food Safety (coordinating body)a
Ireland	Science Committee of the Food Safety Authority of Irelandb	Food Safety Authority of Ireland
Japan	Food Safety Commissionc	Ministry of Health, Labor, and Welfare and Ministryof Agriculture, Forestry, and Fisheries
The Netherlands	National Institute for Public Health and the Environmentd	Food and Consumer Product Safety Authority
The UK	Food Standards Agencye	Food Standards Agency

Sources: Canada, EU, Germany, Ireland, Japan, the Netherlands, and the UK.

Notes:

[a] Germany's 16 federal states are responsible for overseeing compliance with the law, and as such, they are in charge of food and feed safety, animal health and welfare, and plant health. The Federal Office of Consumer Protection and Food Safety coordinates—but does not oversee—the activities of the federal states in these areas.

[b] In Ireland, a Scientific Committee was established in 2000 to aid the Food Safety Authority of Ireland in risk assessment. The committee is made up of scientists from a variety of disciplines whose work for the authority is voluntary.

[c] In 2003, Japan established the Food Safety Commission as a Cabinet-level agency responsible for conducting neutral, scientific risk assessments related to food safety, including the use of food additives, pesticide residues, and the presence of illness-causing bacteria, and other issues. The commission became a fully functioning, independent agency in 2005. Previously, the two ministries responsible for managing food safety—the Ministry of Health, Labor, and Welfare and the Ministry of Agriculture, Forestry, and Fisheries—conducted their own scientific risk assessments. While the Food Safety Commission now assesses risks, the two ministries are responsible for managing these risks.

[d] The Food and Consumer Product Safety Authority's Office of Risk Assessment commissions the National Institute for Public Health and the Environment to conduct risk assessments on its behalf.

[e] The Food Standards Agency also receives advice from 10 scientific committees that provide input, as needed, on various food-related risks.

This office also coordinates food safety surveillance at the federal level. (The 16 individual German states are responsible for food safety legislation and oversight of food inspections performed by local governments.) Canada consolidated public health policy and standard-setting responsibilities, including research, risk assessment, and setting limits on the amount of a substance allowed in a food product, in one agency, Health Canada. Table 2 provides the names of the risk assessment and risk management bodies in each of the selected countries.

Some countries have also separated their risk management agencies from those that promote industry in order to ensure independence. For example, Ireland and the UK, as part of their restructuring several years ago, took risk management away from their ministries of agriculture, which consumers perceived as favoring the food industry over consumer protection. Similarly, prior to Japan's 2003 food safety system restructuring, the Food Agency within the Ministry of Agriculture, Forestry, and Fisheries, which was responsible for food safety, was managed in collaboration with industrial promotion bureaus within the ministry; the Food Agency was abolished when the Food Safety Commission was created.

Inspections of Imports Are Based on Risk, and in the EU and Japan, Importers Bear Some Costs

The selected countries base their inspections of imports on the degree of risk presented by particular food types, and the EU and Japan require that importers bear the cost of disposing of or reinspecting noncompliant food products. Live animals and animal products, such as meat, milk, and fish, are among those that present the highest level of risks because they can transmit serious human and animal diseases. In addition, certain plant products, such as nuts, wheat, corn, beans, rice, and certain spices can present high levels of risks because they may be contaminated by aflatoxins—toxins produced by mold that can damage the liver and may lead to liver cancer.

Fruits and vegetables may also be considered high risk if they contain unacceptably high levels of pesticide residues. Risk may also be considered high if a product is traded in large quantities or if a product or the area it comes from is known to be susceptible to particular plant or animal diseases.

According to the EU, it has shifted its focus from regular, but random, sampling to paying attention to the sources of greatest risk. If the risk of a given food product is not known or quantified, the EU applies what it refers to as the "precautionary principle:" If there are reasonable grounds for suspecting a problem, the commission acts to limit the risk. The EU asserts that it does not necessarily need to wait for proof that there really is a risk.

The EU requires that all imports of live animals and products of animal origin enter the EU only through certain border inspection posts— airports, rail stations, and deepwater ports—of which there are about 300.

The posts, which are under the authority of each member state's official veterinary services, must be notified in advance of the presentation of such consignments; these consignments must undergo an official veterinary check at the post. A member state's customs service cannot release consignments unless they have passed through veterinary controls. When a consignment arrives at a border inspection post accompanied by the correct health certification, three types of checks will be carried out:

- Documentary—for all consignments, inspectors review the accompanying documents.
- Identity—for all consignments, inspectors verify that the identity of the goods corresponds fully with the veterinary documents supplied.
- Physical—for a percentage of consignments, depending on the type of animal product and the country of origin, inspectors physically inspect the consignments to ensure they do not pose a threat to public and animal health. According to EU officials, EU legislation also specifies a minimum number of physical checks to be

carried out per product group (e.g., meat, fish, or dairy) by each member state. A physical inspection may also involve taking samples for laboratory tests.

When all tests and checks are satisfactory, the consignment is issued a Common Veterinary Entry Document and is placed on the EU market.

If a consignment does not comply with EU requirements, it may be rejected. In these cases, EU officials negotiate with the owner of the consignment and the country of dispatch, where appropriate, about whether to destroy the product, to retreat it for uses other than the human food chain, or to return it. Food or feed business operators or their representatives are responsible for the consignment and are liable for any costs incurred by the competent authorities to destroy or redispatch it.

When consignments are not in compliance, all other border inspection posts are notified through the EU's Rapid Alert System for Food and Feed (rapid alert system), an electronic notification system managed by DGSANCO in Brussels. The system alerts all EU member countries of a potential food problem, including either a direct or an indirect risk to human health from food or feed. The rapid alert network involves all member states, the European Community, and the European Food Safety Authority, as well as the non-EU countries of Iceland, Liechtenstein, and Norway.

Each participating country has a rapid alert system contact point to collect information on national notifications and enter them into the database. The exchange of information allows participating states to immediately ascertain whether they are also affected by a problem and take appropriate measures. Since all EU border posts are connected electronically, problems at any one border can quickly be announced to all other border posts via the rapid alert system. Future imports from the same exporting country are then scrutinized more closely.

The EU also maintains a list of food products of nonanimal origin that may represent a human health risk. Cereals and nuts, for example, may appear on the high risk list. Such products undergo control measures, such as health certificates and testing, similar to those required for food products of animal origin. For example, all consignments of pistachios from Iran are sampled and checked. The safeguard measures are lifted once the problem has been addressed.

Food products of nonanimal origin—including fruits, vegetables, cereals, tubers, nondairy drinks, food of mineral origin (such as salt), spices, and condiments—represent less of a risk and as such, do not need to come from approved countries or establishments. These products can come into any EU port of entry. However, they are still subject to certain EU requirements in order to verify that that they comply with EU food standards. Among other things, food business operators in non-EU countries must monitor the safety of products and processes under their responsibility, follow general hygiene provisions for primary production, develop HACCP principles, and register establishments with the appropriate competent authorities. The EU member states' competent authorities are responsible for carrying out regular controls of goods imported into EU territory.

The EU requires that member states ensure that adequate financial resources are available for organizing official controls on imports. Member states may therefore collect fees to cover costs occasioned by these controls. However, they must collect fees for certain activities, including controls for products of animal origin, such as meat inspection, and controls of dairy establishments. Fees are also levied for certain import controls on these commodities.

EU officials stated that the fees may not be higher than the costs borne by the competent authorities.

Japan takes a similarly risk-based approach to inspections. Each year, the Ministry of Heath, Labor, and Welfare produces an imported foods monitoring and guidance plan that, among other things, spells out the quantity and category of inspections to be conducted each year. In fiscal year 2007, for example, the goal was approximately 79,000 random inspections for 124 food groups. If an imported food belongs to a food group that is known to be at an increased risk for contamination from a pathogen, pesticide residue, or animal drug, the ministry issues an order requiring that products with a high violation probability are inspected every time they are imported (lot by lot).

According to the imported foods monitoring and guidance plan, moreover, if the number of imported foods from a specific country, area, or business entity violating the law is above 5 percent of the overall number of foods inspected, and if it is likely that the importation of violating goods will continue, given conditions in the exporting country, the ministry may ban the importation of such goods altogether.

While there is no cost to importers for random inspections at Japanese quarantine stations, if products are required to undergo more intensive inspections as a result of past problems, the importer pays for additional inspections. Japan also imposes financial penalties for importers found to be in noncompliance. According to an expert on the Japanese import system, many Japanese importers therefore require testing certificates from exporters to reduce the potential for violation. In situations where import violations are severe, the Ministry of Health, Labor, and Welfare lists the names of violators on its Web site, which is updated every few weeks.

The Selected Countries Take Steps to Ensure Certain Food Imports Meet Equivalent Safety Standards

The selected countries take steps to ensure that certain food imports meet equivalent safety standards. In the EU, for example, food products of animal origin imported from non-EU countries must meet standards at least equivalent to those of the EU for food quality and hygiene. If such foods are found not to be as safe as those of the EU and do not meet the requirements of EU hygiene regulations, the overseas firm is not allowed to export to the EU. The EU maintains a list of non-EU countries for which it has recognized the capacity of the competent authorities, as well as its animal and public health system but does not maintain such a list for food of nonanimal origin. Among the requirements for approving the export of products of animal origin are the following:

- a country's formal submission of a written application to export to the EU;
- the EU's verification of the exporting country's animal and public health system, such as legislation, control systems, disease surveillance measures, and laboratory facilities;
- the country's submission and approval of a monitoring plan for residues of banned or restricted substances in the EU, including veterinary medicines and growth-promoting hormones; and

- the country's provision of sanitary certification that the products to be exported to the EU meet import requirements.

Inspectors from the EU's Food and Veterinary Office normally visit nonEU countries to verify compliance with these conditions. If compliance is satisfactory, the EU may approve countries and establishments for export to the EU. In addition, non-EU countries must certify and approve business establishments wishing to export to the EU, noting that they meet the relevant EU requirements. The EU maintains lists of these establishments online for all the major categories of animal products (e.g., beef, dairy, fish, or poultry), and compliance is verified during follow-up inspections.

In Canada, the Canadian Food Inspection Agency requires importers of meat and seafood products to meet Canadian standards. Determination of a foreign country's equivalency is based on the approval of a country's system of meat inspection, approval of establishments operating within that system, and review and registration of individual meat products prepared in these establishments. To approve the exporting country's inspection and certification system, the Canadian Food Inspection Agency follows a process of equivalency evaluation, based upon provisions in the Agreement on the Application of Sanitary and Phytosanitary Measures of the World Trade Organization. The agreement requires each member to accept as equivalent sanitary and phytosanitary measures of another member if the exporting member objectively demonstrates to the importing member that its measures achieve the importing member's appropriate level of protection.

Canada's Foreign Country Meat Inspection Systems Evaluation Program requires that imported meat products—unless specifically exempted by Canadian legislation—meet the same standards and requirements as if they were produced in registered establishments in Canada. It also requires that the exporting country's inspection and certification systems, along with the establishments operating under those systems, be approved by the Canadian Food Inspection Agency before meat products can be exported to Canada. The competent authority of the exporting country must issue an official meat inspection certificate for every shipment of meat products exported to Canada. The competent authority is also expected to take appropriate actions if the Canadian Food Inspection Agency notifies it about meat products found to violate Canadian requirements and is to communicate any actions to the agency. The Canadian Food Inspection Agency may require additional examination of subsequent shipments to Canada, with additional certification, for a predetermined number of shipments and/or weight of the certified shipment. The majority of the agency's inspectors are focused on meat products because of the higher risk relative to most other foods. Canada currently allows importation of meat products from 40 countries.

In the case of seafood, Canada enters into agreements with other countries it believes have reliable inspection systems and uses these agreements in concentrating its inspection resources on products and countries representing increased risk. Under some agreements, the Canadian Food Inspection Agency agrees that products from specified processing facilities meet certain standards and therefore are subject to fewer inspections at the border. The agency normally assesses these plants before it adds them to a list. Other agreements represent recognition by the agency that the inspection system in another country is equivalent to the system in Canada. Under these agreements, the competent authority in the other country will inspect and maintain the list of establishments eligible for reduced inspection frequency upon export to Canada.

Canada has an equivalency agreement in place with the EU for meat products and is working toward bringing an equivalency agreement for fishery products into force. The Canada-EU Veterinary Agreement allows equivalency determination according to criteria set out in the agreement that specify gradual levels of equivalency. These levels allow work toward equivalency in products to be tracked over time. The agreement is aimed at recognizing the equivalence of Canadian and EU inspection and certification requirements for trade between the EU and Canada in live animals and animal products.

Japan also requires importers to meet its food safety standards. For example, officials from the Japanese Ministry of Health, Labor, and Welfare or the Ministry of Agriculture, Forestry, and Fisheries engage in bilateral talks with their counterparts in the exporting country to explain Japanese food safety regulations. If a country has no prior record of exporting food to Japan, ministry officials may conduct field surveys to determine whether a country's food safety system can comply with Japanese food sanitary regulations and whether the exporting country's food safety regulations are comparable with Japan's. If Japan has already approved an exporting country and a new facility in that country seeks to export, ministry officials may conduct a pre-export inspection of that facility; if the review is satisfactory, the ministry will issue a certificate to the exporter, copies of which must accompany every shipment of goods to Japan.

Japan also has arrangements with some governments to certify exports of certain high-risk products. According to Japanese officials, under a Japanese-Chinese agreement, for example, the Chinese government certifies Chinese spinach processors, who in turn oversee the practices of local farmers and test the product at three stages of production. Chinese authorities then conduct preshipment tests on the spinach before exporting, confirming that the exporter has observed the proper procedures on pesticide management. The spinach may be inspected again once it arrives in a Japanese port.

Selected Countries and the EU Cite Key Elements of Food Systems as Critical to Effectively Responding to Outbreaks of Foodborne Illness

The selected countries reported that three elements of their food safety systems are critical in helping them respond to outbreaks of foodborne illness. These elements include traceback procedures, cooperative arrangements between government veterinarians and public health officials, and mandatory recall authority. Officials in most of the selected countries told us that with respect to public health, their procedures for tracking the source of foodborne illness outbreaks are generally similar to U.S. procedures.

In general, the selected countries follow the same key steps in addressing outbreaks of foodborne illnesses. These steps include the following:

- *Identification of the outbreak.* In most of the selected countries, this is the responsibility of local medical practitioners, who, after treating victims, also notify the national authorities when there is a suspected outbreak of foodborne illness. The first tests are often conducted at local laboratories. In cases where more sophisticated testing is needed to identify the pathogen and its source, the local laboratories send samples to specialized laboratories—called reference laboratories—that can conduct more sophisticated tests.6 Usually, the national public health monitoring institutes also collect data and confirm the number of illnesses in the outbreak.

- *Coordinated action to manage the outbreak.* In most of the selected countries, local public health authorities manage the outbreak as long as it is confined to a local region. However, if the outbreak crosses provincial or state borders or if the outbreak is very large, the national surveillance institute or health ministry may take over control activities.

The most common foodborne illnesses in the selected countries, listed in alphabetical order, are *Campylobacter, E. coli, Listeria,* norovirus, and *Salmonella.* (Noroviruses are a highly contagious virus transmitted by consumption of contaminated food or water or by direct person-to-person contact).

EU Requirement that All Foods Be Traceable May Accelerate the Identification of an Outbreak Source

All food must be traceable "one step forward and one step back" in EU member states, allowing industry and national governments to quickly track any questionable food products to minimize harm to public health and reduce the economic impact on industry. Food and feed business operators must be able to document where a particular food product came from and where it is going next. Specifically, they must be able to document the names and addresses of suppliers and customers, as well as the nature of the product and date of delivery. They are also encouraged to keep information on the volume and quantity of a product; the batch number, if one exists; and a more detailed description of the product, such as whether it is raw or processed. Food and feed business operators must also have systems and procedures that allow them to provide this information to the competent authorities on demand. (As described in EU guidance, exporters in trading partner countries are not legally required to fulfill the EU's traceability requirement, except in circumstances where there are special bilateral agreements for certain sensitive sectors or where there are specific EU requirements, such as in the veterinary sector.

However, these traceability requirements pertain to EU importers, who should be able to identify their direct supplier in the non-EU country.)

Canada, Japan, and the EU also have mandatory animal identification programs for certain livestock species. In the EU, for example, in addition to farm registration obligations, producers must tag livestock with details of their origin, and when the animals are taken for slaughter, stamp them with the traceability code of the slaughterhouse. The tools used (ear tags, "passports," or bar codes) may vary from country to country but must carry the same information. In addition, to ensure the traceability of animals across borders, the EU established the Trade Control and Expert System, a central database for tracking the movement of animals both within the EU and from non-EU countries. In the event of a disease outbreak, the database ensures that all potentially affected animals can be quickly identified and that authorities can take appropriate measures.[7]

Tracing Dioxin in Milk in the EU

According to EU sources, the EU's traceability system proved useful during an incident that took place in 2004. During standard random monitoring of dioxin levels in milk at a Dutch farm, the national competent authorities found a high level of dioxin. The EU sources noted that the competent authorities immediately barred the farm from trade and began tracing the product through the food chain. They found that the source of contamination was clay, used in food processing to separate higher-quality potatoes from lower-quality ones. The dioxin-tainted clay had contaminated potato peels used for feeding animals. The EU's electronic Rapid Alert System for Food and Feed was used to trigger an exchange of information among national authorities about the problem. EU sources stated that the authorities quickly established that the clay had also been supplied to several food-processing companies located in Belgium, France, Germany, and the Netherlands. The authorities rapidly identified these businesses and barred from trade over 200 farms that had received the potentially contaminated potato peels. According to the EU, because of the traceability system, the contaminated products never reached consumers.

Although Canada does not have mandatory traceability for food, it does have mandatory cattle identification, which it is expanding to include all livestock. Beginning on January 1, 2001, Canadian farmers were required to tag all cattle with a bar-coded ear tag before the cattle left their farm of origin. The Canadian Food Inspection Agency began to fully enforce the program in 2002, with monetary penalties for noncompliance. In 2006, Canada initiated the transition to Radio-Frequency Identification (also known as RFID) tags on all cattle leaving their herds of origin. This tagging system is designed to facilitate the tracing of movement and identification of animals at various stages of the animal production chain, thereby helping to contain and eradicate animal disease.

Japan has a mandatory system in which all beef and dairy cattle must be identified using an ear tag. Information is maintained on an animal's identification number, breed, gender, and production history from the farm of origin through distribution to consumers.

Government Veterinarians and Public Health Officials in Some Countries Cooperate Closely to Trace the Source of Animal-toHuman Diseases

In light of concerns about highly pathogenic avian influenza and BSE, and in recognition of the connection between animal and human diseases, cooperation between public health officials and veterinarians has been critical in tracking the source of zoonotic (animal-to-human) diseases in some countries. For example, according to UK officials, the Veterinary Laboratories Agency, a regional network of 16 laboratories under the Department for Environment, Food, and Rural Affairs is responsible for veterinary research, disease surveillance, and diagnostic service. It has several memorandums of understanding with the Health Protection Agency—the UK agency that monitors outbreaks of infectious diseases—to conduct research. According to Health Protection Agency officials, the staff of these two agencies meets approximately once a month. In addition, staff from these agencies and the

Food Standards Agency meets regularly to review trends in human and animal health. In particular, the Veterinary Laboratories Agency can assist in cases where a direct or indirect animal source is suspected in outbreaks of zoonotic diseases and where veterinary investigation or intervention could help reduce risks to the public. The agency may (1) conduct animal sampling for laboratory cultures, (2) help in identifying management and animal care factors that may have a bearing on human health risks, and (3) provide veterinary epidemiological input, such as data reports of *Salmonella* strains from farm animal surveillance. Strains of animal origin can also be selected for further identification and comparison with human strains. According to UK officials, the UK's Health Protection Agency and the Veterinary Laboratories Agency work closely in the investigation of outbreaks of food poisoning related to food production animals and have in place standardized laboratory and epidemiological methods for disease strain characterization and outbreak investigation. In addition, the Health Protection Agency, the Veterinary Laboratories Agency, and another body, the Centre for Infections (a large research institute) support a joint position to further standardize laboratory methods and harmonize databases.

Health Protection Agency officials told us that communication between public health and veterinary officials has been useful during various outbreaks in the UK. For example, during the investigation of a 2004 outbreak of an antibiotic-resistant strain of *Salmonella* among cattle on an English farm, rapid communication of test results and epidemiological information between the Health Protection Agency and the Veterinary Laboratories Agency led to the containment of the outbreak before it could spread to humans. Officials from the Health Protection Agency likewise said that there are numerous examples of similar collaborative activities between the Health Protection Agency and the Veterinary Laboratories Agency involving both *Salmonella* and a form of *E. coli* known as Verocytotoxin-producing *E. coli.* They also said that the agencies exchange strain typing and epidemiological data on an almost daily basis. They stated that the centralized nature of the UK government facilitates this close cooperation. Similarly, in the Netherlands and Ireland, officials told us that public health officials and veterinarians cooperate closely. In the Netherlands, for example, the Dutch National Institute for Public Health, a government research institute that conducts research projects on public health issues, among other things, collaborates closely with the Dutch Central Veterinary Institute on issues related to zoonotic diseases and animal food products. In Ireland, veterinarians participate in a national zoonoses committee made up of medical experts, public health officials, regional veterinarians, and environmental officers that convenes in the event of a foodborne illness outbreak.

Irish officials told us that during an outbreak of *Salmonella* Agona in Ireland in 2006, collaboration between the veterinary and medical doctors made it easier to trace the pathogen to its source, which was poultry. Moreover, the Irish Department of Agriculture, Fisheries, and Food operates the Central Veterinary Research Laboratory, which is the national reference laboratory for *Salmonella.* The laboratory also carries out typing (identification) of *Salmonella* samples.

All of the Selected Countries Have Mandatory Recall Authority

All of the selected countries have mandatory recall authority—the legal authority to remove, or require another party to remove, a product from the market. This authority enables them to force food producers to take a product off the market if there is a problem with it, such as microbial contamination, or the presence of allergens or non-permitted ingredients.[8]

The EU distinguishes between withdrawals and recalls and has authority for both. Withdrawals occur when the product is still under the control of the producer, and measures are intended to prevent the distribution or display of a dangerous product. Recalls occur when the product is already available to consumers, and measures are intended to have the unsafe product returned. All member states must notify the EU when there is a serious risk to human health.

According to Irish and UK sources, one of the largest mandatory food recalls in the EU took place in February 2005, when the UK's Food Standards Agency discovered that a UK company had used spice contaminated with Sudan Red 1 dye in a variety of processed foods. Sudan Red 1 is an industrial dye used for coloring solvents, oils, waxes, and shoe and floor polishes. It entered EU countries in ground or crushed chili imported from India. Responding to the UK's rapid alert system notifications, other EU countries also recalled products contaminated with the dye.

The Canadian Food Inspection Agency also has mandatory recall authority for unsafe food products, but, according to an agency official, it has only used this authority a total of seven times. Although rarely used, this authority is effective "because it is there," according to a Canadian Food Inspection Agency official, who also said that recall authority has contributed to more effective industry cooperation. According to Canadian officials, one of the most significant outbreaks of foodborne illness in Canada occurred in December 2004, when *Salmonella* linked to mung bean sprouts from a single company sickened 300 people in Ontario. The Canadian Food Inspection Agency made preparations for a mandatory order to be issued because the company was not conducting a "proper" recall on its own. In the end, however, the company agreed to conduct a "proper" voluntary recall.

The Japanese government has mandatory recall authority, but according to Japanese officials, it has rarely used this authority. Typically, the local health centers run by the Ministry of Health, Labor, and Welfare that test food suspected to be the source of an outbreak will "suggest" to a company that it recall its tainted product. According to a Japanese official, if the government communicates in this way to a company, the company feels obliged to recall its products.

The Selected Countries Have Not Evaluated Their Reorganized Food Safety Systems, but Proxy Measures Indicate Improvements

None of the countries we reviewed had comprehensively evaluated the effectiveness of its reorganized food safety system, but most of the selected countries track certain indicators, such as the number of inspections conducted, enforcement actions taken, and foodborne illness outbreaks. Most of these countries had also assessed specific aspects of the country's food safety system. Furthermore, most of these countries use proxy measures, such as public opinion surveys, to assess effectiveness. In addition, industry stakeholders we interviewed cited the benefits of the reorganized food safety system.

None of the Selected Countries Has Comprehensively Evaluated the Effectiveness of Its Reorganized Food Safety System, but They Do Track Certain Indicators

None of the selected countries has comprehensively evaluated the effectiveness of its reorganized food safety systems. One food safety expert noted that it is difficult to determine the effectiveness of a food safety system because it involves proving that something did not happen, i.e., that exporters did not try to ship unsafe food to a country, a shipment of unsafe food did not get past inspectors, and consumers did not eat or drink unsafe food that entered the national food distribution system. An agency official also said that it is difficult to find quantitative data to measure change and performance. In addition, another official said that when the number of foodborne illnesses changes from year to year, it is difficult to know with certainty the cause of the change.

The food safety agencies in the countries we visited track key indicators, such as the number of inspections they conducted and the number of enforcement actions taken. Activities tracked by the Netherlands, for example, include the number of inspections conducted, the number of samples inspected, the number of approvals issued in the livestock and meat sector, international notifications of potential risk, and the number of written warnings issued. The EU also tracks the number of notifications and recalls member states issue under the EU's rapid alert system. Canada likewise tracks recalls. The public health or surveillance institutes of the selected countries monitor the number of foodborne illness outbreaks each year.

Most of the Selected Countries Formally Audit Certain Aspects of Their Food Safety Systems

Although none of the selected countries had comprehensively evaluated the effectiveness of its reorganized food safety system, some of the selected countries had assessed certain aspects of it. For example, Canada's Office of the Auditor General, GAO's Canadian counterpart, has conducted four reviews of certain Canadian Food Inspection Agency activities, including (1) a 2004 study on regulation of plants developed using biotechnology, (2) a 2000 report on the agency's Food Inspection Program, (3) a 1999 report on the agency's management of a particular foodborne illness outbreak, and (4) a 1998 report on the agency's creation. In March 2008, the Auditor General also reviewed selected Health Canada activities, including progress made by Health Canada's Pest Management Regulatory Agency in applying its procedures for evaluating and registering new pesticides and reevaluating older, registered pesticides; it also reviewed the amount of time it takes to get new, possibly safer pesticides to market. (This assessment also evaluated the Canadian Food Inspection Agency's progress in increasing the scope of its program that tests for residues in fresh fruits and vegetables.) The Auditor General found that since an audit conducted in 2003, the national government had made satisfactory progress in selected aspects of managing the safety and accessibility of pesticides, and it had shortened the time it takes to evaluate new pesticides. The Auditor General also reviewed Health Canada's progress in conducting national health surveillance in 2002. It found that Health Canada had made some progress toward resolving some of the weaknesses the auditors identified in a 1999 audit. However, it also found that national surveillance was still weak; many systems still lacked timely, accurate, and complete disease information; and gaps in surveillance continued.

Health Canada is responsible for assessing the Canadian Food Inspection Agency's activities and has completed 10 assessment reports, 9 of which have been published online. The most recent assessments found that the agency was fulfilling its mission, although minor improvements are needed. For example, in 2005, Health Canada reviewed the agency's Fish, Seafood and Production Program's Quality Management Program, a mandatory inspection program for federally registered fish and seafood establishments. The evaluation found that the program was generally effective in enhancing the safety of fish and seafood products. However, Health Canada recommended, among other things, that Canadian Food Inspection Agency managers responsible for the program should conduct trend analysis of complaints and incident data, an action that would enhance the management of emergencies and incidents. The agency agreed with the recommendation.

In the UK, the National Audit Office (GAO's UK counterpart) conducted an audit of the Food Standards Agency in 2003 and found that the agency had made progress in its stated objective of improving public confidence in food safety and standards. For example, according to the audit office, in 2001 and 2002 the Food Standards Agency investigated about 500 incidents with the potential to affect food safety. The agency issued 47 food hazard warnings to local authorities, alerting them to potential health dangers or requiring them to recall food from sale. More recently, the National Audit Office reviewed the agency's interaction with business and rated it highly on adopting innovative alternatives to classic regulation and on having an evidence-based culture. The auditors found that the Food Standards Agency was undertaking many positive initiatives in its risk assessment system. Areas needing further attention included developing a more strategic partnership with local authorities and providing better advice and guidance to small businesses. Overall, the auditors found that the agency was continuing to improve its performance from an already strong base.

Certain agencies within some countries have also conducted-selfassessments. For example, the Canadian Food Inspection Agency has assessed its own performance using criteria developed in collaboration with the Canadian Treasury Board and measuring progress on four strategic outcomes: (1) protecting Canadians from preventable health risks related to food safety or the transmission of animal diseases to humans; (2) protecting consumers through a fair and effective food, animal, and plant regulatory regime; (3) sustaining the plant and animal resource base; and (4) securing Canada's food supply and agricultural resource base from deliberate threats. For each strategic outcome, the agency identified a number of specific targets. According to the agency's 2007 annual performance plan, the agency met or exceeded 31 of its 40 targets. In the UK, the Food Standards Agency conducted an internal review of lessons learned from the 2005 Sudan 1 incident, in which illegal dye was found in food, and the agency's board subsequently conducted a separate review of the incident. The board noted that the agency should take a central role in ensuring more coordinated attention to intelligence gathering and implementing early warning systems, as well as proactively sharing this information with the food industry.

In the EU, the Food and Veterinary Office develops an annual audit plan every year that identifies priority areas and countries it will audit that year. For example, in 2008, the office stated that it intended to conduct 256 audits and inspections, including 65 general audits in six member states. (General audits verify the extent to which countries comply with the multiyear control plans they have prepared.) As part of their audits, the Food and Veterinary Office inspectors may visit producers or processing plants to establish that enforcement mechanisms are effective in practice. If necessary, the Food and Veterinary Office can send out inspectors in response to disease outbreaks both within and outside the EU.

During an audit, the Food and Veterinary Office assesses a member state's compliance with EU requirements for certain aspects of the member state's food safety system. For example, in its June 2005 assessment of Germany's import control system and four operating border inspection posts, the office found that import controls were generally applied correctly in the posts visited, with only minor shortcomings. However, the office also found that (1) supervision of imports that do not comply with EU regulations was inadequate, (2) traceability was not reliable, (3) exit of these noncompliant products from the EU was not ensured, and (4) some of the border inspection facilities had significant deficiencies. If the Food and Veterinary Office finds any shortcomings during its inspection, it makes recommendations to, and requires an action plan from, the member's competent authority for addressing the shortcomings. Together with other EU bodies, the Food and Veterinary Office evaluates this action plan and monitors its implementation and could take legal action to ensure that member states meet their obligations. In response to the Food and Veterinary Office audit of its border inspection posts, for example, Germany said that it had already taken some steps to address the shortcomings identified and would work to address the others.

Most of the Selected Countries Use Proxy Measures to Assess Their Systems, and Stakeholders Generally See Benefits of Reorganization

Among the proxy measures in the selected countries were consumer surveys. Several of the countries, including Canada, Japan, the Netherlands, and the UK, have surveyed their consumers on their views of the food safety system. This emphasis on public confidence in the food safety system comes in the wake of concerns about food agencies' ability to respond to outbreaks of BSE and other potential food contamination problems. For example, in 2003, the UK's Food Standards Agency noted that its effectiveness depended in part on the extent to which the public trusts it to provide reliable and impartial advice—trust that it earns principally by identifying and responding to food safety concerns. Indeed, public confidence in the UK's system for food safety and standards was the agency's first aim, followed by reducing foodborne illness and protecting consumers through improved food safety standards. In 2007, the public's confidence in the agency's ability to protect against foodborne illnesses was an estimated 60 percent, compared with about 44 percent in 2001.

Similarly, in 2005, the EU surveyed consumers to understand how they view risk, particularly food safety risks, in order to inform policy and communicate with the public on risk issues.[9] It found that the public in all 25 EU member states was divided on whether food safety had improved in the past 10 years, with an estimated 38 percent believing it had, 29 percent believing it had stayed about the same, and 28 percent believing it had gotten worse. In some countries, however, views were more favorable. For example, the EU reported that an estimated 67 percent of people in Ireland believed that, overall, food safety had improved over the past 10 years.

Surveys can also be used to understand where the food safety system needs to be improved. For example, according to an official with Japan's Food Safety Commission, part of the commission's risk communication strategy is to survey consumers in order to find out how effectively the government communicates risk—how clearly, accurately, and convincingly. From these surveys, the commission learned that the public generally does not understand the concept of assessing risk.

Consequently, one of the commission's current goals is to better communicate its role to the public and in general improve the clarity of its risk communications.

Germany has taken another approach to gauging public opinion. According to officials with the Federal Office of Consumer Protection and Food Safety, this agency convened stakeholders in November 2007 to discuss the effectiveness the Federal Office of Consumer Protection and Food Safety and the German food safety system in general. About 80 people from federal and state governments and trade associations attended. Comments on the agency's performance were generally positive. In particular, participants approved of the efforts of the national contact point for the EU's rapid alert system. However, they suggested some improvements in the system, and also suggested that the agency provide training to help prepare for Food and Veterinary Office audits. Participants also liked the *Journal of Consumer Protection and Food Safety* that the agency launched in 2006 to provide information, in both German and English, on basic and applied research and on official oversight of current developments in the areas of food and feed, veterinary medicine, and genetic technology. Participants suggested that the agency establish a greater presence at conferences, fairs, and schools and that it be more visible to consumers as a partner.

The views of stakeholders, such as industry organizations and consumer advocacy groups, can also provide insight, albeit anecdotal, on the success of a country's food safety system. We spoke with representatives of stakeholder groups in each of the countries we visited and were told that, in most of the selected countries, the reorganization of the food safety system has been beneficial. In particular, stakeholders said reorganization has improved transparency. For example, one industry stakeholder in Canada said that consolidation greatly sped up the government's decision-making process and provided increased transparency, clarity, and accountability. In Japan, representatives of two consumer groups told us that the creation of the Food Safety Commission as an independent body responsible for risk assessments was a positive step, especially for increasing government transparency. A representative of an industry group in the UK also said that consolidation improved the functioning of the Food Standards Agency. This person believes the agency is now more transparent to industry, and it is easier to consult with agency staff on issues of concern.

Industry stakeholders told us that another benefit of reorganization was having a single point of contact. In the UK, for example, according to a representative of an industry group, the group provides its views to the Food Standards Agency through one-on-one or committee meetings, and has seen changes as a result of these contacts. Because of industry concerns about the way the Food Standards Agency managed a product recall, the agency agreed to notify industry before publishing a mandatory recall and changed preparation instructions for this product. Similarly, Canadian industry representatives told us that the reorganized and consolidated food safety system has had benefits. For example, representatives from two industry groups generally agreed that, with the consolidation, the Canadian Food Inspection Agency now has staff dedicated to food safety issues, a fact that has allowed a working relationship between industry and government to evolve. In addition, a representative from a third Canadian industry group told us that consolidation also helped strengthen the Canadian

Food Inspection Agency's expertise and capability by combining staff from different agencies, although this representative was concerned about how the agency managed recalls.

FOOD SAFETY OFFICIALS IN OTHER COUNTRIES IDENTIFIED ISSUES OF FUTURE CONCERN

Experts in the six countries and the EU identified a number of challenges related to food safety that they expect to face over the next decade, with climate change the most frequently identified challenge. Table 3 summarizes the challenges identified.

Table 3. Emerging Food Safety Challenges Identified by Various Foreign Food Safety Officials

Challenges	Description
Climate change	Climate change may result in new pathogens, such as foodborne viruses, mycotoxins (molds), zoonoses, and changes in biodiversity that can lead to threats to the food chain.
	Climate change may enable pathogens to thrive and spread under new climatic conditions. For example, Listeriosis,especially in older people, seems to be increasing, perhaps because the climate is getting warmer, enabling*Listeria*to thrive.
	Climate change (warmer sea temperatures) may lead to outbreaks of the *Vibrio* bacterium in oysters. Climate change might also bring about changes in new pathogens as the temperature changes, along with crops and associated pests.
Demographic change	Countries are seeing increases in elderly populations, which tend to be more vulnerable than others to foodborne illness.
	Countries are seeing an increase in immigration; many immigrants bring home-prepared foods from overseas. If improperly prepared or preserved, these foods may cause illness.
Foodborne illness and zoonotic diseases	Foodborne illness from *Campylobacter*has increased significantly in the last several years, and it is one of the most frequent sources of food contamination. Scientists' understanding of*Campylobacter*is still limited because it generally occurs in isolated incidents and it is therefore more difficult to study.
	Incomplete knowledge of the nature and transmission of emerging zoonotic diseases (e.g., avian influenza and West Nile virus) is a growing concern, and inadequate veterinary care and public health infrastructure in some countries add to the complexity of managing these diseases. In addition, human and animal interactions are changing, with the potential for disease transmission, including *E. coli*and prions (which are involved in BSE).
	New fungi, pathogens, and diseases will continue to emerge and evolve.

Table 3. (Continued)

Challenges	Description
New types of food and preparation	Popular new types of foods (e.g., ready-to-eat bagged salads) pose new risks. For example, a small amount of contaminated produce that is chopped and placed in multiple bags can affect a large number of people in disparate locations.
	More people are consuming foods that are raw or that do not involve a terminal kill step, suchas cooking.
	Countries are seeing changes in production and processing based on new technologies, such as nanotechnology, genetic modification, and decontamination technologies (e.g., radiation).
Industry and trade development	The consolidation of the food industry, with fewer and fewer major corporations dominating entire food sectors, means that the potential impact of outbreaks and/or recalls is greater.
	The food supply is becoming increasingly global and the volume of international food trade is growing, which means it is increasingly difficult to control all elements of the food chain.
Regulatory and management issues	Assessing the risks of chemical and food additives, which are often imported as nonfood items, is a priority, and the number of contaminants is increasing.
	To focus more on risk, countries need to develop more data, which takes time and money.
	In spite of recent improvements in regulatory regimes, there is still potential for fraud in thesystem; it is difficult to develop a perfect system.
	Resources are sometimes mismatched with problems.
	The current regulatory system is not well suited at present to address certain new innovations, such as genetically modified organisms and nanotechnology.
	There are some differences between EU member countries in how they report information (e.g., zoonoses are reported by some countries as foodborne pathogens and by others as animal illnesses), which makes it difficult compare national statistics.
	Conducting risk assessments is getting more difficult.

Sources: Food safety officials in Canada, the EU, Germany, Ireland, Japan, the Netherlands, and the UK, and documents from these countries' food safety agencies.

As agreed with your offices, unless you publicly announce the contents earlier, we plan no further distribution until 30 days from the report date. At that time, we will send copies to the appropriate congressional committees, the Secretaries of Agriculture and State, the Commissioner of the Food and Drug Administration, the Office of the U.S. Trade Representative, and other interested parties. We will also make copies available to others upon request. In addition, the report will be available at no charge on the GAO Web site at http://www.gao.gov.

If you or your staffs have any questions about this report, please contact me at (202) 512-3841 or shamesl@gao.gov. Contact points for our Offices of Congressional Relations and Public Affairs may be found on the last page of this report. Key contributors to this report are listed in appendix II.

Lisa Shames; Director, Natural Resources and Environment

APPENDIX I: COUNTRY AND EU PROFILES

Canada's Food Safety System

Population and Per Capita Gross Domestic Product (GDP)

In 2007, Canada had an estimated population of 33.4 million, and in 2006 its estimated per capita GDP was US $35,700.

Organization

The Canadian Food Inspection Agency (CFIA), created in 1997, is an independent agency that reports to the Minister of Agriculture and Agri-Food. It is responsible for inspection and quarantine programs for foods, plants, and animals. According to agency officials, Canada consolidated the food safety function in order to reduce overlap and duplication, improve effectiveness and efficiency, save money, and separate risk management from risk assessment.

Canada takes a "gate-to-plate" approach to food safety to safeguard not just the food supply but also the plants and animals upon which safe food depends. Products subject to CFIA's inspection range from agricultural inputs, such as seeds, feeds, and fertilizers; to fresh foods, including meat, fish, eggs, grains, dairy products, fruit and vegetables; and prepared and packaged foods. The government also works with commodity sectors to develop and review food safety plans. CFIA is responsible for all food safety inspections, including inspections of imported and domestic products, export certifications, laboratory and diagnostic support, crisis management, and product recalls. It also inspects foods for quality assurance and is responsible for animal health and plant disease control. At the consumer end of the spectrum, CFIA educates Canadians about safe food-handling practices and various food safety risks through its Web site, food safety fact sheets, and the *Canadian Partnership for Consumer Food Safety Education*, a group of industry, consumer, and government organizations that jointly develop and implement a national program to educate consumers on how to safely handle food. CFIA employs over 6,000 people, including approximately 3,000 inspectors across all business lines. Approximately 10 percent of CFIA's budget comes from user fees.

While CFIA is responsible for risk management, another government organization, Health Canada, under the Minister of Health, is responsible for risk assessment. Health Canada sets the policies and standards that govern the safety and nutritional quality of all food sold in Canada, and CFIA enforces these policies. Health Canada is also responsible for evaluating CFIA's food program effectiveness. Another organization, the Public Health

Agency of Canada, a separate body under the Minister of Health, also conducts national food- and waterborne disease surveillance activities and helps respond to infectious disease outbreaks.

CFIA verifies industry compliance with federal acts and regulations by registering and inspecting slaughterhouses and food-processing plants and testing products. If a food safety emergency occurs, CFIA works with Health Canada, the Public Health Agency of Canada, provincial agencies, and the food industry in implementing an emergency response system.

In 2005, CFIA's border inspection function was shifted to the Canadian Border Services Agency. This agency is responsible for initial inspections of food and agriculture products arriving in Canada. It refers any questionable shipments to CFIA for follow-up action. According to CFIA officials, border guards open and inspect about 2 percent of imports. A CFIA veterinarian inspects most imports of live animals upon entry.

According to Canadian officials, in December 2007, Canada's Prime Minister announced the new Food and Consumer Product Safety Action Plan, which aims to strengthen and modernize Canada's safety system for health, consumer, and food products and to protect the health of Canadians. The Action Plan responds to changes in trade, industry supply chains, and consumer buying patterns, which require a different approach to food safety assurance. Programs focused on prevention, targeting highest risks, rapid response, and regulatory and legislative modernization will be implemented with the (Canadian) $113 million announced in Budget 2008. According to Canadian officials, proposed legislative amendments to Canada's Food and Drugs Act, along with a (Canadian) $62.2 million investment from Budget 2008, will enable CFIA to undertake a series of food safety initiatives, including the following:

- working with industries, provinces, and territories to implement preventive food safety control measures along the food chain;
- putting in place tools to better identify importers, track imports, and work with foreign authorities to verify the safety of foods at their country of origin; and
- increasing authority to monitor risks to Canadians and prevent unsafe products from entering the Canadian marketplace.

Oversight of Imported Food

Certification Programs and Equivalency Agreements

CFIA requires importers of meat and seafood products to meet Canadian standards. Determination of a foreign country's equivalency is based on the approval of a country's system of meat inspection, approval of establishments operating within that system, and review and registration of individual meat products prepared in these establishments. To approve the exporting country's inspection and certification system, CFIA follows a process of equivalency evaluation, based upon provisions in the Agreement on the Application of Sanitary and Phytosanitary Measures of the World Trade Organization. The agreement requires each member to accept as equivalent sanitary and phytosanitary measures of another member if the exporting member objectively demonstrates to the importing member that its measures achieve the importing member's appropriate level of protection.

Canada's Foreign Country Meat Inspection Systems Evaluation Program requires that imported meat products—unless specifically exempted by Canadian legislation—meet the same standards and requirements as if they were produced in registered establishments in Canada. It also requires that the exporting country's inspection and certification systems, along with the establishments operating under that system, be approved by CFIA before meat products can be exported to Canada. The competent authority of the exporting country must issue an official meat inspection certificate for every shipment of meat products exported to Canada. The competent authority is also expected to take appropriate actions if CFIA notifies it about meat products found to violate Canadian requirements and is to communicate any actions taken to CFIA. CFIA may require additional examination of subsequent shipments to Canada, with additional certification, for a predetermined number of shipments and/or weight of the certified shipment. The majority of CFIA's inspectors are focused on meat products because of the higher risk relative to most other foods. Canada currently allows importation of meat products from 40 countries.

In the case of seafood, Canada enters into agreements with other countries it believes have reliable inspection systems and uses these agreements in concentrating its inspection resources on products and countries representing increased risk. Under some agreements, CFIA agrees that products from specified processing facilities meet certain standards and therefore are subject to fewer inspections at the border. CFIA normally assesses these plants before it adds them to a list. Other agreements represent recognition by CFIA that the inspection system in another country is equivalent to the system in Canada. Under these agreements, the competent authority in the other country will inspect and maintain the list of establishments eligible for reduced inspection frequency upon import to Canada.

Canada has an equivalency agreement in place with the European Union (EU) for meat products and is working toward bringing an equivalency agreement for fishery products into force. The Canada-EU Veterinary Agreement allows equivalency determination according to criteria set out in the agreement that specify gradual levels of equivalency. These levels allow work toward equivalency in products to be tracked over time. The agreement is aimed at recognizing the equivalence of Canadian and EU inspection and certification requirements for trade between the EU and Canada in live animals and animal products.

Because of recent problems with Chinese and Vietnamese seafood imports, Canada has established more rigorous testing for specific seafood products from these countries. For example, from 2003 to 2005, Canada imposed a countrywide alert and instituted 100 percent testing of aquacultured fish products from Vietnam after repeatedly finding seafood products tainted with the antibiotic chloramphenicol, according to CFIA officials. The competent authority in Vietnam subsequently agreed to inspect and certify these products for the presence of certain antibiotics.

Foodborne Illness Outbreaks

According to data from the Public Health Agency of Canada, the most prevalent intestinal pathogen in Canada is *Campylobacter*, followed by *Salmonella* and parasitic infections (*Cryptosporidium, Cyclospora, Giardia,* and *Entamoeba*). *E. coli* ranks fourth in prevalence.

Response

If a foodborne illness outbreak occurs, CFIA, in partnership with Health Canada, provincial agencies, and the food industry, operates an emergency response system. This response system can be triggered by a consumer complaint, information from industry or trading partners, or the results of inspection and monitoring activities of CFIA or provincial food inspection agencies. In the event of an outbreak, CFIA investigates to pinpoint the source of the contamination. Health Canada gets involved in food safety emergencies when health risk assessments on food products are required, from either CFIA or the provinces or territories. The Public Health Agency of Canada gets involved in outbreak investigations when outbreaks involve more than one province or have international implications; if an outbreak involves only one province, the agency does not get involved unless its help is requested by the province.

Once a food is identified as a source, CFIA conducts the food safety investigation. On the basis of the results of the outbreak investigation and the food safety investigation, Health Canada (HC) conducts a health risk assessment for the implicated food and CFIA coordinates the risk management actions, one option of which might be to issue a recall. (For provincial outbreaks, the same process applies, except that the provincial health ministries have the lead in the outbreak investigation.) The Public Health Agency serves as an adviser to CFIA and Health Canada in these situations. Health Canada provides risk assessments for all provincial emergency situations except for the province of Quebec. (For products produced and sold only in Quebec, the provincial authorities may conduct their own outbreak investigation and risk assessment and decide on recalls.)

Canadian officials told us that in many ways, their procedures for addressing the public health aspects of foodborne illness outbreaks are similar to those followed by the U.S. Centers for Disease Control and Prevention (CDC).

In 2006 and 2007, according to CFIA data, CFIA conducted 2,915 food safety investigations, of which 246 resulted in voluntary recalls. CFIA has mandatory recall authority for food, which it has used a total of seven times. Though infrequently used, according to a CFIA official, this authority has contributed to more effective industry cooperation. This official also said that mandatory recall is rarely used precisely "because it is there." According to a Canadian industry representative, the mandatory food recall process is an important part of the food safety system because it is the last stop in the supply chain.

International Coordination

CFIA has a memorandum of understanding with the U.S. Food and Drug Administration to cooperate on food recalls and exchange information. In addition, Canada participates in the CDC's PulseNet, a network of public health and food regulatory agency laboratories.

Recent Incidents

According to food safety officials, one of the most significant outbreaks of foodborne illness to occur in Canada was a 2004 outbreak of *Salmonella* in mung bean sprouts from a single company. Health Canada conducted the health risk assessment for this incident, and the Public Health Agency got involved at the request of the Ontario government. The outbreak affected 300 people in the province of Ontario. CFIA made preparations for a mandatory order to be issued because the company was not conducting a "proper" recall on its own. In the end, however, the company agreed to conduct a "proper" voluntary recall. CFIA put a hold on other products by the same company.

In 2006, moreover, Canada was affected by the same *E. coli* in spinach incident that occurred in the United States. One person in Canada was sickened by the tainted product. CFIA and Health Canada collaborated with the U.S. Food and Drub Administration (FDA) and the state of California to assess and reduce the risk to Canadian consumers, and Health Canada assisted with tracing the product back to the source of contamination. U.S. spinach was recalled from Canadian store shelves, and Canada subsequently required U.S. spinach producers exporting to Canada to participate in an on-farm quality assurance program.

Although Canada does not have mandatory traceability for food, it does have mandatory cattle identification, which it is expanding to include all livestock. Beginning on January 1, 2001, Canadian cattle producers were required to tag all cattle with a bar-coded ear tag before the cattle left their farm of origin. The Canadian Food Inspection Agency began to fully enforce the program in 2002, with monetary penalties for noncompliance. In 2006, Canada began the transition to Radio-Frequency Identification (also known as RFID) tags on all cattle leaving their herds of origin. This tagging system is designed to facilitate the tracing of movement and identification of animals at various stages of the animal production chain, thereby helping to contain and eradicate animal disease.

Efforts to Measure Effectiveness of the Food Safety System

Performance Measures

The Canadian government has not comprehensively evaluated the results of its 1997 reorganization. A CFIA official told us that it is difficult to find quantitative data to measure systemwide change and performance.

Evaluations and Audits

Although there have been no comprehensive assessments of the Canadian food safety system, certain aspects have been formally reviewed. For example, Canada's Office of the Auditor General, GAO's Canadian counterpart, has conducted four reviews of certain CFIA activities, including (1) a 2004 study on regulation of plants developed using biotechnology, (2) a 2000 report on CFIA's Food Inspection Program, (3) a 1999 report on CFIA's management of a particular foodborne illness outbreak, and (4) a 1998 report on CFIA's creation. The Auditor General has also reviewed selected Health Canada activities, including progress made by Health Canada's Pest Management Regulatory Agency in applying its procedures for evaluating and registering new pesticides and reevaluating older registered pesticides and the amount of time it takes to get new, possibly safer, pesticides to market.

(This assessment also evaluated CFIA's progress in increasing the scope of its program testing for residues in fresh fruits and vegetables.) The Auditor General found that since an audit conducted in 2003, the federal government had made satisfactory progress in selected aspects of managing the safety and accessibility of pesticides, and it had shortened the time it takes to evaluate new pesticides. The Auditor General also reviewed Health Canada's progress in conducting national health surveillance in 2002. It found that Health Canada had made some progress toward resolving some of the weaknesses the auditors identified in a 1999 audit. However, it also found that national surveillance was still weak; many systems still lacked timely, accurate, and complete disease information; and gaps in surveillance continued.

Health Canada is responsible for assessing CFIA's activities and has completed 10 assessment reports, 9 of which have been published online. The most recent assessments found that CFIA was fulfilling its mission, although minor improvements were needed. For example, in 2005, Health Canada reviewed CFIA's Fish, Seafood, and Production Program's Quality Management Program, a mandatory inspection program for federally registered fish and seafood establishments. The evaluation found that the program was generally effective in enhancing the safety of fish and seafood products. However, Health Canada recommended, among other things, that CFIA managers responsible for the program should conduct trend analysis of complaints and incident data, which would enhance the management of emergencies and incidents. CFIA agreed with the recommendation.

CFIA has also assessed its own performance using criteria developed in collaboration with the Canadian Treasury Board and measuring progress on four strategic outcomes: (1) protecting Canadians from preventable health risks related to food safety or the transmission of animal diseases to humans; (2) protecting consumers through a fair and effective food, animal, and plant regulatory regime; (3) sustaining the plant and animal resource base; and (4) securing Canada's food supply and agricultural resource base from deliberate threats. For each strategic outcome, CFIA identified a number of specific targets. According to CFIA's 2007 annual performance plan, the agency met or exceeded 31 of its 40 targets.

Public Opinion Surveys

According to a CFIA report, public opinion research conducted in October 2006 and March 2007 suggested that CFIA was meeting its objective of ensuring that the public is aware of food safety risks. In the survey, 82 percent of Canadians said that they had heard about a food recall in the last year. According to CFIA, the research also indicated a positive link between Canadians' awareness of food recalls and their confidence in the food supply. In addition, in a September 2007 survey conducted by a third party on 29 federal departments using 11 indicators, CFIA and Health Canada were among those departments with the most public confidence.

Stakeholder Perspectives

The views of industry stakeholders who interact frequently with CFIA can also provide insight, albeit anecdotal, on the effectiveness of a country's food safety system. Industry representatives we spoke to in Canada generally believed that CFIA was effective and that consolidation of the food safety system had been beneficial. For example, one industry stakeholder stated that his organization was glad there was a single government body responsible for enforcing food safety policy and regulations. This individual further told us that as a result of consolidation, there were now CFIA staff dedicated to food safety issues, a fact that has allowed a working relationship between industry and government to evolve, a point echoed by a second industry group. His group also supported CFIA's focus on risk-based inspections.

A third industry group representative said that consolidation also helped strengthen agency expertise and capability by combining staff from different agencies. However, this person also expressed concern about CFIA's management of recalls.

Other Relevant Issues

Emerging trends and challenges. Officials identified the following concerns:

- The consolidation of the food industry, with fewer and fewer major corporations dominating entire food sectors, means that the potential impact of outbreaks and/or recalls is greater.
- The popularity of new types of foods (e.g., ready-to-eat bagged salads) poses new risks.
- Imported foods and processes are a concern, especially those, such as produce, that do not involve cooking to kill pathogens.
- Climate change, and the warmer sea temperatures that result, may lead to outbreaks of the *Vibrio* bacterium in oysters. Climate change might also result in new pathogens, new crops, and associated pests.
- Incomplete knowledge of the nature and transmission of emerging zoonotic diseases (e.g., bovine spongiform encephalopathy (BSE, otherwise known as mad cow disease), avian influenza, West Nile virus, new strains of rabies), is a growing concern, and inadequate veterinary care and public health infrastructure in some countries add to the complexity of managing these diseases.

The EU's Food Safety System

Population and Per Capita GDP

The European Union (EU) consists of the following 27 member countries: Austria, Belgium, Bulgaria, Cyprus, Czech Republic, Denmark, Estonia, Finland, France, Germany, Greece, Hungary, Ireland, Italy, Latvia, Lithuania, Luxembourg, Malta, the Netherlands, Poland, Portugal, Romania, Slovakia, Slovenia, Spain, Sweden, and the United Kingdom. Together, the countries have a population of about 490 million people. The EU's 2007 estimated average per capita gross GDP was US $32,900.

Organization

Since January 2006, the EU food safety system has been fully integrated and is regulated by EU legislation that applies to all EU member countries and importers. However, food safety in Europe was historically part of agriculture policy under the EU's Directorate General for Agriculture. Two events in the late 1990s—the crisis with BSE and the discovery of dioxin in chicken products—drove the EU to comprehensively reform its food safety legislation. The EU created a separate body, the Directorate General for Public Health and Consumer Protection (referred to as DG-SANCO), focused on food safety and consumer protection. DG-SANCO, headquartered in Brussels, Belgium, is independent of the EU's agricultural policy.

DG-SANCO oversees three key areas: food safety, public health, and consumer affairs. The food safety mandate is broad, covering, among other things, animal health and welfare, veterinary inspections, plant health, food labeling, contaminants, and pesticide residues. DG-SANCO is divided into six directorates spread over three locations: Brussels; Luxembourg; and Grange, County Meath, Ireland. The Brussels office is involved in risk management. This includes the development of the EU policy on food safety, animal health and welfare, and plant health, and the daily management of food safety legislation. Luxembourg is home to a DG-SANCO group on public health and risk assessment. The Grange office houses the Food and Veterinary Office (FVO), which, through audits, inspections, and related activities, oversees member states' compliance with EU requirements for food safety and quality, animal health and welfare, plant health legislation, and imports from non-EU countries exporting to the EU. FVO also contributes to the development of EU policy on food safety, animal health and welfare, and plant health, and the development of effective control systems for food safety, animal health and welfare, and plant health.

Other entities playing important roles in the EU's food safety system include the following:

- The European Centre for Disease Prevention and Control (ECDC), based in Stockholm, Sweden, was established in 2005 and is the EU agency responsible for strengthening Europe's defenses against infectious diseases. Its mission is to identify, assess, and communicate current and emerging threats to human health posed by infectious diseases. The Center works with national health protection bodies across Europe to strengthen and develop continentwide disease surveillance and early warning systems. Its mission is centered on transmissible diseases to humans, and it collaborates with the European Food Safety Authority (EFSA), in particular in the field of zoonoses (ECDC transmits to EFSA the data it collects on foodborne diseases; EFSA includes these data in its annual report on zoonoses). ECDC also cooperates with the U.S. Centers for Disease Control.
- *EFSA is the main scientific agency for food and feed safety.* Based in Parma, Italy, EFSA provides independent scientific advice on all matters with a direct or indirect impact on food safety—including animal health and welfare, plant protection, genetically modified organisms, and nutrition. Its work falls into two major areas: risk assessments and risk communication, but its tasks also include data collection (for example, the annual zoonoses report). At the request of the European Commission as well as member states and the European Parliament, EFSA assesses the risks associated with the food chain, including, for example, risk assessment related to food or feed additives submitted for premarket approvals, microbiological risk, contaminants, animal health and welfare, and plant health. These risk assessments inform the policies and decisions of EU risk managers, who establish limits on these substances. EFSA also communicates to the public the results of its scientific work. Because its mission is independent risk assessment, EFSA is separate from the DGSANCO structure. EFSA cooperates closely with the scientific bodies responsible for risk assessment in the various member states and with the U.S. Food and Drug Administration. The EFSA Advisory Forum is composed of a representative from each of the member states' national bodies responsible for risk assessment. The forum facilitates the sharing of scientific information between the national authorities and EFSA and ensures close cooperation with the national scientific bodies to avoid duplication and to promote common scientific views on risk assessment and risk communication.

At the national level, each EU member state has one or more agencies charged with implementing EU regulations, referred to as the "central competent authority" or "competent authority." For example, in the UK, the Food Standards Agency is the competent authority for food and feed safety, while the Department of Environment, Food, and Rural Affairs is the competent authority for animal health and welfare and plant health issues. Each member state is expected to prepare a multiyear control plan that contains general information on the structure and organization of the systems for feed and food control. This plan includes the designation of competent authorities and their tasks at the central, regional, and local level. The member states are required to provide the European Commission, the executive branch, or governing body, of the EU, with an up-to-date copy of their multiyear control plans on request.

Regulatory Framework

The EU has adopted an integrated farm-to-fork approach to food safety that aims to protect human life and health while also taking into account the protection of animal health and welfare, plant health, and the environment. Under this framework, food law and feed law cover all stages of production, processing and distribution.[1] Food and feed operators have primary responsibility for food safety; member states ensure surveillance and control of these operators, and the EC tests the performance of member states' control capacities and capabilities through audits and inspections.

In the EU, food and feed business operators have primary responsibility for food safety, while member states provide oversight over these operators at all stages of production. Business operators are responsible for the food and feed (such as cattle fodder or pet food) that they produce, transport, store, or sell. They must (1) be able to rapidly identify any supplier or consignee, (2) immediately inform the competent authorities if they have reason to believe their food or feed is not safe, (3) immediately withdraw a product from the market if they have reason to believe the product is not safe, (4) apply HACCP principles[2] in their processes and ensure that controls are applied at critical points,[3] and (5) cooperate with the competent authorities in actions taken to reduce risk. The competent authority in each member state is responsible for monitoring producers to ensure that they are meeting these obligations. The EU's FVO then assesses the performance of the member states' competent authorities, countries aspiring to join the EU (referred to as candidate countries), and non-EU countries intending to export to the EU (referred to as third countries), to verify the effectiveness of national control systems for meeting EU standards in the areas of food safety, animal health and welfare, and plant health.

Feed suppliers, for example, must apply HACCP principles, register with their national competent authorities to help ensure traceability, and comply with specific microbiological criteria, such as for levels of *Salmonella*, molds, and yeast. The competent authorities in each country approve certain feed operators (i.e., those manufacturing and/or selling certain feed additives) by visiting the facility before they start up any activity to ensure that the operators meet EU standards, and once the operator is approved, the competent authority provides oversight and imposes penalties for noncompliance.

In turn, FVO inspects the competent authorities' oversight and provides recommendations when there are shortcomings. It also inspects countries aspiring to join the EU, and non-EU countries intending to export to the EU, to verify the effectiveness of national control systems to implement EU standards in the areas of food safety, animal health and welfare, and plant health. As for imported feed, importers must ensure that the feed meets EU standards.

According to EU sources, the primary law laying out the regulatory framework for food safety in the EU is the General Food Law of 2002. Subsequent legislation merged, harmonized, and simplified detailed and complex hygiene requirements previously contained in 17 directives covering the hygiene of foodstuffs and the production and marketing of products of animal origin. According to these sources, the EU's food legislation framework includes the major regulations and directives described in table 4.

Table 4. Major EU Laws, Regulations, and Directives

Regulation	Major provisions
General Food Law (Regulation [EC] 178/2002)	Covers the general principles and requirements of food law and procedures in matters of food safety and includes the following key provisions: (1) Safety: Business operators shall not place on the market unsafe food or feed; (2) Responsibility: Business operators at all stages of production shall ensure that food or feed satisfy the food law; (3) Traceability: Business operators shall be able to identify anyone from whom they have been supplied a food or food component; and (4) Emergency: Business operators shall immediately initiate withdrawals of food or feed from the market if they have a reason to believe that it is not in compliance with food safety requirements.
Hygiene I (Regulation [EC] 852/2004)	Covers the general rules for food business operators on the hygiene of all foodstuffs, noting that primary responsibility lies with business operators, food safety starts with primary production, and implementation of HACCP should reinforce business operator responsibility.
Hygiene II (Regulation [EC] 853/2004)	Covers specific rules for food business operators for foods of animal origin, including processed and unprocessed foods, and covers rules for importers of foods of animal origin.
Hygiene III (Regulation [EC] 854/2004)	Covers specific rules for the organization of specific controls for products of animal origin intended for human consumption, in particular for businesses producing meat, raw milk, eggs, or fishery products, and includes detailed inspection tasks.
Hygiene IV Directive [EC] 2002/99	Covers the general animal health rules governing all stages of production, processing, and distribution within the European Community and the introduction from non-EU countries of productsof animal origin intended for human consumption. The stated aim is to prevent the spread of animal diseases as a result of placing animal produce on the market.
Council Directive [EC] 97/78	Covers the principles governing the organization of veterinary checks on products of animal origin entering the EU from third countries.
Regulation [EC] 882/2004	Covers official controls performed to ensure the verification of compliance with feed and food laws, animal health, and animal welfare rules.

Source: EU documents.

DG-SANCO provides training to member states to harmonize their food safety regimes and to ensure uniform application. The implementation of EU legislation in member states is reviewed by other EU members and by FVO. EU legislation is mostly in the form of regulations or decisions that are directly applicable in the member states. In other cases, the EU legislation takes the form of directives, which the member states must translate into national law. Directives establish the target objective(s) and allow member states to decide on the most appropriate measures and adapt them to their situations in order to reach the defined objective(s).

EU member states may also institute their own country-specific food safety regulations, as appropriate for their particular situations, provided that the level of protection defined at the EU level is not jeopardized and that the additional measures proposed do not impede the free circulation of goods among the member states.

The EU also emphasizes the importance of being able to trace food "one step forward and one step back" to quickly track any questionable food products. Each food and feed business operator must be able to identify its suppliers and which businesses it supplied. Specifically, the operator must be able to document the names and addresses of the suppliers and customers, as well as the nature of the product and date of delivery. The operators are also encouraged to keep information on the volume and quantity of a product; the batch number, if there is one; and a more detailed description of the product, such as whether it is raw or processed. Food and feed business operators must also have systems and procedures that allow them to provide this information to the competent authorities on demand. (Exporters in trading partner countries are not required to fulfill the EU's traceability requirement, except in circumstances where there are special bilateral agreements for certain sensitive sectors or where there are specific EU requirements, such as in the veterinary sector. However, these traceability requirements pertain to EU importers, who should be able to identify their direct supplier in the non-EU country.)

According to EU sources, the EU's traceability system proved useful during an incident that took place in 2004. During standard random monitoring of dioxin levels in milk at a Dutch farm, the national competent authorities found a high level of dioxin. EU sources noted that the competent authorities immediately barred the farm from trade and began tracing the product through the food chain. They found that the source of contamination was clay, used in food processing to separate higher-quality potatoes from lower-quality ones. The dioxin-tainted clay had contaminated potato peels used for feeding dairy animals. The EU's electronic Rapid Alert System for Food and Feed was used to trigger an exchange of information among national authorities about the problem. According to EU sources, the authorities quickly established that the clay had also been supplied to several food-processing companies located in Belgium, France, Germany, and the Netherlands. The authorities rapidly identified these businesses and barred from trade over 200 farms that had received the potentially contaminated potato peels. EU sources noted that because of the traceability system, the contaminated products never reached consumers.

EU producers must also tag livestock with details of their origin, and when the animals are taken for slaughter, stamp them with the traceability code of the slaughterhouse. The tools used (ear tags, "passports," or bar codes) may vary from country to country but must carry the same information. In addition, to ensure the traceability of animals across the EU, the EU established the Trade Control and Expert System (TRACES), a central database for tracking the movement of animals both within the EU and from third countries. In the event of a disease outbreak, TRACES ensures that all potentially affected animals can be quickly identified and that authorities can take appropriate measures.

Oversight of Imported Food

Import Controls

The EU's guiding principle is that all food products in the EU should be safe, regardless of origin. However, imported products require specific controls, owing to different animal, public, and plant health situations in countries of origin. Animal products such as meat, milk, fish, and honey, as well as live animals, present the highest level of risks because they can transmit serious human and animal diseases. Certain plant products, such as cereals and nuts, also present higher levels of risks because they may be contaminated by aflatoxins. "Shelf-stable" products, such as canned, processed, and dried foods present lesser risks; control requirements are thus tailored accordingly.

Equivalency Agreement/Certification Programs

One of the key features of EU regulations is that products of animal origin imported from non-EU countries (referred to as third countries) must meet safety standards at least equivalent to those of the EU. If such food is found not to be as safe as that of the EU, the overseas firm is not allowed to export to the EU. For example, the EU maintains a list of third countries in which the capacity of the competent authority has been recognized, along with the country's animal and public health system and status, but the EU does not maintain such a list for food of nonanimal origin. On the basis of this recognition, third countries' competent authorities propose establishments to be approved for export of products of animal origin to the EU. Among the requirements for approving the export of products of animal origin are the following:

- formal submission of a written application to export to the EU;
- verification of the exporting country's animal and public health system, such as legislation, control systems, disease surveillance measures, and laboratory facilities;
- submission and approval of a monitoring plan for residues of banned or restricted substances in the EU, including veterinary medicines and growth-promoting hormones; and
- provision of sanitary certification that the products to be exported to the EU meet import requirements.

FVO normally visits countries to verify compliance with these conditions. If compliance is satisfactory, the EC may formally decide to approve countries and establishments for export to the EU. In addition, third countries must certify and approve business establishments wishing to export products of animal origin to the EU, noting that they meet the relevant EU standards. Lists of these establishments are maintained online by the European Community for all the main categories of animal products (e.g., beef, poultry, fish, or dairy), and compliance is verified during follow-up FVO missions. To help reduce problematic imports, DGSANCO provides technical assistance to developing countries. In particular, DG-SANCO trains people overseas on hygiene and HACCP.

Inspections

The EU bases its inspections of imports on the degree of risk presented by particular food types. According to the EU, it has shifted its focus from regular, but random, sampling to paying attention to the sources of greatest risk. Risk may be high because a particular product is traded in large quantities, or because a product or the area it comes from is known to be susceptible to a particular plant or animal disease. If the risk of a given food product is not known or quantified, the EU applies what it refers to as the "precautionary principle:" If there are reasonable grounds for suspecting a problem, the commission acts to limit the risk. The EU asserts it does not necessarily need to wait for proof that there really is a risk.

Because of countries' differing risk profiles, the EU has different inspection methods for food products of (1) animal origin, (2) nonanimal origin, and (3) high-risk foods of nonanimal origin.

First, all imports of live animals and animal products must enter the EU through its roughly 300 approved border inspection posts, which include airports, rail stations, and deepwater ports. The posts are under the authority of each member state's official veterinary services. A member state's customs service cannot release consignments unless they have passed through veterinary controls. The system thus requires the cooperation of veterinary authorities and customs officials. The border inspection posts must be notified in advance of the presentation of such consignments, which must undergo an official veterinary check at the inspection post. When a consignment arrives at a post, three types of checks are carried out:

- Documentary: A documentary check is carried out on all consignments.
- Identity: An identity check is carried out on all consignments to verify that the identity of the goods corresponds fully with the veterinary documents supplied.
- Physical: A physical check is carried out on a percentage of consignments on the basis of the type of animal or animal product and the country of origin to ensure it does not pose a threat to public and animal health. According to EU officials, EU legislation also specifies a minimum number of physical checks to be carried out for each product group (e.g., meat, fish, or dairy) by each member state. A physical inspection may also involve taking samples for laboratory tests.

When all tests and checks are satisfactory, the consignment is issued a Common Veterinary Entry Document and is placed on the EU market. In cases where testing is carried out because of unfavorable results of previous tests on the animal product or when a problem is suspected, the consignment will not be cleared or allowed to leave the border inspection post until the border authorities receive the results of the new tests.

If a consignment does not comply with EU requirements, it may be rejected. In these cases, EU officials negotiate with the owner of the consignment and the country of dispatch, where appropriate, about whether to destroy the product, to retreat it for uses other than the human food chain, or to redispatch it. Food or feed business operators or their representatives are responsible for the consignment and are liable for any costs incurred by the competent authorities to destroy or redispatch it. In addition, if consignments are not in compliance, all other border inspection posts are notified through the Rapid Alert System for Food and Feed. This electronic notification system, managed by DG-SANCO, alerts all EU member countries to a potential food problem, including either a direct or an indirect risk to human health from food or feed. The rapid alert system involves all member states, the EC, and EFSA, as well as Iceland, Liechtenstein, and Norway (non-EU countries). Each participating country has a rapid alert contact point to collect information on national notifications and enter them into the database. The exchange of information allows participating states to immediately ascertain whether they are also affected by a problem and take appropriate measures. Since all EU border posts are connected electronically, problems at any one border can quickly be announced via the rapid alert system to all other border posts. Future imports from the same exporting country are then scrutinized more closely.

Second, food products of nonanimal origin—including fruits, vegetables, cereals, tubers, nondairy drinks, food of mineral origin (such as salt), spices, and condiments—do not need to come from approved countries or establishments and can come into any EU port of entry. However, they are still subject to certain EU control requirements in order to verify that they comply with EU food safety standards. Among other things, food business operators in third countries must monitor the safety of products and processes under their responsibility, follow general hygiene provisions for primary production, develop HACCP principles, and register establishments with the appropriate competent authorities. In the EU, the competent authorities of the member states are responsible for carrying out regular controls of the goods imported into EU territory. Controls are determined based on potential risks.

Finally, the EU maintains a list of food products of nonanimal origin that may represent a health risk to humans. As noted above, cereals and nuts, for example, may appear on the high-risk list. Such products undergo control measures, such as health certificates and testing, similar to those required for food products of animal origin. For example, all consignments of pistachios from Iran are sampled and checked. The safeguard measures are lifted once the problem has been addressed.

Problems with imports are normally brought to light by inspections carried out by the FVO, checks at border inspection posts, checks carried out during the course of "market surveillance" by member states,[4] business or consumer groups, or media reports. The following actions are available to address these problems:

- circulate information through the rapid alert system to all member states, especially their border inspection posts, to enable a higher level of surveillance;
- request that the exporting country take corrective action, such as deleting the exporting establishment from the authorized list for export to the EU;
- introduce additional requirements, such as a higher level of testing at border inspection posts, retention of consignments awaiting laboratory confirmation of noncontamination, and additional certification requirements through "safeguard decisions"; and
- ban exports to the EU outright.

These measures are normally introduced in full consultation with the member states. In recent years, safeguard decisions have been taken in relation to products from a wide range of third countries, including China (all animal products banned in 2002) and Brazil (100 percent testing of poultry and meat products for veterinary residues). In urgent cases, the EU can also take safeguard measures on its own initiative, pending confirmation by the member states.

With respect to actions that can be taken domestically in response to an import problem, the EU distinguishes between withdrawals and recalls under the rapid alert system and has authority for both. Withdrawals occur when the product is still under the control of the producer and consist of measures aimed at preventing the distribution or display of a product that is dangerous to the consumer. Recalls occur when the product is already available to consumers and consist of measures aimed at achieving the return of an unsafe product. All member states must notify the EU when there is a serious risk to human health.

The EU requires that member states ensure that adequate financial resources are available for organizing official controls on imports. For that purpose, member states may collect fees or charges to cover the costs of these controls. However, they must collect fees for certain activities, including controls of products of animal origin, such as meat inspection, and controls of dairy establishments. Fees are also levied for certain import controls on these commodities. EU officials said that fees may not be higher than the costs borne by the competent authorities.

Foodborne Illness Outbreaks

According to EFSA, in 2005 the most frequently reported zoonotic pathogen in humans within the EU was *Campylobacter*, followed by *Salmonella.* Other common zoonotic pathogens include Verotoxigenic *E. coli,* [5] *Yersinia,*[6] *Listeria*, and *Brucella.*[7] *Salmonella, Campylobacter,* and foodborne viruses—especially calicivirus—were the most prevalent causes of foodborne outbreaks in the EU in 2005.

Response

Responsibility for investigating and controlling outbreaks of foodborne illness rests with local or regional authorities in most of the EU member states. National epidemiologists collect and analyze outbreak data and cooperate with other responsible bodies, such as the environmental health office or the regional veterinarian, to implement control measures. For larger outbreaks, or for those that cover more than one region, the member state's national surveillance institute, which monitors and investigates public health issues, often assists. The ECDC is not involved in outbreaks confined to one member state, except for providing training, guidelines, and possible expertise when requested. However, the country investigating an outbreak informs the ECDC if it finds that the contamination may affect other EU citizens because, for example, the food product is distributed in EU countries, or if the outbreak is likely to spread to other EU countries. The investigating country informs the ECDC through the Early Warning Response System— a computer database that deals with communicable diseases. ECDC assesses risk at the EU level to confirm a threat and then (1) works with other entities to ensure a coordinated approach to investigation and control; (2) cooperates closely with other EU agencies, particularly EFSA; (3) ensures proper communication with the EU and the public; and (4) assists the member states involved.

Data from all foodborne illness outbreaks are reported to EFSA and published annually. Cross-border outbreaks are not reported separately. In case of a foodborne illness outbreak, the member states must carry out epidemiological investigations. EFSA also provides guidance on what information should be reported in case of a foodborne illness outbreak.

ECDC manages a computerized database—Enter-net—an international surveillance network for human gastrointestinal infections. It involves all 27 EU countries, as well as Australia, Canada, Japan, South Africa, Switzerland, and Norway. Network participants include the microbiologists in charge of each country's national reference laboratory for *Salmonella* and *E. coli* infections, and each country's epidemiologist is responsible for the national surveillance of these diseases. The network conducts international surveillance of salmonellosis and *E. coli,* including antimicrobial resistance. Limited data on each laboratory-confirmed case of *Salmonella* or *E. coli* infection identified by the national reference laboratories are transferred to the central databases at the Enter-net hub. These records include microbiological and epidemiological data, which are analyzed on a regular basis and reported to all participants. The central database allows Enter-net to monitor trends in infection and recognize unusual events that can be seen only when the data are pooled internationally. The Enter-net database has led to a number of recalls, including, for example, peanuts from China.

When more than one EU member state is involved in an outbreak, human data are communicated to other member states through the Early Warning and Response System, a database managed by the European Commission with the support of the ECDC and used by public health authorities in member states and in European Economic Area (EEA) countries.[8] The system is a forum for exchanging information on the details of specific events caused by communicable diseases and the public health measures planned or undertaken at national level to respond to those events. The database is confidential and can be accessed only by the officially nominated public health authority in member states, the commission, and the ECDC.

Information on any food involved in an illness outbreak is immediately communicated through the rapid alert system. There are also networks of EU reference laboratories linking national reference laboratories for each of the major foodborne pathogens. These networks provide support to member states' competent authorities in analyzing suspect food and exchanging information on the molecular typing of isolates (samples).

The epidemiological investigation of foodborne outbreaks is an important tool for identifying the major causes of foodborne infections in humans. It is a major source of information used when deciding on priorities for the control of foodborne infections in the EU.

Recent Incidents

According to EU officials, the EU has had some recent problems with dye and chemical contamination of food, but there have not been any EU-wide incidents of foodborne illness outbreaks to date.

Efforts to Measure the Effectiveness of Food Safety Systems

Performance Measures

According to EU officials, performance measures for the EU include annual reports from EFSA on trends in foodborne illness, reports by individual member states on their effectiveness, and an EU health indicators database.

Evaluations and Audits

FVO audits are the key EU instruments to ensure that member states and non-EU countries are complying with regulations. Under the EU's farm-to-fork approach, FVO must examine the entire chain. Each year FVO develops an inspection program that identifies priority areas and countries it will audit that year. During the audit, it assesses a member state's competent authorities and compliance with EU requirements. Competent authorities must have their own audit authorities, which FVO also audits. As part of their reviews, the FVO inspectors may visit producers or processing plants to establish that enforcement mechanisms are effective in practice. If necessary, FVO can send out inspectors in response to disease outbreaks both within and outside the EU. FVO makes recommendations to the country's competent authority to address any shortcomings found during the inspections. The competent authority in each member state is then asked to present an action plan to the FVO on how it intends to deal with any identified shortcomings. Together with other EU bodies, the FVO evaluates this action plan and monitors its implementation. According to FVO staff, if an audit turns up deficiencies, the commission could put in place safeguard measures that, for example, block trade from a particular country if the audit finds there is immediate harm to public, animal, or plant health. The commission can also issue an alert to all member states through the rapid alert system. As a last resort, the commission could take legal action to ensure that member states meet their obligations.

In 2006, FVO carried out 255 inspections, of which 68 percent were related to food safety, 14 percent to animal health, 13 percent to animal welfare, and 5 percent to plant health. Sixty-three percent of the audits were in EU member countries, 26 percent were in non-EU countries, and 11 percent were in EU candidate countries.

Public Opinion Surveys

The EU periodically surveys citizens in its member countries on a variety of issues as part of the Eurobarometer series.[9] According to a 2005 Eurobarometer survey published in 2006, an estimated 38 percent of people in the EU stated that, overall, food safety had improved, 29 percent that it had stayed about the same, 28 percent that it had worsened, and 5 percent did not know. In addition, 47 percent of those surveyed stated that public authorities' actions in the EU with regard to food safety risks are usually appropriate, 33 percent that the actions are insufficient, 8 percent that the actions go beyond what is needed, and 12 percent did not know. Finally, according to the Eurobarometer survey, an estimated 59 percent of people in the EU agreed that food produced in the EU is safer than food imported from elsewhere, 27 percent disagreed, and 13 percent did not know.

Other Relevant Issues

Officials we spoke with at the DG-SANCO and FVO identified the following ongoing and future challenges to the EU's food safety system:

- The EU is looking to develop a more risk-based veterinary imports control program to identify the greatest risks associated with imported food, so that it can focus more on problem areas. Officials believe that it is possible to have a more flexible approach to veterinary controls in some areas without diminishing the overall approach. However, in order to focus more on risk, the EU needs to develop more data, and EU officials currently are looking to improve data availability. The development of data takes time and money.
- Despite regulatory improvements, there is still potential for fraud in the system.
- Resources are sometimes mismatched with problems.
- The food supply is becoming increasingly global, which means it is more difficult to control all elements of the food chain.
- The current regulatory system is also not well suited to address certain innovations, such as genetically modified organisms, certain agricultural crops, and nanotechnology.

- Some items, such as dyes, which are chemicals, are imported as nonfood items but can be used as additives in certain processed foods.
- There are also differences between the EU member countries in how they report information. For example, zoonoses are reported by some countries as foodborne pathogens and by others as animal illnesses.
- The number of contaminants, such as mycotoxins, as well as unauthorized additives, is increasing.
- Conducting risk assessments is also getting more difficult. New legislation has moved to risk-based approaches. Member states have more leeway on how they define risk.

Germany's Food Safety System

Population and Per Capita GDP

In 2007, Germany had a population of approximately 82.4 million, and in 2006 it had an estimated per capita GDP of US $31,900.

Organization

In 2002, the Federal Office of Consumer Protection and Food Safety (BVL) and the Federal Institute for Risk Assessment were established within the portfolio of the Federal Ministry of Consumer Protection, Food, and Agriculture. The German government took this action in response to numerous crises, including dioxin-contaminated chicken feed, misuse of antibiotics in pig feed, and the emergence of BSE in Germany in the late 1990s. The reorganization separated risk assessment from risk management. Prior to the reorganization, three federal ministries—for public health, agriculture, and environmental protection, overseeing a total of 18 agencies—were responsible for food safety.

Germany's 16 federal states are responsible for overseeing compliance with laws, and as such, they are in charge of food and feed safety, animal health and welfare, and plant health. Local authorities in each state are in charge of control and enforcement, and the federal states oversee inspections performed by local governments. To harmonize food safety activities among the states, the German government and federal states have established a set of standard operating procedures for the control of food establishments and the sampling of food products, among other things. As a result of this decentralized structure, BVL coordinates—but does not oversee—the activities of the federal states in these areas. BVL conducts surveillance (not audits) to ensure the states adhere to the EU regulations for food safety.

BVL's main focus is risk management. Other responsibilities include cooperating with the Federal Ministry of Consumer Protection, Food, and Agriculture in the areas of food safety, veterinary affairs, and consumer protection by providing data and support. BVL also provides logistical and organizational support to the states on food safety-related matters and houses the national and EU reference laboratories for residues, including veterinary medicines, for contaminants, and the National Reference Laboratory for Genetically Modified Organisms. The agency is also Germany's central contact point for the EU's Rapid Alert System for Food and Feed and for the EU's Food and Veterinary Office. BVL has approximately 430 employees.

The Federal Institute for Risk Assessment is in charge of risk assessment and risk communication. It provides scientific opinions on food and feed safety and animal health, as well as assessments of the health effects of chemicals, and risk assessments on genetically modified animals, plants, and feedstuffs. Its research results and recommendations are an important decision-making aid for a number of public agencies, including the Federal Ministry of Consumer Protection, Food, and Agriculture and BVL. The Federal Institute for Risk Assessment is also the primary German point of contact for the European Food Safety Authority. The institute houses 14 national reference laboratories related to food safety and hygiene.

The Robert Koch Institute is responsible for disease prevention and control. It is also responsible for scientific investigation, epidemiological and medical investigation, and analysis of dangerous diseases. It also collects, maintains, and reports epidemiological data at the federal level.

Each German state also has a ministry that oversees the control, planning, and coordination in all areas of food, feed, and veterinary matters in the state. Each state also has one or more authorities that oversee food safety and/or veterinary matters at the district or municipal level. In addition, five German states have provincial governments that supervise food-related matters at the provincial level—between the state and local level— and provide oversight over local authorities. Although the Federal Ministry of Consumer Protection, Food, and Agriculture is the national-level competent authority for import controls on animals and food of animal origin, the individual states implement the veterinary import controls, and local authorities oversee Germany's 22 border inspection posts.

Oversight of Imported Food

According to BVL, Germany imports about 47 million tons of food per year, 19 percent of which comes from developing countries.

Import Control

Germany's regulations are fully harmonized with the EU's. For a more detailed summary of the EU food safety requirements, see the EU profile.

Inspections

See the EU profile for more detail.

Equivalency Agreements/Certification Programs

See the EU profile for more detail. According to German officials, Germany has some of its own laws overseeing food safety matters, including the Law on Food and Feed and certain other legislative acts pertaining to foods of animal origin and certain other specific products. According to these officials, some of Germany's most important food safety regulations include the following:

- a regulation for the execution of provisions of community food hygiene laws as a national executive order requiring implementation of EU regulations on food safety and other directives on adapting and consolidating national provisions concerning food import and market regulations, labeling and sanitary rules, and distribution;
- an import regulation for foodstuff of animal origin;

- product-specific regulations, such as those for wine, honey, and milk; and
- general administrative procedures.

The 16 federal states do not have their own food safety laws, but their regulations and administrative rules apply to their responsibility for enforcing food safety legislation.

The federal states also do not impose fees for regular controls—only for controls detecting infringements.

Foodborne Illness Outbreaks

According to data from the Robert Koch Institute, the most commonly reported intestinal pathogen in Germany in 2006 was norovirus, with 75,766 reported cases, followed by *Salmonella,* with 52,267 reported cases. *Campylobacter* was the next most common pathogen in Germany, with 52,035 reported cases. In addition, there were 6,470 cases of *E. coli* and 508 cases of *Listeria* infection.

Response

Multiple agencies in Germany are involved in managing an outbreak of foodborne illness. Local health agencies are the primary points of contact when an outbreak occurs. These agencies identify, treat, and report the illness to the Robert Koch Institute. The institute's epidemiological department collects data and identifies and confirms the number of illnesses. The institute is also the primary conduit for communication to the public throughout an outbreak. If the outbreak does not spread to a neighboring county or federal state, the local county health official retains responsibility for managing it. However, if the outbreak does spread, the Robert Koch Institute manages it, in collaboration with the local authority. The Federal Institute for Risk Assessment collaborates with the Robert Koch Institute to determine what the illness is, including the strain of the pathogen and the source of the outbreak. Local laboratories send any samples to the Federal Institute for Risk Assessment's reference laboratories for more sophisticated testing. The institute also has food and veterinary experts who assist in the investigation. (In the context of foodborne illness outbreaks, most of the food scientists are veterinarians specializing in food microbiology.) BVL helps track the source of the outbreak, provides information to other national agencies and the states, coordinates activities at the federal level, conducts tracking and tracing, and coordinates a recall if necessary. However, in Germany, it is the federal states that have the recall authority; BVL does not issue recalls. German officials told us that their procedures for addressing the public health aspects of foodborne illness outbreaks— in terms of identifying pathogens and tracking diseases—are generally similar to those followed in the United States by the Centers for Disease Control and Prevention.

International Coordination

During an investigation of an outbreak of foodborne illness, BVL is responsible for notifying the EU's rapid alert system and for sending information received from other EU member states via the rapid alert system to competent authorities in the states. In 2006, Germany issued 425 rapid alert notifications, including 2 related to microbial contamination and 20 related to potentially pathogenic organisms. The Robert Koch Institute is the competent German body providing scientific advice to European Centre for Disease Control.

A scientific officer from the Robert Koch Institute is member of the Center's Advisory Forum, where information on health threats is exchanged.

Recent Incidents

According to a report by the Robert Koch Institute, on August 15, 2007, the institute detected an outbreak of *Salmonella* Panama in several German states during its routine computerized analysis of state-reported monitoring data. In all, 10 states reported *Salmonella* Panama cases. On the same day that they identified the outbreak, Robert Koch Institute officials asked the states to investigate the issue at the local level, including having the local health officials ask the victims' parents to participate in a telephone interview so the institute could learn more about the child's illness and the food the family had eaten. Laboratories were asked to send *Salmonella* Panama samples to the national *Salmonella* reference laboratory in the state of Saxony-Anhalt.

A month earlier, the Robert Koch Institute had learned that during the course of semi-annual monitoring, a worker at a meat-processing plant had been diagnosed with asymptomatic *Salmonella* Panama. The plant produced, among other things, minisalami sticks, a snack popular with children.

The institute then included consumption of minisalami sticks in questions about what had been eaten by the children who became ill. In several instances, parents separately told interviewers that their children had eaten minisalami sticks. To confirm the connection between the minisalami and the *Salmonella* Panama infection, institute staff conducted a case-control study, using 22 victims of the July outbreak as the "cases" and people from 20 affected communities as the controls.

To identify the control cases, the institute asked certain local offices in the affected regions to select from their databases up to 30 families with children in three different age groups. Local officials used a statistical procedure called frequency matching to select 62 control cases.

As part of a telephone survey, officials asked the parents of both the "case" (i.e., victim) and control subjects about their shopping and eating activities in the week prior to the outbreak. The institute then included consumption of minisalami sticks in questions about what the sick children had eaten. The experts found that in the 7 days before the outbreak, there was a high statistical correlation in the cases between consumption of minisalami and *Salmonella* Panama infection.

While the Robert Koch Institute was conducting the surveys, the reference laboratory identified the specific strain of *Salmonella* involved in the outbreak and confirmed that all 11 samples from the cases belonged to the same strain, as did the sample from the asymptomatic worker at the salami plant and a coworker's 10-month-old grandchild, who had become ill. BVL also queried the EU's rapid alert system to see if there had been any case of *Salmonella* Panama between January 1, 2006 and August 2007, and found none. The local competent authorities also examined minisalami samples from the processing plant thought responsible for the outbreak for *Salmonella* but found none and did not find any in minisalami products taken from shops in two states where the firm's products were sold.

In early September, staff from the local food safety authority and the Federal Institute for Risk Assessment again inspected the salami manufacturer. The competent authorities also conducted a thorough review of the firm's records. No shortcomings were found in hygiene procedures. Officials nonetheless concluded that the minisalami sticks were the most likely cause of the outbreak, even though the pathogen was not found in tests of the product.

In summarizing the incident, the Robert Koch Institute pointed out that this outbreak was discovered only through the nationwide aggregation of institute-collected data and computerized analysis, because the number of victims in any one state was too low to signal an outbreak. Furthermore, the case-control telephone survey enabled officials to conduct an almost real-time epidemiological analysis.

In addition, according to the institute, close cooperation among the Federal Institute for Risk Assessment, BVL, the Robert Koch Institute, the national reference laboratory, and local authorities contributed to rapid investigation and management of the outbreak.

Efforts to Measure the Effectiveness of Food Safety Systems

Although Germany had not conducted a formal review of its reorganized food safety system at the time of our review, BVL met with relevant stakeholders in November 2007 to discuss how the German food safety system and BVL are working. Participants included consumers, politicians, administrators, nonprofit organizations, industries, scientists, and representatives from the EU, who discussed how BVL had performed over the 5 years since it was created. Among the themes discussed were data management and analysis, cooperation between the federal government and the states, international cooperation, and research and scientific work.

Overall, participants believed that BVL had been meeting its objectives, and views were generally positive. In particular, participants approved of the efforts of the national contact point for the EU's rapid alert system. However, they suggested some improvements in the system, and also suggested that BVL provide training to help prepare for FVO audits. Participants also had positive things to say about the BVL press office, and suggested that BVL allow its home page to be reviewed by users and by external media experts. Participants furthermore spoke highly of BVL's *Journal of Consumer Protection and Food Safety*, which was launched in 2006 to provide information, in both German and English, on basic and applied research and on official oversight of current developments in the areas of food and feed, veterinary medicine, and genetic technology. Finally, participants suggested that BVL establish a greater presence at conferences, fairs, and schools and that it be more visible to consumers as a partner for information and questions.

Performance Measures

According to BVL officials, measures used to evaluate performance include quality management systems within competent authorities, targets set through control and monitoring plans, data found in annual reports on food safety, and evaluation of rapid alert system notifications. BVL's performance is evaluated by the German Federal Court of Auditors, GAO's German counterpart.

Evaluations and Audits

BVL cannot audit or evaluate the state-level food safety systems. However, some states audit other states' local and regional food safety systems upon request.

Moreover, between 2001 and 2007, FVO conducted 53 performance audits of certain aspects of Germany's food safety system and most made recommendations to German officials. In June 2005, for example, the office assessed the import control system and four operating border inspection posts in Germany.

It found that import controls were generally applied correctly in the border inspection posts visited, with only minor shortcomings. However, it also found that supervision of imports that do not comply with EU regulations was inadequate, traceability was not reliable, and the exit of these noncompliant products from the EU was not ensured. Furthermore, it found significant deficiencies at some of the border inspection post facilities. FVO audits have been conducted on such topics as BSE, food hygiene, and animal welfare. The office discusses any problems it detects at the state level with BVL and the states.

Public Opinion Surveys

Officials from BVL stated that the agency is in constant dialogue with stakeholders and evaluates daily consumer mails and queries related to food safety and consumer protection (including on economic issues).

According to a 2005 Eurobarometer survey published in 2006, an estimated 37 percent of people in Germany stated that overall, food safety had improved over the past decade, 37 percent that it had stayed about the same, 21 percent that it had worsened, and 5 percent did not have an opinion.

In addition, an estimated 56 percent of the Germans surveyed stated that usually public authorities' actions in the EU with regard to food safety risks were appropriate, 28 percent that actions were insufficient, 8 percent that the actions went beyond what is needed, and 8 percent did not have an opinion. Finally, an estimated 60 percent of the Germans surveyed agreed that food produced in the EU was safer than food imported from elsewhere, 30 percent disagreed, and 10 percent did not know.

Other Relevant Issues

Stakeholder Perspectives

The views of stakeholders who interact frequently with BVL can also provide insight, albeit anecdotal, on the effectiveness of a country's food safety system. In Germany, a representative of an industry group told us that overall the consolidated food safety system represented an improvement over the previous system. This person also said that the EU's rapid warning system was working well, although there was room for improvement in some areas.

Furthermore, one of the positive outcomes of the consolidation, in this person's view, was the establishment of a working group of representatives from the 16 states who meet to discuss problems of food law interpretation.

According to this person, one of the challenges of the German food safety system was the different interpretations of law at the state and local levels. For example, public warnings and information can vary among the state governments during food crises, and some states took different views on whether a product should be recalled.

Finally, this industry representative noted that the EU's traceability requirements made firms more proactive in protecting their brand names.

Emerging Trends and Challenges

Officials we spoke with identified the following areas of concern with regard to ongoing and future challenges to the country's food safety system:

- Climate change may affect foodborne illness, in that illness can spread under new climatic conditions.
- New fungi, pathogens, and diseases will continue to emerge.
- Genetically modified organisms will continue to be developed, but there is zero tolerance for them in Germany.

Ireland's Food Safety System

Population and Per Capita GDP

In 2007, Ireland had a population of approximately 4.1 million, and in 2006 its estimated per capita GDP was US $44,500.

Organization

Before Ireland reorganized its food safety system, about 50 different public agencies were in charge of food control, with little coordination among their activities. Responsibilities were shared between the Department of Agriculture and Food (now known as the Department of Agriculture, Fisheries, and Food—DAFF), the Department of Health and Children, 33 local authorities, 8 health boards, the Department for the Marine and the Department of Trade. With no central system of coordinating food safety control activities, there were overlaps and gaps in the functions of the different agencies. Some of the government departments had dual roles of promoting the industry and overseeing food controls, raising conflict-of-interest concerns.

The Food Safety Authority of Ireland (FSAI) was created in 1998 to oversee the enforcement of food safety regulations. An independent, science-based body under the jurisdiction of the Minister for Health and Children, FSAI coordinates the enforcement of food regulations among various state agencies; sets food standards that are based on science and risk assessment; manages risk in association with other agencies and the Irish food sector; and communicates risks to consumers, public health professionals, and the food industry. It is the central competent authority for Ireland under EU legislation. FSAI has 87 employees who oversee a total of about 2,500 people working in 39 other government agencies as part of the integrated national system. (About 1,200 members of this workforce focus exclusively on food safety issues, while others, such as veterinarians, work only a few days per week on food safety matters.) Twenty-five staff work at the three Irish border inspection posts. In all, FSAI and its partner agencies oversee food safety in nearly 45,000 food establishments.

FSAI has service contracts with the 39 entities—such as DAFF, the Sea Fishery Protection Agency, the Health Service Executive, the National Standards Authority—to oversee specific elements of the system. For example, DAFF enforces food safety legislation for meat, milk, and egg products, and inspects live animals and products of animal origin coming through Ireland's three border inspection posts from non-EU countries, while the Health Service Executive inspect imports of food of nonanimal origin. Only specific products of nonanimal origin known to present a risk are restricted to specific points of entry. FSAI does not provide money to these government agencies for their work but instead establishes the terms of work, such as conducting a set number of inspections annually on the basis of the risk level of the food product. Each agency is audited to make sure it is carrying out its contractual obligations. FSAI's authority extends from the farm gate to the final consumer; its jurisdiction is only food safety, not on-farm hygiene or feed control. (The latter is overseen by DAFF, separately from the FSAI contract.)

FSAI is charged with investigating and managing food-related incidents in Ireland and is the country's point of contact for the EU's rapid alert system. In 2006, FSAI conducted 76 investigations related to food safety, 16 percent of which were related to microbial contamination.

One of the largest food recalls in Irish history took place in 2005, when FSAI oversaw the recall of 67 products contaminated with a chili powder containing carcinogenic industrial dye called Sudan Red 1 that was used as an ingredient in a variety of processed foods. The dye entered EU countries in ground or crushed chili imported from India; Ireland was notified by its counterpart in the UK, the Food Standards Agency, about the discovery in a primary ingredient used in the manufacture of other foods. FSAI then worked with official agencies and the food industry to ensure that all contaminated products were traced and removed from Irish retail stores. It advised consumers to either dispose of the product or return it to the store where it was purchased. FSAI also posted a list of the affected food products on its Web site.

Two other entities are of particular importance to the food safety system:

- The Health Service Executive, created in 2005, runs the health services in Ireland. It is also responsible for import controls on foods of nonanimal origin. Within the executive is the Health Protection Surveillance Centre (HPSC), which was established in 1998 to collect, interpret, and disseminate data on infectious disease and to provide data on foodborne illness to the relevant authorities.
- A Scientific Committee was established in 2000 to assist FSAI in assessing risk. The committee is made up of scientists from a variety of disciplines whose work for FSAI is voluntary. Among other things, the committee clarifies scientific and technical issues relating to food safety and hygiene. FSAI then manages risk on the basis of the committee's assessments.

Regulatory Framework

According to Irish officials, most of Ireland's food safety legislation comes from EU legislation, but some flexibility is allowed on how member states apply the food safety requirements within their national territory (in particular, for producers supplying small quantities of foods within their local areas). Ireland is examining the areas for which "national rules" can be applied to determine what national legislation should be introduced. Under consideration is the reintroduction of a national ban on the sale of raw milk in Ireland. In the area of labeling, Ireland has introduced national legislation that, according to Irish officials, requires all beef sold in Irish restaurants and catering outlets to include information on the country of origin. This would apply in addition to the EU beef labeling regulations.

Oversight of Imported Food

Import Controls

Ireland's regulations are fully coordinated with the EU's. For a more detailed summary of the EU food safety requirements, see the EU profile.

Inspections

Ireland's regulations are fully coordinated with the EU's. See the EU profile.

Equivalency Agreements/Certification Programs

Ireland's regulations are fully coordinated with the EU's. See the EU profile.

Foodborne Illness Outbreaks

Ireland applies veterinary inspection fees to importers. Fees currently charged contribute a small proportion of the total import control budget. According to an Irish official, as of April 2008, the fee structure was being reviewed to ensure that it aligns with the EU Food Hygiene legislation.

According to Irish sources, the most common gastroenteric pathogen in Ireland is *Campylobacter,* of which there were 1,815 cases in 2006—more than four times the number of *Salmonella* infections (422). Other sources of foodborne illness in Ireland in 2006 were *E. coli* (158 cases), *Listeria* (7 cases), and norovirus (1,639 cases).

Response

Outbreaks in Ireland are generally managed at the local level, but HPSC gets involved if there is a large national outbreak or an international outbreak affecting Ireland. If someone becomes ill with 1 of 67 diseases that must be reported to public health officials, the local public health authority is immediately notified, and a local environmental or public health officer interviews the patient about where he or she had been and what was eaten and forwards the information to HPSC.

To determine the cause of an outbreak, HPSC examines a sample of the pathogen to ascertain whether it is normally associated with food (microbiological evidence); determines whether other people have been afflicted by the same strain (epidemiological evidence); and looks at the hygiene of the food institution that produced the food (environmental evidence) if the source is thought to be food. If the foodborne illness appears to be an isolated case, no additional work is conducted. However, if a similar case occurs, samples of the bacteria are sent to reference laboratories for more precise typing.

HPSC uses a surveillance database, called the Computerized Infectious Diseases Reporting System, to combine and link epidemiological data from laboratories and hospitals so that all notifiable diseases can be tracked. The Health Service Executive (HPSC's parent organization) notifies FSAI in the case of an outbreak and provides FSAI with information on the outcome of any investigations. It also shares these data with the European Centre for Disease Control in Stockholm. Irish officials told us the procedures they follow are generally similar to those followed by the U.S. Centers for Disease Control and Prevention for monitoring foodborne illness.

DAFF's Veterinary Research Laboratory Service also provides a range of services in relation to identifying and addressing zoonotic diseases. As part of this, the DAFF Central Veterinary Research Laboratory is the national reference laboratory for *Salmonella* and carries out typing of *Salmonella* samples from official control samples and from samples taken by food business operators of their own products.

International Coordination

In the case of an outbreak, FSAI, as Ireland's competent authority, sends out the necessary data alerts to the public and follows up after the outbreak.

Recent Incidents

Detailed information on recent outbreaks was not provided.

Efforts to Measure the Effectiveness of Food Safety Systems

An FSAI official told us that FSAI was working on a consolidated report on overall performance of the food safety system, but as of April 2008, the report was not available.

Performance Measures

According to an Irish official, FSAI's service contracts require that inspection frequencies be risk-based, so FSAI can measure performance against these requirements.

Evaluations and Audits

FSAI's audit and compliance unit periodically audits the work of all the contracted agencies to make sure they are meeting the terms of their contracts in such areas as the number of inspections and tests conducted, number of staff, and corrective actions to address previous audit findings (e.g., of food businesses or by the EU Food and Veterinary Office). Together, FSAI and the audited agency work to resolve any identified problems. If FSAI uncovers a problem with how an agency fulfills the terms of its contract, the two agencies meet to discuss it to prevent future occurrences. FSAI also monitors the contracts through regular reporting on inspection frequencies and outcomes and through food sampling and analysis.

If noncompliance with a service contract is found to be particularly egregious, FSAI could also report it to the head of an agency, but this has not yet happened. In addition to FSAI audits, all of the agencies with service contracts to FSAI either have established—or will be establishing—internal audit systems, according to an Irish official.

If FSAI finds breaches in food businesses' implementation of the EU and Irish food law, FSAI and the official agencies can take legal action against the food business, which may result in fines, and in extreme cases, prison sentences, but issuing enforcement orders and subsequently "naming and shaming" on the FSAI Web site is FSAI's main compliance tool.

The EU's Food and Veterinary Office has also conducted a number of audits of various aspects of the Irish food safety system. Between 2001 and 2006, the office conducted 31 audits in Ireland on such topics as on-farm animal welfare, import controls and border inspection posts, and traceability of beef and beef products, among others. As part of its evaluations, the Food and Veterinary Office provided some recommendations for improvement in areas where it identified gaps. In 2005, for example, the office audited Irish import controls and border inspection posts. Auditors found that the import control system was well defined and generally applied in a uniform way in all the Irish border inspection posts, but on two occasions, implementation of certain EU legislation had been delayed.

Major deficiencies identified in a 2003 audit had been for the most part corrected, with a few exceptions, according to the Food and Veterinary Office report. However, the office noted that Irish border inspection posts used a simplified customs clearance procedure for all consignments handled by customs agents that did not flag the need for veterinary checks required for products of animal origin. The Irish central competent authority for food safety follows up on any recommendations in Food and Veterinary Office reports to make sure that the corrective actions are taken.

Public Opinion Surveys

According to a 2005 Eurobarometer survey published in 2006, an estimated 67 percent of people in Ireland stated that overall, food safety had improved over the past decade, 14 percent that it had stayed about the same, 11 percent that it had worsened, and 8 percent did not know. In addition, an estimated 52 percent stated that usually public authorities' actions in the EU with regard to food safety risks are appropriate; 23 percent, that the actions are insufficient; 7 percent, that the actions go beyond what is needed; and 18 percent did not know. Finally, an estimated 65 percent agreed that food produced in the EU is safer than food imported from elsewhere, 13 percent disagreed, and 22 percent did not know.

Stakeholder Perspectives

The views of stakeholders who interact frequently with FSAI and the agencies it oversees can also provide insight, albeit anecdotal, on the food safety system's effectiveness. In Ireland, we spoke with representatives of one industry and one consumer group. Representatives of the industry group said that the reorganization that created FSAI had a positive impact and that its new umbrella structure is working well. In particular, they believed that this structure opened lines of communication between government and industry. They also approved of the approach FSAI took a few years ago concerning a major recall of a chocolate product. Nonetheless, they expressed concern that FSAI has little authority over local inspectors and needs more control over the service contracts with the agencies it oversees. A representative of the consumer group stated that, overall, consumers have great respect for FSAI and that the hygiene of food production had improved with consolidation of the system a few years ago. However, this representative believes the government could do more to educate the public on food safety issues.

Other Relevant Issues

Emerging Trends and Challenges

Irish officials identified the following issues as areas of concern:

- Resources for the number of inspections required were limited, and inspectors were concerned that they must rely to a certain extent on statements by importers, which means there is potential for fraud in the system.
- The possible increased risk of botulism among migrant workers from Eastern Europe, who may import home-produced foods that are not transported under refrigerated conditions, is a concern.

Japan's Food Safety System

Population and Per Capita GDP

In 2007, Japan had an estimated population of 127.4 million, and in 2006 its per capita GDP was estimated to be US $33,100.

Organization

Several food safety-related crises in the past decade, including outbreaks of *E. coli* and concern over the BSE crisis, drove Japan to comprehensively reform its food safety system. In 2003, Japan established the Food Safety Commission (FSC) as a cabinet-level agency responsible for conducting objective, neutral, scientific risk assessments related to food safety, including the use of food additives, pesticide residues, the presence of illness-causing bacteria, and other issues. FSC became a fully functioning, independent agency in 2005. Previously, the two ministries primarily responsible for managing food safety—the Ministry of Agriculture, Forestry and Fisheries (MAFF) and the Ministry of Health, Labor and Welfare (MHLW)—conducted their own scientific risk assessments. FSC, MAFF, and MHLW are the three agencies responsible for food safety at the national level.

While FSC assesses risks, MHLW and MAFF are responsible for managing these risks. MHLW is responsible for setting standards for food processing and manufacturing and monitoring imported and domestic food throughout the supply chain. It also operates quarantine stations throughout Japan, which are responsible for ensuring the safety of food entering the country, as well as regional health centers, which are responsible for dealing with cases of foodborne illness. In 2007, MHLW employed 334 inspectors, up from 314 the previous year. MAFF is the ministry primarily responsible for setting regulations for food labeling, setting nutritional standards for food produced in Japan, establishing nutritional guidelines for the Japanese public, and ensuring Japanese agricultural products comply with the World Trade Organization's (WTO) Sanitary and Phytosanitary (SPS) Measures.

The National Institute of Infectious Diseases conducts research on contagious diseases. It serves as Japan's reference laboratory for infectious diseases and is responsible for collecting information on such diseases from the local public health centers. It also monitors incidents of infectious diseases around the country. In the event of an outbreak, the institute performs epidemiological investigations.

Oversight of Imported Food

Import Controls

Japan imports about 60 percent of its food. It uses a risk-based approach in inspecting imported food entering the country and also emphasizes the role of the exporting country in ensuring the safety of the food it exports. MHLW produces an Annual Imported Foods Monitoring and Guidance Plan intended to promote intensive, effective, and efficient inspections of imported foods at the border and also provides guidance to importers. The plan also spells out the quantity and category of inspections to be conducted each year. In fiscal year 2007, for example, the goal was approximately 79,000 random inspections for 124 food groups. According to the plan, food safety should be secured by appropriate measures in every stage of the domestic and overseas food supply chain. On the basis of this principle, the plan lays out measures for ensuring the sanitation of food imports in three stages: (1) in the exporting countries, (2) at entry into Japan, and (3) through internal distribution.

Inspections

Thirty-one quarantine stations at ports of entry throughout Japan are responsible for inspecting food imports. They are primarily responsible for reviewing import notifications and certificates. Some quarantine stations house Imported Food Inspection Offices, which are responsible for conducting more advanced technical tests, such as microbiological sampling. In addition, two specialized stations are responsible for conducting the most technically complicated tests. Quarantine stations randomly select shipments for monitoring on a daily basis; such tests are paid for by the Japanese government. In fiscal year 2006, MHLW conducted nearly 80,000 random inspections and found 360 violations.

Port of entry inspections beyond routine document checks depend on a variety of factors: companies' past violations; whether Japan has certified the exporting companies; and information on exporting countries, including the types of agreements they have with Japan, resource materials, and manufacturing methods. Japan maintains this information in a national database. Additionally, Japan has specific concerns related to certain contaminants, such as aflatoxin and agro-chemicals. If an imported food belongs to a food group that is known to be at a higher risk for contamination (e.g., from a pathogen, pesticide residue, or animal drug), MHLW issues a Ministerial Inspection Order, which, according to Japanese sources, requires that products with a high violation probability be inspected at every time of importation (lot by lot). Japan prohibits the importation and distribution of products that fail to pass inspection; importers bear the cost of that inspection, and future inspections from that country are strengthened. In 2006, for example, Japan required compulsory testing of 100 percent of Vietnamese shrimp imports after inspectors repeatedly found chloramphenicol, a banned antibiotic, in shipments of Vietnamese shrimp. Moreover, according to the Imported Foods Monitoring and Guidance Plan for fiscal year 2007, if the number of imported foods from a specific country, area, or business entity violating the law is above 5 percent of the overall number of those inspected, and if it is likely that the importation of violating goods will continue, given conditions in the exporting country, MHLW may ban the importation of such goods altogether.

Testing under the Ministerial Inspection Order includes laboratory testing for pathogens, which the importing company pays for. Violation information is entered into the database the quarantine stations use in making future inspection decisions. If a violation is found under a Ministerial Inspection Order, the shipment may be recalled, disposed of, or shipped back to the exporter (at the expense of the importer in Japan).

The importing company is asked to investigate the cause of the violation, and before resuming importation must test a sample of the product. Companies with repeat violations will not be allowed to export to Japan, and the Japanese government publishes violations on its Web site. In fiscal year 2006, there were over 100,000 inspections conducted under the MHLW Ministerial Inspection Order, uncovering 681 violations. Overall, in 2006, Japan inspected 11 percent of declared products coming into its ports. (This figure includes both random inspections and Ministerial Inspection Order examinations.)

If MHLW believes that certain foods represent a particularly significant hazard, it can issue a comprehensive prohibition on the importation of those foods, which means that these high-risk items can be barred from Japan without even undergoing an inspection. According to an MHLW official, this type of prohibition has never been issued.

Japan also provides the option for first-time exporters to submit their products to voluntary inspections, giving these exporters an opportunity to demonstrate that their products pose a low health risk. Before sending the first shipment to Japan, these exporters send samples of their products to private Japanese companies approved by MHLW for testing and analysis. On the basis of the outcome of these preliminary tests, the exporter is either rejected or approved to proceed with the first shipment. If an exporter is approved and subsequently exports to Japan, the first shipment will be subject to routine random monitoring; if the exporter did not go through with voluntary inspection, the first shipment would be subject to a Ministerial Inspection Order.

Japan has also created a "Positive List" of substances that must be controlled in all imported foods stuffs.[10] If an importer violates the positive list, MHLW will subsequently test 30 percent of all products coming to Japan from the violating country for 1 year. For a second violation, Japan imposes 100 percent "hold-and-test," meaning that all goods from the violating country will be held and tested for 2 years and a minimum of 300 imports.

In addition to government programs, there are Japanese private sector initiatives to help ensure food safety. For example, according to an official from the umbrella organization for the many private food cooperatives in Japan, all growers that supply products to co-ops are required to prove that they adhere to "Good Agricultural Practices," as well as specific regulations of the co-op, such as those for pesticide usage. Co-ops have their own specifications— separate from the government— for acceptable materials, additives, and labeling requirements, including detailed nutritional information. Some growers also provide the co-ops with information about their products (e.g., location of farm, names of the farmers, types of pesticides used, dates of planting, dates of cultivation, dates of packaging and shipping). Consumers can then access this information using a cell phone to scan the barcode on the product packaging. The Japanese Consumers Cooperative Union also has its own programs to ensure the safety of imported foods that are independent of the government. For example, it conducts its own inspections of overseas firms from which it imports foods and tests incoming products twice a year.

As a result of a food safety scare in early 2008, when frozen dumplings imported from China were found to be contaminated with a dangerous level of pesticides, the Japanese government announced its plans to implement various new food safety measures in several areas, including (1) establishing a new consumer agency to oversee work currently being handled by multiple ministries, and (2) establishing a director-general position in the MHLW, MAFF, and other government bodies to oversee the distribution of information related to foodborne illness. In addition, public health centers will be required to be open 24 hours a day, and prefectural governments will be required to notify the health minister when there is a case of poisoning,[11] (3) increasing testing for all imported foods, with special attention to agriculture residues in processed foods, and (4) requiring stricter labeling requirements. At the time of our review, these measures had not yet become law.

Bilateral Agreements/Certification Programs

According to Japanese sources, Japanese officials from MAFF and/or MHLW engage in bilateral talks with their counterparts in the exporting country to explain Japanese food sanitary regulations. If a country has no prior record of exporting food to Japan, MHLW officials may conduct field surveys to determine whether a country's food safety system can meet Japanese food sanitary regulations and whether the exporting country's food safety regulations are comparable to Japan's. If Japan has found an exporting country's food safety system and food safety regulations satisfactory, and a new facility in that country seeks to export to Japan, MHLW officials may conduct a pre-export inspection of that facility. If the review is satisfactory, MHLW will issue a certificate to the exporter, copies of which must accompany every shipment of goods to Japan.

According to Japanese officials, under Japan's bilateral agreement with China to screen spinach imports, the Chinese government certifies Chinese spinach processors (exporters), who in turn oversee the practices of local farmers (including requiring them to, among other things, keep records on pesticide purchase and usage) and test the product at three stages of production. Chinese government authorities then conduct preshipment tests on the spinach before exporting, confirming that the exporter has observed the proper procedures on pesticide management. The spinach may be randomly inspected again once it arrives in Japanese ports. Chinese exporters of 19 other products, including tea leaves and frozen vegetables, are likewise required to register with the Chinese government, and blowfish and meat from China also require certification of processing. Japan has certification programs in place with other countries as well. For example, after concerns about high levels of antibiotics in Thai shrimp came to light, MHLW worked with the Thai government to identify shrimp exporters that were subsequently included on a "safe list" as being reliably able to comply with Japanese requirements for antibiotic levels.

Foodborne Illness Outbreaks

Response

MHLW operates a network of regional health centers in partnership with local governments, which are responsible for the day-to-day operation of the centers. In cases of foodborne illness, these centers work with hospitals to identify the cause and the source of contamination. They will notify MHLW only if the number of patients with the same symptoms exceeds 50. According to MHLW officials, the most recent outbreaks over the past 2 years have been confined to single prefectures. In these cases, MHLW coordinates the work of the participating groups (e.g., hospitals, health centers, and food manufacturers), oversees data collection, and communicates with the public. The Japanese government has mandatory recall authority for unsafe food products, but according to a Japanese official, it has rarely exercised this authority. Typically, the government (specifically, MHLW-run local health centers responsible for testing food that is suspected to be the source of an outbreak) will "suggest" to companies that they recall their product. According to this official, if the government communicates in this way to a company, the company feels obliged to recall its products.

With regard to animal tracking, Japan has a mandatory system in which all beef and dairy cattle must be identified using an ear tag. Information is maintained on an animal's ID number, breed, gender, and production history from the farm of origin through distribution to consumers.

Recent Incidents

Japanese officials did not identify any major outbreaks of foodborne illness.

Efforts to Measure the Effectiveness of the Food Safety System

Performance Measures

Japan does not have a systematic assessment mechanism in place to measure the effectiveness of its food safety system, and officials we contacted from the Board of Audit of Japan, GAO's counterpart organization, told us that they had not referred to the Japanese food safety system in the annual audit report or other reports. (Each year the Board of Audit prepares an audit report showing the results of all audits conducted that year and sends it to the Cabinet with the audited final accounts of revenues and expenditures of the state. The Cabinet then submits both of them to the Diet. The Audit Report is used in the Diet (legislative) session for deliberation on the state's final accounts and for future administration by the financial authorities.) However, Japanese officials indicated that some components of the system are subject to review under certain conditions.

Evaluations and Audits

The FSC conducts investigations to ascertain whether its assessment results have been appropriately reflected in the food safety policies implemented by the risk management agencies (MHLW and MAFF). Also, according to FSC and MHLW officials, if there is a food safety-related emergency, such as a natural disaster that affects the food supply, bioterrorism, or an outbreak of foodborne illness, FSC is responsible for monitoring and reporting on how effectively MHLW handles the crisis. However, Japanese officials noted that such a scenario has not occurred, so no assessments had been conducted to date.

Public Opinion Survey

MAFF and FSC conduct public opinion surveys. A staff member from a Japanese nongovernmental organization told us that the August 2007 and February and March 2006 surveys conducted by MAFF indicate that consumers perceive imported foods in general to be unreliable and untrustworthy. A private organization, the Japanese Consumers Cooperative Union, also conducted some consumer surveys and noted that surveys from 2005 to the present have shown that the most important consumer concerns are country of origin (for imported foods), the trustworthiness of all suppliers (domestic and foreign), and the overall quality of the product. Food additives are a major concern for consumers, as is pesticide residue on food. The surveys generally indicate that Japanese consumers are more concerned about food additives and chemicals than about microorganisms.

Stakeholder Views

The perspectives of stakeholders can be useful in providing some insight into the effectiveness of a country's food safety system. In Japan, we spoke to representatives of two consumer organizations about their perceptions of the Japanese food safety system. Both individuals told us that the creation of the FSC has been a positive step, increasing transparency between government and stakeholders. One of these people told us that, previously, expert committee meetings within ministries were closed, but now they are open to the public, a change that is viewed as positive. A representative of the other consumer group stated that the government needs to improve its risk communication to the public; for example, many Japanese consumers are still highly suspicious of imported beef and do not fully understand the safety measures in place for beef.

Other Relevant Issues

Officials in Japan identified the following areas of concern with regard to ongoing and future challenges to the country's food safety system:

- Assessing the risks of chemical and food additives is a priority. At the time of our review, FSC was reviewing the potential public health risks of approximately 800 chemicals.
- Foodborne illness from *Campylobacter* has increased significantly in the last several years and is one of the most frequent sources of food contamination. In response to this, FSC has initiated risk assessments relating to microorganism contamination of food, starting with *Campylobacter*.
- The volume of international food trade is growing, and imported food is increasingly harder to track.
- Human/animal interactions are changing, with potential for disease transmission, including *E. coli* and prions (which are involved in BSE).

The Netherlands Food Safety System

Population and Per Capita GDP

In 2007, the Netherlands had a population of approximately 16.6 million, and in 2006 its estimated per capita GDP was US $32,100.

Organization

In response to public concern about food safety stemming from the dioxin contamination of animal feed, the BSE crisis, and other animal diseases, as well as the EU's proposed food safety legislation, the Netherlands created the Food and Consumer Product Safety Authority (VWA) in July 2002. Consumers, parliament, and interest groups had demanded a single powerful organization to investigate and monitor food and product safety. Two organizations, the Inspectorate for Health Protection and Veterinary Public Health and the National Inspection Service for Livestock and Meat were combined into one agency under VWA as of January 1, 2006.

VWA, an independent agency in the Ministry of Agriculture, Nature, and Food Quality, is responsible for assessing and communicating risk and managing food safety incidents. It monitors food and consumer products to safeguard public health and animal health and welfare. It also enforces food-related legislation, coordinates inspection activities throughout the country, and conducts research; each of VWA's five regional divisions has its own laboratory to carry out routine microbiological and chemical analyses for food safety controls. One of VWA's regional departments (southwest) is in charge of managing the Netherlands' seven border inspection posts and overseeing imports of foods of animal origin. VWA inspectors work with Dutch customs agents, who carry out documentary checks on imports. VWA is also the contact point for the EU's Rapid Alert System for Food and Feed and for the EU Food and Veterinary Office. In 2006, VWA had a total of 1,750 employees. (The previous year, it had transferred its meat inspectors to private bodies.)

The National Institute for Public Health and the Environment (RIVM) is a government research institute that conducts research on public health (infectious diseases, care, prevention, and food safety), medicines, nutrition, and the environment for VWA, as well as for a number of other inspection services and Dutch ministries. RIVM assists VWA and the Dutch government in developing food safety policy and conducts formal risk assessments for VWA. The formal risk assessments are commissioned through VWA's Office of Risk Assessment, to which the results are reported. VWA then advises the inspectorate and/or the ministries. RIVM houses several of the Dutch national reference laboratories as well as both the Dutch and EU community reference laboratories (on *Salmonella* and on residues). The institute also collaborates closely with the Dutch Central Veterinary Institute (part of Wageningen University and Research Centre) on issues related to zoonotic diseases and animal food products. RIVM's Centre for Infectious Disease Control, established in 2005, conducts surveillance on infectious diseases; collects data on health, illness, and disease; and provides early warnings on threats to public health.

The RIKILT Institute for Food Safety (RIKILT), part of Wageningen University and Research Center, is a private research organization that also performs research for the Dutch government on food and feed. It is a reference laboratory for pesticide and veterinary residues, feedstuffs, and genetically modified organism analyses. RIVM is responsible for conducting risk analysis for food (fork), while RIKILT is responsible for assessing feed and food quality (farm). RIVM, RIKILT, and the Central Veterinary Institute are "house institutes" of VWA. They all assist VWA and the Dutch government in developing food safety policy and conduct formal risk assessments commissioned by VWA's Office of Risk Assessment.

Meat inspection in the Netherlands is conducted by official veterinarians, who are employed by VWA either as permanent staff or as staff hired on a temporary basis. In the past, their assistants were employed by VWA as well, but these posts were privatized a few years ago. However, because these assistants work under the oversight of official veterinarians, meat inspection in the Netherlands is still in public hands.

Oversight of Imported Food

Import Controls

The Netherlands' regulations are fully harmonized with the EU's. For a more detailed summary of the EU food safety requirements, see the EU profile.

Inspections

See the EU profile VWA's annual budget is about 165 million euros, with 40 million to 43 million euros paid by producing companies and 5 to 6 million euros from import control fees based on usage. The port of Rotterdam is the largest port in Europe and one of the largest in the world. The money Dutch customs officials receive from the EU's import tax is sent to the EU treasurer in Brussels after the Netherlands deducts 10 percent, which is the fee for administering the Dutch ports. (EU member states are required to give a certain percentage of their GDP to the EU, so any additional costs on import controls not covered by fees can be deducted from their annual payment to the EU).

Equivalency Agreements/Certification Programs

See the EU profile.

In addition to government initiatives, a Dutch official told us that some private companies have programs in place to promote food safety. KLM airlines, for example, has a program called "OK to Forward" to conduct document checks before a company ships certain live animal products and before KLM accepts these products on its airplanes. This is an additional quality control and assurance procedure put in place to prevent problems at the port of entry.

Foodborne Illness Outbreaks

Campylobacter is the most frequent cause of gastroenteritis in the Netherlands. In 2006, there were 3,401 confirmed cases. In 2006, there 1,667 confirmed cases of *Salmonella.* (Dutch epidemiological studies indicate that if unconfirmed cases were included, the number would likely be much higher). There were 69 reported cases of *Listeria.* According to Dutch sources, *E. coli* has been comparatively rare in the Netherlands, with 78 cases reported in 2004.

Response

Any instance of foodborne illness is first reported to VWA through local public health services, which are responsible for controlling the illness. If more than one local public health service is involved, RIVM's Preparedness and Response Unit, a branch of the Centre for Infectious Disease Control, takes charge of control activities. VWA and the regional public health laboratories may become involved in investigating samples. Moreover, at VWA's request, RIVM provides epidemiological resources to assist in tracing the illness. A committee for managing the crisis, called the outbreak management team, is also set up to bring all knowledge together to get the best possible advice. The Ministry of Agriculture takes the lead during a crisis related to contaminated food or animal products, but if a person is infected with a pathogen, the Dutch Ministry of Public Health takes over because it is then considered a public health issue.

(Two persons infected with the same strain of a pathogen is considered an outbreak in the Netherlands). However, if there is a large and widespread epidemic, the Ministry of Internal Affairs will take over.

Dutch officials told us that on the public health side, their procedures for addressing foodborne illness outbreaks are similar to those followed in the United States by the Centers for Disease Control and Prevention for identifying pathogens and tracking diseases. However, they noted that there is greater integration of veterinary and public health in the Netherlands.

VWA has mandatory recall authority under EU legislation, but it has not used this authority very often. According to Dutch officials, when a recall is needed, VWA will first ask the affected company to recall the product by putting information in the newspaper, and the company is subsequently held accountable if there are any further issues with its product.

International Coordination

In the event of an outbreak, VWA would send out notifications to other EU member states using the Rapid Alert System for Food and Feed. In 2006, the Netherlands issued 55 rapid alert notifications, including 1 related to microbial contamination and 3 related to potentially pathogenic microorganisms. RIVM is very involved in the networks of the European Food Safety Authority and the European Centre for Disease Control. In addition,

RIVM reports results of the Dutch human laboratory surveillance for *Salmonella, Campylobacter,* and *E. coli* on a monthly basis to the EU network, Enter-net.

Recent Incidents

No information on recent outbreaks was provided.

Efforts to Measure the Effectiveness of Food Safety System

At the time of our review, the Dutch government had not formally evaluated its reorganized food safety system.

Performance Measures

Indicators tracked by VWA include the number of inspections conducted, samples inspected, EU approvals in the livestock and meat sector, international notifications of potential risk, and written warnings issued. Of the approximately 145,000 inspections conducted in 2005, the greatest number were in the area of meat and fish.

Evaluations and Audits

Although there had been no formal evaluations of the impact of consolidation on the Dutch food safety system at the time of our review, the EU Food and Veterinary Office had conducted 45 audits of certain aspects of the Dutch food safety system between 2001 and 2007. For example, in March 2006, the office audited the Netherlands' import control system for products of animal origin and live animals and the application of import requirements in two border inspection posts. It found that overall the Netherlands has a well-organized system that complies with EU requirements, as well as good cooperation between veterinary services and customs. However, the Food and Veterinary Office also found that the EU requirement that the border inspection post and its inspection centers be in the same customs-designated area was not applied at the Rotterdam post, and that even though the movement of consignments to the inspection centers is controlled using a customs transit procedure, this procedure was not in conformance with EU legislation or consistent with practices at other large EU border inspection posts. Furthermore, the Food and Veterinary Office noted some shortcomings with respect to supervising the destruction of confiscated illegal imports of certain products of animal origin.

Public Opinion Surveys

According to VWA, public confidence in food safety is the highest in Europe, at 80 percent. Moreover, according to a 2005 Eurobarometer survey published in 2006, an estimated 52 percent of people in the Netherlands stated that overall, food safety had improved over the past decade, 33 percent that it had stayed about the same, and 12 percent that it had worsened; 4 percent did not know. In addition, an estimated 53 percent stated that usually public authorities' actions in the EU with regard to food safety risks were appropriate, 22 percent that the actions were insufficient, and 17 percent that the actions went beyond what is needed; 7 percent did not know. Finally, an estimated 57 percent agreed that food produced in the EU was safer than food imported from elsewhere, 34 percent disagreed, and 10 percent did not know.

Stakeholder Perspectives

The views of stakeholders who interact frequently with government food safety bodies can also provide qualitative insight, albeit anecdotal, on the effectiveness of a country's food safety system. In the Netherlands, we spoke to representatives of one consumer organization and one product board, which is a government-authorized trade association. A representative of the consumer organization stated that VWA and RIVM responded well in 2005 to the Sudan Red 1 incident, in which an industrial dye was found in certain imported food products. During the outbreak, communication to the public, facilitated by VWA, was quite good. However, this person also said that it is sometimes difficult to know who takes the lead for communicating with the public during a food safety crisis—it can be VWA, RIVM, the Ministry of Agriculture, or the Ministry of Public Health. In this person's view, government communication during a crisis could be improved, and there should be a designated point of contact for providing information during a crisis. The industry representative told us that a 2006 reorganization of VWA that moved meat inspectors out of VWA and into private, accredited inspection firms that VWA audits has been successful, in that "people with the right qualifications are doing their job well."

Other Relevant Issues

According to VWA documents, the agency is concerned with the following ongoing and future challenges to the country's food safety system:

- climate change, including the potential for new foodborne viruses, mycotoxins (molds), new pathogens, and new plants and insects that can lead to threats to the food chain;
- demographic change, such as immigration, and the impact of age on risks (children and the elderly tend to be more susceptible to illness than others);
- sociocultural trends, including changes in lifestyle and behavior and the segmentation of society;
- globalization (large-scale movements of humans, animals, and goods increase the risk of the introduction and rapid spread of pathogens); and
- changes in production and processing based on new technologies, such as nanotechnology, genetically modified organisms, and decontamination technologies.

The UK's Food Safety System

Population and Per Capita GDP

In 2007, the United Kingdom (UK), consisting of England, Northern Ireland, Scotland, and Wales, had an estimated population of about 61 million, and its estimated per capita GDP in 2006 was US $31,800.

Organization

The Food Standards Agency (FSA) was created in 1999 as the lead food safety body. Prior to this, food safety responsibilities were divided among several central government departments, such as the Ministry of Agriculture, Fisheries, and Food and the Ministry of Health, as well as local authorities. FSA was founded in response to (1) the loss of public confidence in the government's handling of food safety issues, such as BSE and *Salmonella* in egg products; and (2) perceived conflict of interest in the Ministry of Agriculture, Fisheries, and Food, which also promoted UK agriculture. FSA is responsible for developing and implementing food laws in the UK and is the UK's competent authority for EU food and feed legislation. FSA also conducts scientific research to guide the implementation of its key responsibilities and conducts surveys on nutrition and diet to document changes in eating habits. It is the main UK body in charge of assessing the risk of food. The agency employs about 2,350 staff, including 1,600 inspectors in the Meat Hygiene Service, an executive agency within FSA that inspects premises where fresh meat is processed. According to FSA officials, the focus of the agency's inspections is on processes. For example, farmers are to employ HACCP measures to ensure food safety.

Another independent government agency, the Health Protection Agency (HPA) was established in 2005 following reorganization of the UK's public health laboratory system. HPA is an "arm's length body," independent of government.

It is responsible for managing infectious diseases, disease outbreaks, radiological health, and emergency planning. If a foodborne illness outbreak covers a wide area, HPA initiates investigations to determine the contaminant and identify the source and provides information to FSA to manage risk. HPA has a network of approximately 3,000 staff at three major centers and smaller regional and local centers throughout England and works with locally based colleagues in Northern Ireland, Scotland, and Wales. It also has a central office based in London.

The infectious disease side of HPA is divided into three areas of responsibility: the Centre for Infections, based at Colindale, in north London, the laboratory and epidemiological center for characterizing disease strains and for coordinating national epidemiological investigations; Local and Regional Services, which coordinates outbreak investigations at the local level; and the Regional Microbiology Network, which is the laboratory equivalent of Local and Regional Service and is the frontline service for identifying the causes of disease.

Other key agencies in the UK's food safety system include the following:

- Department for Environment, Food, and Rural Affairs, which manages animal health and welfare and plant issues, including imports from non-EU countries for products of animal origin.
- Veterinary Laboratories Agency, a regional network of 16 laboratories under the Department of Environment, Food, and Rural Affairs that are responsible for veterinary research, disease surveillance, and diagnostic services.
- Animal Health, which is responsible for operating the UK's 23 border inspection posts for products of animal origin and live animals. Animal Health is responsible for ensuring that these posts meet the required standards and that veterinary checks are correctly and consistently implemented across the UK.
- Her Majesty's Revenue and Customs oversees customs procedures to import goods and releases consignments after Animal Health and other requirements have been met.
- Local authorities (district and county authorities) that enforce legislation on imported food. There are a total of 468 local authorities in the UK.

Some private sector industry organizations in the UK also participate in voluntary food safety efforts. For example, according to a UK industry representative, the Assured Food Standards Association sets voluntary standards for industry on agricultural products.

That is, it provides guidance for primary producers growing vegetables or raising animals for meat. The British Retail Consortium, a trade association, offers HACCPbased certification for processed foods.

In addition, an association for smaller producers, called SALSA (Safe Food for Local Suppliers Association), is a membership organization made up of the National Farmers Union and other agriculture-related nongovernmental organizations that tries to improve small-scale production processes.

Oversight of Imported Food

Import Controls

The UK's regulations are fully coordinated with the EU's. For a more detailed summary of the EU food safety requirements, see the EU profile.

Inspections

The UK's procedures for inspections are fully coordinated with the EU's. See the EU profile for more detail.

Equivalency Agreements/Certification Programs

See the EU profile for more detail.

Foodborne Illness Outbreaks

According to a UK official, EU legislation is implemented through the UK's food safety laws, for example, by implementing additional EU import control measures where there is a serious risk to public or animal health.

According to HPA data, *Campylobacter* is the most commonly reported bacterial cause of infectious intestinal disease in England and Wales. In 2006, there were 46,603 reports of *Campylobacter,* 12,633 reports of *Salmonella,* and 1,003 reports of *E. coli* O157.[12]

Response

An outbreak of foodborne illness is defined in the UK as either two or more linked cases of the same disease or when the observed number of cases unaccountably exceeds the expected number. General medical practitioners are required to notify the local authority—usually the Consultant in Communicable Disease Control, who is now a member of the Local and Regional Services Directorate of the HPA—of cases or suspected cases of food poisoning. These consultants are asked to report outbreaks through HPA's central reporting system. In cases of an outbreak extending beyond a local area, or in the event of serious localized outbreaks, the environmental health officers of the local authority are required to inform the FSA.

Routine surveillance can help detect outbreaks, and the HPA has established a baseline for the expected number of cases of infection that generally occur at any given time. (All reports for a current week are compared with reports from the past 5 years to see if there are any exceedances of the baseline.) If HPA's reference laboratories determine that the total numbers of laboratory-confirmed cases have exceeded this baseline, they notify FSA. The Veterinary Laboratories Agency may provide assistance to outbreak control teams if a direct or indirect animal source is implicated in outbreaks of intestinal (or other zoonotic) diseases and where veterinary investigation or intervention could help reduce risks to the public. The agency may (1) conduct animal sampling for laboratory cultures, (2) help in identifying management and animal care factors that may have a bearing on human health risks, and (3) provide veterinary epidemiological input, such as data reports of *Salmonella* strains from farm animal surveillance. Strains of animal origin can also be selected for further identification and comparison with human strains. The HPA and the Veterinary Laboratories Agency work very closely in the investigation of outbreaks of food poisoning related to food production animals and have in place standardized laboratory and epidemiological methods for strain characterization and outbreak investigation. In addition, the HPA's Centre for Infections and the Veterinary Laboratories Agency support a joint post targeted at the further standardization of laboratory methods and the harmonization of databases.

UK officials told us that in many ways, their procedures for addressing the public health aspects of foodborne illness outbreaks are similar to those followed by the U.S. Centers for Disease Control and Prevention, except that the UK reference and veterinary laboratory systems are more centralized than in the U.S. system. The UK officials also believed that the particularly close working relationship between the HPA and the Veterinary Laboratories Agency is different from the U.S. system and has proven useful in addressing foodborne illness outbreaks. Moreover, the close working relationship between the HPA's gastroenteric and epidemiological teams has also been beneficial during outbreaks.

When an outbreak occurs in the UK, an outbreak control team investigates the incident. The team consists of a consultant on communicable disease control, an environmental health officer, and a consulting microbiologist. Depending on the size and nature of the incident, other individuals, such as representatives of the FSA, the Meat Hygiene Service, the Veterinary Laboratories Agency, a consultant in infectious diseases, a toxicologist, a food examiner/microbiologist, and others, may also become involved. The team follows an outbreak control plan that describes, among other things, the roles and responsibilities of each team member and information on arrangements for care of patients and for media liaison.

During an outbreak, FSA works with the local authority in charge of the affected food producers, industry, and other government agencies and departments to determine an appropriate risk management strategy. FSA can also issue a food alert to local authorities who enforce the law, and it publishes these alerts on its Web site. It can force the producer to recall the product, although FSA officials said they have rarely used their recall authority, because it is the food business operator's responsibility to ensure the safety of the food the operator places on the market, and it is usually the operator who takes action to recall unsafe food. In 2006, FSA dealt with a total of 1,342 food safety-related incidents, including 146 related to microbial contamination. Ten (about 1 percent) of the incidents addressed in 2006 were classified as high risk, that is, they had the potential to cause death or serious illness; they were complex (affecting a large number of products or required a high level of resources to manage); and/or they were widespread and likely to generate a high level of public concern.

International Coordination

As the designated UK point of contact for the EU's rapid alert system, FSA notifies other EU member nations about food problems it has identified. HPA coordinates with its European counterparts using an EU database called Enter-net; this database makes it possible for scientists to track pathogen strains throughout Europe.

Recent Incidents

In 2006, there was a major outbreak of *Salmonella* in chocolate products produced by Cadbury Schweppes, a large British candy manufacturer. Although no one died from the outbreak, over 130 people—mainly children—became ill. According to HPA officials, the incident came to light when, during routine surveillance, HPA discovered an increase in exceedances of the baseline level of *Salmonella* and determined that it was witnessing a major outbreak of *Salmonella* Montevideo, a rare strain of the *Salmonella* bacterium. A private food laboratory sent the HPA some *Salmonella* samples for identification. According to HPA sources, HPA scientists used a range of analytical techniques to trace the bacteria to Cadbury's chocolate products. They then notified FSA, and an outbreak control team was assembled, consisting of representatives from HPA, FSA, other government departments, and local authorities. To determine whether the outbreak had extended beyond the UK, HPA electronically transmitted a molecular profile of the outbreak strain to over 50 countries 2 days after recognition of the outbreak. (This electronic transmission was done through the EUfunded Enter-net network for the surveillance of *Salmonella*, Verocytotoxin-producing *E. coli,*[13] and *Campylobacter.*[14]) For its part, FSA used the EU's rapid alert system to communicate the distribution information of affected products outside the UK. HPA scientists also communicated with their Veterinary Laboratories Agency counterparts, who found the same *Salmonella* strains in poultry. Local authorities determined that a leaking pipe had dripped *Salmonella*-contaminated water into the candy manufacturer's products. No direct connection to poultry was found, but the laboratory findings strongly suggested that the animal source of the contaminating strain was poultry. Following identification of the outbreak in children, the time between the initiation of laboratory studies and withdrawal of the product was 8 or 9 days. In all, the bacteria had contaminated 30 different Cadbury products; over 1 million chocolate bars were removed from the market at a cost of over £30 million (about $60 million).

According to HPA officials, the established interactions between the HPA and the Veterinary Laboratories Agency, including standardized methods of strain typing and rapid communication of epidemiological findings (such as those described above) facilitated investigations to determine the animal source of the contaminating strain. HPA officials told us that such communications have been useful in several other outbreaks, including, for example, the investigation and containment of a 2004 outbreak of multiple antibiotic-resistant *Salmonella* Paratyphi B variant Java among cattle on an English farm. Rapid communication of typing results and epidemiological information between the HPA and the Veterinary Laboratories Agency resulted in containment of the outbreak before it could spread to humans.

According to HPA, there are numerous examples of similar collaborative activities between the HPA and the Veterinary Laboratories Agency involving both *Salmonella* and Verocytotoxinproducing *E. coli*, with typing and epidemiological data being exchanged on an almost daily basis. The reporting of outbreaks to the HPA is done on a voluntary basis. There is no lower size limit on the number of cases affected for a report to be generated; HPA would follow up on single cases of severe diseases, such as botulism or listeriosis.

Efforts to Measure the Effectiveness of the Food Safety System

At the time of our review, the UK had not conducted a review of its reorganized food safety system. However, FSA, the UK's National Audit Office (the UK equivalent of GAO), and the EU's Food and Veterinary Office have reviewed individual aspects of the system.

Performance Measures

Performance measures for FSA include the number of illness reported and consumer surveys on food safety issues. For example, FSA reported in 2006 that incidents of foodborne illness declined by 19.2 percent between 2001 and 2006. According to FSA statistics, this reduction equates to 1.5 million fewer people suffering from foodborne illness, 10,000 fewer in the hospital as a result of this illness, and an estimated total cost savings of more than £750 million (nearly U.S. $1.5 billion). FSA staff attributed this decline to, among other things, (1) an ongoing decline in *Salmonella* incidences as a result of efforts in the farming industry to reduce contamination of eggs, including improved biosecurity measures and vaccination of laying hens, and (2) measures undertaken to keep slaughterhouses clean and reduce cross-contamination. For example, HACCP measures were introduced in slaughterhouses, and new, clean henhouses were being used on many farms; and (3) FSA made efforts to educate the public on preventing *Campylobacter* contamination.

Evaluations and audits

The UK's National Audit Office, GAO's counterpart in the UK, conducted an audit of FSA in 2003 and found that the agency had made progress in its stated objective of improving public confidence in food safety and standards. For example, according to the office, in 2001 and 2002 the FSA investigated about 500 incidents with the potential to affect food safety. FSA issued 47 Food Hazard Warnings to local authorities, alerting them to potential health dangers or requiring them to recall food from sale. The audit office also made some recommendations for further progress.

More recently, the National Audit Office assessed the extent to which FSA implemented a set of principles, referred to as the Hampton principles, that include the following:

- Regulators, and the regulatory system as a whole, should use comprehensive risk assessment to concentrate resources on the areas that need them most.
- No inspection should take place without a reason.
- Regulators should provide authoritative, accessible advice easily and cheaply.
- All regulations should be written so that they are easily understood, easily implemented, and easily enforced, and all interested parties should be consulted when they are being drafted.

The National Audit Office review team concluded that, in many respects, FSA regulated in accordance with the Hampton principles. The office rated FSA highly on adopting innovative alternatives to classic regulation and on having an evidence-based culture. Many positive initiatives were being undertaken by FSA in its risk assessment system. Areas to develop further included developing more of a strategic partnership with local authorities and providing better advice and guidance to small businesses. Overall, the National Audit Office found that FSA was continuing to improve its performance from an already strong base.

After the 2005 Sudan Red 1 incident in which illegal dye was found in food, FSA conducted an internal review of the lessons learned. In January 2007 the FSA Board established an independent panel to review the lessons learned following the incident, what changes had been introduced as a result, and how well different parts of the food chain, including manufacturers, retailers, enforcement authorities, and FSA, are able to identify emerging issues and prevent them from developing into food incidents in future. The board made recommendations to both FSA and industry. Among other things, it recommended that FSA take a central role in ensuring more coordinated attention to intelligence gathering and implementing early warning systems, as well as proactively sharing this information with the food industry.

In addition to reviews conducted by UK agencies, the EU's Food and Veterinary Office conducted 71 audits in the UK between 2001 and 2007 and provided recommendations for corrective measures in certain areas.

For example, a 2006 report on import controls and border inspections found a largely functioning import control system in place, but also found that there were some weaknesses, such as in implementing a training program for contract/part-time officials. In addition, it found some general shortcomings related to implementation of the border control system, such as not all live animals arriving at the border inspection posts were checked as required, and veterinary checks on some species were being carried out by technical staff instead of by official veterinarians. Other Food and Veterinary Office audits have included reviews of import controls on food of animal origin, animal welfare on farms, and foot-and-mouth disease.

Public Opinion Surveys

FSA annual consumer surveys between 2001 and 2007 show a marked decline in the public's concerns about foodborne illness, from 71 percent to 57 percent. FSA surveys also indicated that public trust in FSA was an estimated 60 percent in 2007, compared with 44 percent in 2001. The survey likewise found that FSA was seen as a reliable source of information for both food safety and healthy eating by the majority of those who use it, although it was used and considered reliable more for food safety than for healthy eating.

According to a 2005 Eurobarometer survey published in 2006, an estimated 47 percent of people in the UK stated that overall, food safety had improved over the past decade, 30 percent that it had stayed about the same, 17 percent that it had worsened, and 6 percent did not know. In addition, an estimated 50 percent stated that usually public authorities' actions in the EU with regard to food safety risks were appropriate, 24 percent stated that the actions were insufficient, 12 percent stated that the actions went beyond what is needed, and 13 percent did not know.

Finally, an estimated 47 percent agreed that food produced in the EU is safer than food imported from elsewhere, 32 percent disagreed, and 21 percent did not know.

Stakeholder Perspectives

The views of industry and consumer groups can serve as an informal indicator of the effectiveness of a country's food safety system. In the UK, we spoke to representatives of two industry organizations. A representative of one such organization stated that he thought consolidation of the UK's food safety system had resulted in improvements; a representative from another organization said that FSA listens more to industry concerns now. According to one representative, FSA is now more transparent to industry, and it is easier to consult with the agency on issues of concern. Nevertheless, this person believed that FSA could do a better job of sharing information. Another industry stakeholder noted that FSA acted "disproportionately" to a recent recall.

Other Relevant Issues

Emerging Trends and Challenges

Officials we spoke with identified the following areas of concern with regard to ongoing and future challenges to the country's food safety system:

- Pathogens continue to evolve.
- People are changing the types of foods they eat and the ways they prepare them.
- More people are eating out, and food preparation in small restaurants and by caterers carries more risk.
- Demographic changes mean that there are and will continue to be more elderly people in the UK, and these people tend to be more vulnerable to foodborne illness than others.
- There is an ever-increasing international market for foods, particularly produce. Although only a very small proportion of such foods is contaminated with an organism capable of causing disease, the scale of food importation, particularly from countries where standards are not as stringent as in the UK, has resulted in an increasing number of international outbreaks. Such outbreaks have been regularly identified by the Enter-net network, and international intervention measures have been introduced on numerous occasions.
- Incidences of foodborne illness caused by *E.coli* or *Campylobacter* have continued to increase at a steady rate in 2006. Scientists' understanding of *Campylobacter* is still limited because it generally occurs in isolated incidents (i.e., it is not an "outbreak" bacterium) and is therefore more difficult to study.
- Listeriosis, especially in older people, seems to be increasing, not just in the UK but around the world. The reason for this increase is unclear and is likely to reflect multiple factors, including perhaps the fact that a warmer climate enables *Listeria* to thrive.
- Many immigrants, both from other EU member states and from non-EU countries, bring home-prepared foods into the UK from overseas. If improperly prepared or preserved, these foods may cause illness.

End Notes

[1] GAO, *High-Risk Series: An Update*, GAO-07-310 (Washington, D.C.: January 2007).

[2] GAO, *Food Safety: Experiences of Seven Countries in Consolidating Their Food Safety Systems,* GAO-05-212 (Washington, D.C.: Feb. 22, 2005).

[3] Department of Health and Human Services, U.S. Food and Drug Administration, *Food Protection Plan* (Washington, D.C.: 2007).

[4] Interagency Working Group on Import Safety, *Action Plan for Import Safety* (Washington, D.C.: 2007).

[5] Primary producers, that is, farmers, hunters, and fishermen, are not required to apply HACCP principles. However, guides to good practice encourage the use of appropriate hygiene practices at farm level.

[6] Reference laboratories are specialized laboratories that assist in surveillance for, and investigation of, foodborne illness outbreaks. They use standardized equipment and methods to analyze samples isolated from humans, animals, and suspected foods. These laboratories generally have expertise in specialized areas in which there is a need for precise analytical methods and definitive diagnostic results. For example, a reference laboratory may conduct DNA "fingerprinting" of a pathogen such as *Salmonella* or *E. coli* to identify the precise strain of the pathogen. Networks of reference laboratories allow public and animal health scientists to identify patterns and determine whether a foodborne outbreak is occurring even if the affected persons are geographically far apart.

[7] For information on the U.S. animal identification system, see GAO, *National Animal Identification System: USDA Needs to Resolve Several Key Implementation Issues to Achieve Rapid and Effective Disease Traceback*, GAO-07-592 (Washington, D.C.: July 6, 2007).

[8] For information on recall authority in the United States, see GAO, *Federal Oversight of Food Safety: High-Risk Designation Can Bring Needed Attention to Limitations in the Government's Food Recall Programs*, GAO-07-785T (Washington, D.C.: Apr. 24, 2007) and GAO, *Food Safety: USDA and FDA Need to Better Ensure Prompt and Complete Recalls of Potentially Unsafe Food*, GAO-05-51 (Washington, D.C.: Oct. 6, 2004).

[9] This information comes from the EU's Eurobarometer—a series of surveys regularly performed on behalf of the European Commission since 1973. Eurobarometer produces reports of public opinion across the member states on a variety of EU-related topics, including social conditions, health, culture, and environment.

End Notes for Appendix I

[1] Stages of production, processing, and distribution mean any stage, including import, from and including the primary production of a food through storage, transport, sale, or supply to the final consumer and, where relevant, the importation, production, manufacture, storage, transport, distribution, sale and supply of feed.

[2] Hazard Analysis and Critical Control Point (HACCP) is a science-based safety system for certain food products designed to improve the safety of food by having industry identify and control biological, chemical, and physical hazards in products before they enter the market.

[3] Primary producers, that is, farmers, hunters, and fishermen, are not required to apply HACCP principles. However, guides to good practice should encourage the use of appropriate hygiene practices at the farm level.

[4] Market surveillance refers to the routine monitoring of the rapid alert system's Web site and other sources to see if any products are being recalled.

[5] Some forms of *E. coli* bacteria can produce toxins capable of killing a special type of cell called a Vero cell. These *E. coli* have thus become known as verotoxin or verocytotoxin *E. coli* (VTEC). VTEC O157 is the type most frequently associated with human disease.

[6] *Yersinia* is a bacterium that causes an infectious disease called Yersiniosis. Infection is most often acquired by eating contaminated food, especially raw or undercooked pork products. Drinking contaminated unpasteurized milk or untreated water can also transmit the infection. Occasionally, infection occurs after contact with infected animals.

[7] Bacteria of the *Brucella* family can cause an infectious disease called Brucellosis. Various *Brucella* species affect sheep, goats, cattle, deer, elk, pigs, dogs, and several other animals. Humans are generally infected by eating or drinking something that is contaminated with *Brucella*, breathing in the organism, or having the bacteria enter the body through skin wounds. The most common way to be infected is by eating or drinking contaminated milk products.

[8] The European Economic Area consists of the EU member states, the European Community, and Iceland, Liechtenstein, and Norway. Switzerland is not part of the EEA.

[9] Eurobarometer is a series of surveys regularly performed on behalf of the European Commission since 1973. It produces reports of public opinion across the member states on a variety of EU-related topics, including social conditions, health, culture, and environment.

[10] The allowable residue of any chemical in a food commodity entering or produced in a country is known as the Maximum Residue Level (MRL) and is expressed in parts per million (ppm); in Japan, these MRLs are compiled into a master list called the Positive List. This is the list of allowable substances eligible for

marketing in Japan. Foods containing residues exceeding the MRL levels on the positive list are prohibited from being sold or used as food in Japan.

[11] A prefecture in Japan is a subnational jurisdiction, a governmental body larger than a city, town, or village. Japan has 47 prefectures.

[12] This paragraph refers to *reports* rather than *cases* because, according to UK officials, for every case of *Salmonella* reported nationally, there are about three other cases in the community. For *Campylobacter*, the multiplier is about 10, and for *E.coli* O157, it is about 2.

[13] Some forms of *E. coli* bacteria can produce toxins capable of killing a special type of cell called a Vero cell. These *E. coli* have thus become known as verotoxin or verocytotoxinproducing *E. coli* (VTEC).

[14] At the time of the outbreak the epidemiological and laboratory hub of Enter-net was based in the Department of Gastrointestinal Infections of the HPA, at the Centre for Infections, Colindale. In September 2007, Enter-net was subsumed into the newly formed European Centre for Disease Control, based in Stockholm, Sweden. Although not a member of Enter-net, the United States is party to all Enter-net communications regarding outbreaks and strain typing.

INDEX

A

B

C

D

E

F

J

K

L

M

N

O

P

Q

R

S

T

U

V

W

X

Y